With Rhodes in Mashonaland

David Christiaan De Waal

Nabu Public Domain Reprints:

You are holding a reproduction of an original work published before 1923 that is in the public domain in the United States of America, and possibly other countries. You may freely copy and distribute this work as no entity (individual or corporate) has a copyright on the body of the work. This book may contain prior copyright references, and library stamps (as most of these works were scanned from library copies). These have been scanned and retained as part of the historical artifact.

This book may have occasional imperfections such as missing or blurred pages, poor pictures, errant marks, etc. that were either part of the original artifact, or were introduced by the scanning process. We believe this work is culturally important, and despite the imperfections, have elected to bring it back into print as part of our continuing commitment to the preservation of printed works worldwide. We appreciate your understanding of the imperfections in the preservation process, and hope you enjoy this valuable book.

[*By permission of Messrs. Elliott & Fry.*

THE RIGHT HON. CECIL J. RHODES.

WITH RHODES IN MASHONALAND.

BY

D. C. DE WAAL, M.L.A.

TRANSLATED FROM THE ORIGINAL DUTCH BY

JAN H. HOFMEYR DE WAAL.

IN TWO PARTS.

J. C. JUTA & CO.,
CAPE TOWN. | PORT ELIZABETH.
JOHANNESBURG.
AND
36, BASINGHALL STREET, LONDON, E.C.
1896.

[Entered at Stationers' Hall.]   [All rights reserved.

Afr 8250.16

LONDON:
PRINTED BY WILLIAM CLOWES AND SONS, LIMITED,
STAMFORD STREET AND CHARING CROSS.

PREFACE.

THE contents of this book appeared a few years ago as a series of articles in the *Zuid Afrikaansche Tijdschrift,* a Dutch monthly magazine published in Cape Town. As Charterland or Rhodesia (as it has recently been named) was then, so to speak, a new-born babe to which the political eye of South Africa was turning with keen interest, the description of our travels was eagerly and appreciatively read.

The reader will find the account to consist of facts written in plain words. I have neither indulged in florid language, nor do I make any claim to correct literary style. When I penned the contents of this volume, I did not in the least contemplate their being printed in English. Shortly after their publication in their original form, I was asked by numbers of my English friends to have them translated and published in book form. To this request I have at last yielded, and I trust the book will please them and all others who care to know something about the nature and history of Mashonaland—the future Eldorado.

The second part of the book, which contains an account of our second trip to the interior, will, I believe, be generally accepted as the more interesting of the two, so I hope the reader will not lay aside and criticise the book until he has perused the whole of it.

If worthy of being read, the following pages should be of interest not only to South Africans, but to the English public generally, as Rhodesia is certain in the near future to become one of the foremost dependencies of Great Britain.

In conclusion I may point out that Mr. Rhodes, Sir H. B. Loch, Mr. Sivewright, Captain Bower, and Dr. Jameson, as mentioned in this book, are now respectively the Right Hon. Cecil J. Rhodes, Lord Loch, Sir James Sivewright, Sir Graham Bower, and Dr. Jameson, C.B.

DAVID C. DE WAAL.

CAPE TOWN,
December, 1895.

CONTENTS.

PART I.

OUR FIRST TRIP.

CHAPTER I.

We set out—My travelling companions—Met by Mankoraan—The chief's complaints—Sir Henry's presents are rejected—Vrijburg—We witness a Kafir wedding at Mafeking—A visit to Montsioa 1

CHAPTER II.

Having parted from the Governor and his company, we start—Our waggons and their attendants—We spend our first night with an old hunter, and he and his household enlighten us as to Lobengula and his country—"Nelmapius" is best left alone—Willow Park . . . 12

CHAPTER III.

Buispoort—Travellers' tales not all gospel—We outspan at a German missionary's—More harrowing details about the chief of the Matabele—A literal dance of death—We have our first misadventure—Kafir beer better than Nelmapius 18

CHAPTER IV.

The banks of the Limpopo—Mr. Rhodes a good shot—Mr. Venter fails to imitate a lion—An unsuccessful wild duck hunt—Arrive at Palla's Camp, and again meet the Governor 24

CHAPTER V.

Hunting in clay—A visit to a Transvaal shopkeeper, and a look at a boa constrictor—How Grobbelaar met his death—Major Sapte's compass not so useful as horses' hoofs—I receive very sad news from home—Pietje upsets Mr. Venter 29

CHAPTER VI.

We arrive at Sofala—Journeying through a kloof—Too large a company has its drawbacks—Mr. Rhodes shows the strength of his resolution, and gets drenched—The meeting with Khama—The chief's differences with the armers—Khama's wife—Reflections on the country . 35

CHAPTER VII.

Leave Tjopong—We outspan, and I go a-fishing—A man saved from drowning—A talk with Sir Henry Loch . 42

CHAPTER VIII.

An adventure with a lion—The weather not what we expected—Mr. Rhodes reminds me of my grandfather—Sunday in the camp—Sir Henry goes out hunting, and Mr. Venter and I spend the morning tree measuring—We lose our way, and meet some game which we fail to secure—The Premier the best sportsman . . . 46

CHAPTER IX.

"The place of death"—Macloutsi—Though man proposes, God disposes—A review of the British Bechuana police—Telegraph facilities—A separation which Sir Henry Loch disapproves—Mr. Rhodes wishes to see Mashonaland, and we go forward 52

CHAPTER X.

A dark night and a recalcitrant driver—We find we have an invalid in the company—We go on and pass through a country deserted through fear of Lobengula—A letter of warning from the Governor 58

CHAPTER XI.

We arrive at the Tuli River—Other tourists there besides ourselves—Our ideas considered impracticable—Mr. Rhodes gives up his project with regret—The story of a brave lion-hunter 62

CHAPTER XII.

A bad night—Solomon fears he is going to die—Traces of hyænas and snakes—We come to an African Paradise—Mr. Venter and I go in search of milk, and are nearly torn to pieces—We cross the Crocodile, and have an interview with Mr. Greeff—A proposed big hunt . . 69

CHAPTER XIII.

We divide our forces—The prospect of a delicious supper—I meet with some curious wild animals—An interview with crocodiles—The return of our hunters—An adventure with a tiger—Mr. Greeff tells an exciting story. 76

CONTENTS.

CHAPTER XIV.

Mr. van Aarde's farm—Too tired to run after koodoos—A difference about our journey, and Mr. Lange has to give way—Cremataart River and the trees there . . . 83

CHAPTER XV.

Fascinating scenery—The River Nile, so called—We make another effort to buy milk—The Kafir women as bad as the dogs—A delusive hill—The Premier is dissatisfied, but the oxen are not—A born hunter and his family—Salt-waggons from Zoutpansbergen 87

CHAPTER XVI.

A carriage and four horses—Mr. Barend Vorster—Mr. Adendorff and his concession—A tiresome invitation which has to be accepted—We reach Pietersburg, and read sad tidings in the newspapers—We do not enjoy our quarters, and decide to leave—Expensive hospitality—We hear more than we desire of the concession . . 92

CHAPTER XVII.

The concession again—A sumptuous lunch—Makapaan's Poort—The cave of the Kafirs—A fearful death—We reach Potgieter's Rust—Kafirs on the way to the gold fields—The advantages of Kafir labour . . . 101

CHAPTER XVIII.

No hurry to reach Pretoria—An officer meets us with an invitation—We enter in procession, and sleep, after two months' travelling, under a roof—Nelmapius gives me a headache in Pretoria—The gold mines of Johannesburg—I am treated discourteously by a post-office clerk at Kimberley—Home at Capetown once more . . 106

PART II.

OUR SECOND TRIP.

CHAPTER I.

Introduction—We leave Capetown for Port Elizabeth—The Premier shuns a public demonstration—The mosquito in Durban—On board ship—Beetles as company—Mr. Rhodes does not mind them, but I do, and crack my crown in consequence 117

CHAPTER II.

Still in the *Norseman*—We arrive at Delagoa Bay—The character of the Portuguese residents—Why Delagoa Bay is unhealthy—Back to our berths—Beetles preferable to dirt—The manœuvres of our pilot—An awkward predicament—At Inhambane—We hire Kafir boys, but the Governor disapproves—The Premier waxes wrathful and gains his point 124

CHAPTER III.

We depart from Inhambane—The pilot proves an unsuccessful acrobat—We reach Beira Bay—In trouble once more about our Kafirs—Captain Pipon to the rescue —The Governor outwitted 134

CHAPTER IV.

Our first sight of hippopotami—Native canoes—A lovely night—We row to the shore and have a water-buck hunt—Major Johnson the "man of the day"—We reach Naves Ferreira—Notes on the Portuguese inhabitants and the native Kafirs 143

CHAPTER V.

Unloading under difficulties—Pikenin astonishes us with an acrobatic feat—"Crocodile Nest"—Supper at Mapandas—A novel way of destroying rats—Off again and meet some game on the way—Outspan at Muda—Our night's rest disturbed by lions 149

CHAPTER VI.

Vexatious trouble with the horses—Buffaloes—A natural zoological garden—A dash in a crocodile pool—Lions dangerously close—Rest at last—Mr. Rhodes shoots a zebra—A wild rush—The Premier chased by a "lion". 159

CHAPTER VII.

Sarmento—The apes watch us bathing—We have to abandon one of our carts—Packing and unpacking—Difficulties grow and I am attacked with despondency—We resolve to give up our second cart also—A lion kills one of our horses—Beautiful palms, but bad water . . . 170

CHAPTER VIII.

A dreary search for water—Anxious hours in the dark—A happy meeting—The Major challenges me to a rash plunge—We meet Bowden, who appears ill—I lose my dearly-loved pony 179

CHAPTER IX.

Annoyance at the hands of our boys—We pass a Portuguese Lema; he travels in state—How the natives salute one another—Traces of the tsetse-fly—No pleasure in a bamboo forest—I lose some of my baggage—Chimoyo at last 189

CHAPTER X.

Bartering with Kafirs—Our followers begin to feel fatigued—I stick to my portmanteau in spite of Mr. Rhodes' generous offers—Major Johnson is charged by a wild ox—How a Kafir smokes—A lovely halting-spot . . 192

CHAPTER XI.

An historical show—The scene of a battle—Massi-Kessi—On the track of the ancient gold-seekers—We plan to sleep outside the tent, but are discovered by our Premier—Some thrilling lion stories 199

CHAPTER XII.

We cross the Umtali Mountains—A good night's rest—Our Kafir boys leave us, but Pikenin and Matokwa choose to stick by their present masters—An accident to Pikenin—I am thrown into a pool—Our boys frighten the Kafir women—A Kafir burial-place . . . 208

CHAPTER XIII.

Beautiful farm sites—Eccentricities of Kafir hair-dressing—We take shelter from the storm—Left without food—Major Johnson loses his bet 215

CHAPTER XIV.

Marandella's kraal—A touch of fever—More thunderstorms—We enter Salisbury, and I inspect the stores awaiting me there—Misfortunes and losses—Captain Tyson more generous than is needful—My tent-mate . . . 221

CHAPTER XV.

Salisbury—A visit to the auction sales—The Premier has dissatisfied deputations to deal with—Many officers but no privates—£35 worth of champagne at a sitting—Unpleasant visitors—King Solomon's mines . . 227

CHAPTER XVI.

Lord Randolph Churchill—An ancient gold-seeker—Political discussions—I grow warm, and give the English ex-Chancellor my views without fear or favour—The Blue Rock Reef—Dr. Jameson and I inspect an old mine—Lord Randolph shows he can cook 234

CHAPTER XVII.

The Rothschild Mines—Output of gold—How Lobengula treated his advisers—Traces of the Phœnicians—Lemon-trees—Crossing the Hunjani River—Hunting the Setsiebies bucks—I prefer to shoot nothing to being shot—We have to return empty-handed 240

CHAPTER XVIII.

Hunting again—The Premier Nimrod this time—Adventure with a crocodile—Mr. Scott's narrative—Our oxen missing, and we are all out of humour—A tropical storm 246

CHAPTER XIX.

The Umfuli River—Ant-heaps a thousand years old—The climate of Mashonaland—The Makalaka Kafirs—A meeting in the wilds with friends—Young colonists—Captain Tyson's stores are replenished—We receive a visit from Mr. Selous and travel on the road he constructed—More lion stories 251

CHAPTER XX.

Remarks on Mashonaland—The natives' fear of the Matabele—A profitable exchange—The houses of the Mashonas—Their fondness for rats as food, and surprise that we do not share it—How the climate compares with other parts of South Africa 257

CHAPTER XXI.

Formation of rocks at Fort Victoria—Lord Randolph Churchill's opinion of the Mashonaland Gold Mines—Will not accompany us to the ruins of Simbabe—I cannot understand such conduct in a news-correspondent—He invites the Premier and myself to be his travelling companions, but we refuse 263

CHAPTER XXII.

We start for Simbabe—A perilous ford—The great Simbabe temple—We find our arrival is expected, and don't altogether like our reception at first—Explanations make all clear—We climb the walls—An early cup of coffee . 268

CHAPTER XXIII.

Inspecting Simbabe—Mr. and Mrs. Bent's discoveries—Early history of Simbabe—Supposed to be built by Solomon—The connection of the Moors with Simbabe—Early gold fields—Sun worshippers there probably—The ancient prosperity of Simbabe to be surpassed in the future . 275

CHAPTER XXIV.

We return to our travels—The thriving condition of the Simbabe Kafirs—Their pretty children—The little ones suspicious of the meat-tins—One of our animals taken ill—A visit to Dickens' Gold Reef—Stamping the quartz—Dr. Jameson displays his horsemanship and comes to grief 284

CHAPTER XXV.

A new team—Mr. Lange, Captain Tyson and I are teamsters—A mad rush down hill—A bathe in the Crocodile's pool—Providential Pass; in the haunts of the gold-seekers—Long's Reef—Mr. Long can give reasons for his actions—Lord Randolph much in error . . . 289

CHAPTER XXVI.

Again on the march—An accident to my portmanteau—I am sad in consequence—A hard alternative before Roeping and January—We interview Chibe to learn the truth about the Adendorff Concession—An uphill climb—Chibe does not confirm the Concession—We learn more details about Lobengula—My new boy . . . 296

CHAPTER XXVII.

Captain Tyson's dip—How Mr. Vluggi lost his way—A grim game—A meeting with some disappointed diggers—The scene of young Hackwell's death—A hunt before breakfast, in which we see traces of much game, but shoot none—I shoot an alligator—Captain Tyson proposes a race—I accept the challenge and come off victorious . 310

CONTENTS.

CHAPTER XXVIII.

Secluded huts—Evidence of a struggle between animals—A view of a huge crocodile—Captain Tyson deceived—He has a nasty fall—At the Boobi River—A needed bath—The snake hunts the cayman and the boys hunt the snake—Van Riet's wonderful adventure . . . 321

CHAPTER XXIX.

A koodoo shot—Mr. Rhodes' light waggon—I over-persuade my companions, and we all start together for Bechuanaland—Pikenin leaves me—On the track of our previous journey—An invitation at Macloutsi in which I am not included 330

CHAPTER XXX.

We leave Macloutsi—Meet Khama—At Palapye—The chief's grievances—I do not enjoy the *rôle* of John Gilpin, and reproach my companions—A little excusable exaggeration in my complaints—Captain Tyson and Mr. Lange left behind—Matabele boys—Arrival at Notwani . . 339

CHAPTER XXXI.

Plenty of room in the coach—Lord Randolph and the mules—My anxiety not to disturb his lordship's rest—A rapid run to Mafeking—The troubles of fame—Mr. Rhodes makes a speech at Fourteen Streams—At Kimberley . 345

WITH RHODES IN MASHONALAND.

PART I.

CHAPTER I.

We set out—My travelling companions—Met by Mankoraan—The chief's complaints—Sir Henry's presents are rejected—Vrijburg—We witness a Kafir wedding at Mafeking—A visit to Montsioa.

On the 2nd of October, 1890, the Hon. C. J. Rhodes, M.L.A., Mr. M. M. Venter, M.L.A., and myself—in company with the Governor of the Cape Colony, Sir Henry Loch, and his party—left Kimberley by special train for the north at half-past eight in the morning, and arrived at Taungs, Mankoraan's chief town, at one.

There we pitched a large tent and had our lunch under it. Shortly afterwards, Mankoraan and eighteen of his indunas, with a retinue of a thousand men on horseback, made their appearance at our camp. They came to welcome the Governor, and to confer with him on certain matters regarding their land. The scene of their approach was an imposing one, and the subsequent interview very interesting. Mankoraan, who, upon the invitation of the High Commissioner, was the first to speak, started at once complaining in bitter terms that sufficient land had not been left to him and his people, and said that, if better provision were not made for them, they would starve, etc., etc. The Governor then pointed out to him that, according to the last census returns, not only had his property as well as the number of his people during recent years vastly increased, but his kingdom had never before been in so prosperous a condition, and that, had the English Queen not taken him and his tribe under her protection, they would very probably by that time have been expelled from the land by the stronger negro tribes, as had been the case with Massouw.

Mankoraan shook his head. "No," grumbled he, "the Queen has not protected us, but has deprived us of our land and handed much of it over to the Transvaal."

"But," asked Sir Henry, "what is it that you want? Do you want us to retake the land already granted to the Transvaal, and so plunge into war with that country?"

"Well, I can't help it if that follows," he replied, "but I *must* have more land."

"If you had fallen under the protection of the Transvaal, would you have been better off than you are?" the Governor asked.

"Certainly," was the answer; "I would have been treated far better."

The Governor now was silent for a while. Indignation at the ingratitude of the negro chief was to be read upon his countenance.

At length he replied, "I shall mention your complaints to Sir Sidney Shippard" (the Administrator of Bechuanaland), "and see what he can do for you."

He then turned to the counsellors of the black ruler and told them that if they had anything to ask or state he would lend a willing ear. The brother of Mankoraan thereupon took up the word and grumbled like the latter—"too little ground! too little grass!" This was indeed the gist also of all the succeeding speeches.

The royal deputation having exhausted their complaints, the High Commissioner, to prevent if possible the existence of any ill-feeling, offered to make Mankoraan a small present—giving him his choice of either a horse, a saddle and bridle, a watch and chain, a telescope or a rifle.

"No, thanks," said Mankoraan, shaking his head; "I shall take nothing for nothing. If I want anything I'll pay for it, for if I accept your present you will only deprive me of more land."

"I think Mankoraan has mistaken me," said Sir Henry to the interpreter, so as to clear away any possible misunderstanding. "I mean to give him a *present*, not to *change* with him."

"Oh, I understood the Governor well enough," replied the chief, "but I repeat I will have nothing from him for nothing."

At this the High Commissioner changed colour. "Tell the chief," he said, "that Her Majesty's

High Commissioner *gives*, but does not *take*, and tell him that because of his uncourteous reply he shall get nothing—and now you may all go," concluded His Excellency.

His black majesty thereupon rose with his odoriferous advisers, shook Sir Henry's hand and those of some others, and left the tent. They mounted their horses, and off they went, horses and riders, in a cloud of dust.

Upon the departure of those honourable visitors and their followers, we had to decide between two things—to sprinkle the tent with eau-de-Cologne in order to remove the odour the Kafirs had left behind, or to haul down the tent altogether and proceed on our journey. We chose the latter course.

Naturally, our topic for the next hour or so was the attitude of Mankoraan. Our Premier was of opinion that the sooner the people of Mankoraan be compelled to work for the farmers instead of being allowed to cluster together in thousands and do nothing, the sooner they would learn to their advantage that it was the duty of every man, be he black or white, to earn his bread by toil—and shepherds and labourers were just then what farmers were most in need of. I, too, felt —and Mr. Venter shared the feeling with me—that there existed far too much ungratefulness and impoliteness in Mankoraan and his men towards their benefactors. They should be forced to do labour under the farmers. The sooner Bechuanaland is annexed to the Cape the better, not only for those lazy lords personally, and the country in which they live, but for the general civilisation and prosperity of the land.

The veld and cattle there appeared in excellent

condition, and instead of finding Bechuanaland—as I had always previously had an idea it was—a land of limestone, baboons and vultures, I found it a grand country for cattle and sheep-farming, as well as, to some extent, for agriculture.

We were now travelling through narrow passages, past hills, across valleys, and over plains. Mr. Venter repeatedly expressed his amazement at the wonderful adaptability of the veld for cattle, and he is a man whose judgment should carry especial weight, for he is a great authority on stock-farming, being himself a stock-farmer who owns many thousands of acres of land in the Colesberg and Philipstown districts. But one did not need to be an expert in grass to discover the excellent quality of the veld we were now speeding over: anyone who was not blind and who knew anything at all about veld could see it for himself. Almost all the way from Kimberley to Vrijburg the land is excellently suited for cattle and sheep.

At half-past four, and within about a mile and a half from Vrijburg, we had to leave the train, as the railway had not yet been completed to the village. All was life here. Dozens of vehicles stood ready to convey to the village the party that had just arrived. Pretty spring waggons, waggonettes, dogcarts, landaus and spiders, all drawn by fine strong horses, were to be seen; and amongst the number who came to bid us welcome many a gentleman in tile, gloves and eye-glass, and in every respect dressed in the latest fashions, was to be observed. "Goodness me!" I thought, "how do *we* with our grey broad-brimmed felt hats look in contrast with them!"

We drove off to the little town, and there numbers of flags were waving in honour of the visiting party. Having listened to the addresses read to the Governor —a lot of ceremonial nonsense—each hurried to his boarding-house to take, what the dusty way had caused him sorely to need—a good bath. Mr. Venter and myself put up at Advocate Allen Fraser's,* who, together with his gracious wife, treated us exceedingly well.

At evening we took a stroll through the village and were surprised at seeing such fine strong buildings, such big hotels and commercial houses, and so neat a townhouse. The following morning we went to see the prison, a building ornamental to the place and certainly one of the finest of its kind in South Africa. To the principal springs of Vrijburg we also paid a visit, and they too excited our admiration. At a small expense the town might be very abundantly provided with water. The soil there is fertile: almost anything would grow and thrive in it. Indeed, I think that Vrijburg is bound in the near future to become an important city whence hundreds of tons of wool will yearly be exported. We met several farmers there who had come from various districts to see the Governor, and to express their desire of having Bechuanaland annexed to the Cape Colony. They told us that they found Bechuanaland one of the finest countries for cattle and sheep they had seen. Some of them besought us to visit their farms in order to ascertain for ourselves the nature of the land. A Mr. Steijn assured us that, in spite of a drought of eight months' duration which his

* Adv. Fraser died last year (1895).—*Translator.*

part of the country had just been undergoing, he was plentifully supplied with milk and butter, and his cattle were as fat as they could be. Besides, his last crop had yielded him thousands of oatsheaves, and he was expecting between 400 and 500 bags of corn; this two other farmers confirmed. And, I must say, not a single farmer out of the dozens with whom I came in contact described Bechuanaland otherwise than most favourably as a country for cattle, sheep and cultivation. Thus Mr. Venter's opinion regarding the productive character of the land was amply affirmed.

The farmers expressed their desire to establish a branch of the Africander Bond in Bechuanaland, but they somewhat feared doing so owing to the country being a Crown Colony. With the aid of Advocate Fraser, however, and the assent of Sir Sidney Shippard, who will certainly have no objection to it, I am sure that ere long British Bechuanaland will also have a branch of the Bond; this would be the cause of greater political life amongst the farmers, and we would then hear more of them and their country than we do now.

Before leaving Vrijburg we were entertained at a dinner at which some interesting speeches were delivered. The speech of our Governor was appreciated much, but that of our Premier more, for his was a political one. Numerous other speeches followed, some very selfish and some strongly Jingoistic—some pleaded for their pockets and some for the continuance of Bechuanaland* as a Crown Colony rather than its

* Bechuanaland was annexed to the Cape Colony during the last session (1895) of the Cape Parliament.—*Translator*.

being annexed to the Cape, where there were so many Bondsmen who had so much to say! The speeches that pleased us most were those delivered in true South African spirit by Advocate Fraser and Attorney Wessels, whose sensible arguments carried no small amount of force with them, and at the same time revealed the men we were some day to find the representatives of Bechuanaland in the Cape Parliament.

On leaving Vrijburg we entered upon another fine, fruitful tract of country, and on our way we met several farmers, amongst whom was a Mr. Rood, formerly of the Colesberg district, who, together with his wife and a couple of children, was living in the open veld in a waggon and tent. We asked him what he thought of the veld. "Oh," said he, "the veld is as good as at Colesberg, and here I have an unlimited extent of land at my disposal, whereas in the old colony my land had become too narrow for me. As to my cattle and sheep, they are in a very good condition."

"And have you sufficient water for your cattle?" we next inquired.

He assured us that he had more than he needed, and that water was to be got anywhere at a depth of six or eight feet. "The land is flat and even," he continued, "and rains are very copious from December till the end of March. Every farm is plentifully supplied with water; should there not be enough on the surface, dams might easily be laid out."

Mr. Venter and myself then partook of coffee with the kind old gentleman and his wife, and we left him highly pleased. Afterwards, we passed through Maribogo, a large Kafir town, rich in soil and in cattle and sheep as well as in water.

The following Sunday night, the 5th of October, we lodged at the Messrs. Worsey's hotel, on this side of the historical town of the chief, Moshette. This town was the capital of the chief who, some years previously fought against the chief, Montsioa, and only gained the best of the war when some irresponsible Boers came to his assistance; but, later, was again attacked by Montsioa and completely overcome. Out of this war arose the subsequent dispute about Land Goschen and Rooigrond, with which were connected the names of Great Adriaan de la Rey, Van Niekerk, Bethell, McKenzie, etc.; and the quarrel did not terminate until British troops, under command of Sir Charles Warren crossed the border, and Mr. Rhodes, as mediator, brought about an amicable settlement of the matter between England and the Transvaal. It is chiefly through the instrumentality of our Prime Minister that McKenzie and his rabble were prevented from playing the master over the land.

We journeyed from Kunana over a meadowy region, and arrived at Mafeking, about a hundred miles from Vrijburg, at eight o'clock. This little town also was in a bustle at the coming of the Governor. A grand dinner was given to His Excellency in the evening; it lasted till past midnight — no wonder most of us complained of headache the following day. At Mafeking, too, we were struck at the fine new buildings, the well laid-out streets, the large stores and shops and the pretty townhouse and prison. A few years before, this place was nothing more than an insignificant hamlet, and now it was on the road to becoming a large flourishing city.

Messrs. Rhodes, Lange, Venter and myself saddled our horses and rode to call on the old chief, Montsioa. The sun was just setting when we found the aged negro-ruler sitting in front of his little house on a small chair surrounded by some friends. Mr. Rhodes had a long and interesting chat with him on what had happened during the siege of his town. The veteran chief showed us some bullet-holes in his house made by the enemy as they were forcing their way into his town, who, however, were again beaten back. His recollections of the war were still very vivid; and the name of Rhodes, too, he remembered well. The Premier had meanwhile been sitting on another little chair, and when he bade the chief good-bye, the latter gave him it as a remembrance of the visit. With this little present Mr. Rhodes was much taken up, and frequently made use of it on his further journey. To return his kindness, the Premier handed Montsioa a few sovereigns for his church.

Whilst this meeting was taking place, great rejoicing was going on amongst the young people in the Kafir town owing to a wedding that was taking place between a white Kafir—called by some "one of Bethell's sons,"—and a tall black girl. Their chief amusements were music and dancing. The bride and bridegroom, typical barbarians, danced with wilder vigour than the rest. There was something attractively romantic, however, in the celebration, and it was certainly very interesting to look upon such a number of different faces of Kafir youth of both sexes.

On the eighth of the month we departed from Mafeking, leaving behind us everything that was not absolutely necessary on our journey. The Governor and his party with their waggons and horses had already left when we started. The two parties—that of the Governor and that of the Premier—chose different directions for their journey; the latter preferred to travel through British Bechuanaland into Khama's country, whilst we selected travelling *viá* Marico, Transvaal.

CHAPTER II.

Having parted from the Governor and his company, we start—Our waggons and their attendants—We spend our first night with an old hunter, and he and his household enlighten us as to Lobengula and his country—"Nelmapius" is best left alone—Willow Park.

WE set out from Mafeking with three neat spring-waggons, each drawn by a team of eight strong mules, and each supplied with both a driver and a rein-holder. Besides these, we had a folding cart drawn by four first-rate mules (the driver of which also held the reins) and five ponies which were ridden by our attendants, Bandmaster (our waiter) and Peter (our young guard). Tonie was our cook. The *tourists* were— beside the Premier—Mr. Venter, Mr. Eduard Lange (brother of the advocate), and myself. To Mr. E. Lange the charge of the waggons was entrusted. In this way we had already travelled from Vrijburg, where we overtook our waggons, which had been sent in advance from Kimberley, and this arrangement having been found to work well, we hoped to continue our journey in this manner for the rest of the trip.

The first night after our parting with the Governor we spent at De Putten, a farm of which an old Mr.

Viljoen is the proprietor, situated close to the border of the Transvaal. This grey-haired gentleman of over eighty, who seemed particularly taken up with Mr. Venter's company, told us a great deal about Mashonaland. He himself had been an inhabitant of Mashonaland, he said, since 1849. Hunting had always been his chief pursuit, and through it he had naturally gained great experience of the country. Three of his sons, who had fallen victims to fever in the low land, lay buried there.

"But," said he, "I *love* Mashonaland! it is the prettiest country that I ever saw. I am acquainted with the Cape Colony, the Free State, and the Transvaal, but Mashonaland beats them all."

"Why did you not *stay* there, then?" inquired Mr. Venter.

"Well, because I was afraid that war would break out, and I should not have liked my horses, oxen and sheep to fall into the hands of the Kafirs. Rhodes's people have crossed into the land of Lobengula, and have planted forts there as if the land is their own, but this the fearless Kafirs will not tolerate. As for Lobengula, he is as deceitful a devil as his uncle Dingaan used to be, who murdered the brave Piet Retief and his men, and followed up the slaughter by attacking the defenceless Boer camp and mercilessly massacring every mother and child in it. Oh, I know that nation too well; they are as false as they are tyrannical. Look how little they value the lives even of their own people, and how they constantly plunder the weaker tribes and carry off the women and children! But when the month of February is past, and if war by that time has not been declared, I shall return to that beautiful country."

"It is a pity, old friend," observed Mr. Venter "that age has already such a hold on you, else you might assist Mr. Rhodes in the event of war breaking out."

"Old?" repeated the grey-haired man with an air of pride; "if Rhodes wants to fight that tyrant, who has been playing the bully for so long a time, then I and all of us shall go and help him, and I think I will fell more of those cruel naked animals than any of you will."

"Yes," added the old lady, who had been listening with keen interest to the conversation, "what my husband says I can confirm. He seldom misses a shot, and he still rides his horse like a young man."

"But," said Mr. Venter, "do you think it is *right* of Mr. Rhodes to deprive the Matabele of their land?"

"Certainly," she replied with emphasis, "and none but he *can*. That unfeeling, treacherous Lobengula, who has slain his brothers and captains out of mere covetousness of their wealth, should be brought to his wits! But all have been afraid of him; now, however, Rhodes has come, and he is not afraid, and a man who is not afraid we must assist. But then, we want him to grant our people farms, and will he do that?"

"Oh, yes," answered Mr. Venter, "of that I am convinced."

"Then I am sure," the old lady replied, "that both my husband and my children would be glad to join in the war."

We left them and returned later in the evening. The old couple had already gone to bed, but a son of theirs and a son-in-law (Mr. Fourie) were still up enjoying a pipe. These latter, also, could not speak enough about the excellence of Mashonaland, and affirmed every word that had been told us by their father and mother. They, too, appeared very desirous to *trek* to Mashonaland. They wished from the bottom of their hearts that war should arise between the heartless Matabele chief and the "chief" of the Chartered Company.

"But," I asked, "don't you think it would be very difficult to subdue Lobengula?"

"No," was the reply, "Lobengula is such a tyrant, and he is so hated by all Kafir tribes, even by a portion of his own, that I have no doubt some 1500 or 2000 men would immediately be in arms against him if called to assist in putting him down. All are aware, too, that he possesses a magnificent country, rich and extensive; and, just as our aged father and ourselves are willing to take up our guns to assist in depriving him and his nation of all power, so there are thousands of farmers in the States and in the Colony prepared to do the same if only they are rewarded for their trouble."

"But," I next asked, "do you not think it would be unjust to expel him from his land?"

"Decidedly not," the two unanimously answered. "You people from the Cape are not aware," continued one of them, "of the cruel, inhuman deeds Lobengula and his men have committed, and are still committing." Then we were told a little of the shocking Matabele history, which was afterwards also related to us by a missionary, and to which I shall return.

Perceiving the influence Morpheus now began to exert on our informants—revealed by yawns and stretchings—we bade them " good-night" and retired to our waggons.

The following morning I arose with a terrible headache due to that mealie-mixture called "Nelmapius," which we had drunk the night before. I never could drink that stuff—and I know of very few who could—without suffering some bad effect. Such a headache as I had that day I don't remember ever having before. Since then I have never again touched a drop of the liquor,—at least, not knowingly.

Well, to return to our travel, the sky that morning was dark with threatening clouds and the air severely cold. Leaving De Putten, we crossed the Transvaal border into the Marico district, and at ten o'clock arrived at Mr. Taylor's, Willow Park, a lovely farm provided with abundant water and with rich arable land, a great part of which was under cultivation. Trees, too, were plentiful there. These, together with the large comfortable dwelling-house, combined to make the place a most pleasant abode.

After partaking of a substantial breakfast, we took a walk about Mr. Taylor's place. The gardens, the fruit trees, the fine lands—all looked beautiful indeed. And Mr. Taylor was not behind the times in the farming implements he employed; he had his own threshing-machine and corn-mill. He had just mown his fields, had gathered thousands of oatsheaves, and was expecting some eight hundred bags of corn. He told us he would not accept less than £11,000 for his farm.

On returning from our walk Mr. Taylor had his spider and cart inspanned, and brought us to the pretty mission-station of Ikalafijn, situated in a large valley between two hills. The neatly-built Kafir huts and the fine gardens surrounding them make a very pretty appearance. The brook, that feeds the town of a population of about ten thousand, runs through it. Its inhabitants, exclusively Kafirs, wear clothes, and in all respects the village is a credit to Missionary Janssen in particular, and to the Transvaal in general. In the missionary's garden some fine lemons, citrons and oranges were to be seen. We ate some and were provided with a quantity for our journey. Thence we returned to Willow Park.

CHAPTER III.

Buispoort—Travellers' tales not all gospel—We outspan at a German missionary's—More harrowing details about the chief of the Matabele—A literal dance of death—We have our first misadventure—Kafir beer better than Nelmapius.

We left Willow Park at three in the afternoon and arrived towards evening at Buispoort, a narrow vale between two hills, and very densely wooded. There we spent the night.

Continuing our journey the following morning, our next outspan-place was at Mr. Niemand's. That gentleman told us that a brother of his, shortly before, whilst attempting to cross the Limpopo, was drawn into the water by a crocodile and never seen again.

From there we passed on to Mr. Kirton's, which we reached within half-an-hour, and here we were sorry to discover that we had made a mistake in outspanning at Mr. Niemand's, for Mr. Kirton had not only forage ready for our horses and mules, but had a breakfast prepared for us. Unfortunately we had already had our morning meal at Mr. Niemand's.

Departing from Mr. Kirton's in the afternoon, we passed through a tract of country well wooded and grown with a tall dry grass fit for cattle. We left Mr. Rhodes at Mr. Kirton's, he arranging to follow us a little later on, which he did two hours afterwards.

We rested the night at Brakfontein. It had been warm during the day, so our horses and mules were weary and thirsty, and to our disappointment we learnt from some transport-riders that the water there was very brackish and would certainly injuriously affect our animals if they drank too much of it. But, when once the poor creatures got to the water, they drank as much as they could hold; yet they were able to consume at evening as much forage as usual, and they trot away the following morning with no less vigour than they did the morning before. When one travels he should not attach much weight to all the alarming representations of danger made to him.

The following morning we outspanned at a German missionary's, close to a Kafir location, Vlijsfontein by name. We were invited into the house and almost forced to take breakfast there whether we cared to do so or not. The missionary was poor—a fact of which there was no want of indication—but a man more genial and kindhearted it is impossible to imagine. He spoke Kafir fluently, and conducted service for the natives in a small temple every morning. His pay he received from Germany.

He had many interesting stories to tell us about Lobengula. He knew that monarch well, and had several times been in his town. Not long ago, said the missionary, Lobengula had given a dancing-feast to his people that lasted three days. One of the chief's fondest young wives, who had taken a lively part in it, became tired of dancing and therefore begged him to allow her a little rest and refreshment. This the king refused, with the command, "Dance on!" It was then already noticeable that "Lo Ben" was displeased with the desire of his favourite. She obeyed his order, but returned to him a little while afterwards and said to him:

"I should like to know whether you, if you were in my place, and were compelled to dance without stopping, and without eating or drinking, would have been able to do it."

At once the peevish king was in a rage, scolded her, commanded his counsellors immediately to assemble, and sentenced her to death. The poor girl fell down at the monarch's feet, prayed for pardon, and told him she had not intended to offend him by what she had uttered. She caressed him and in every possible way endeavoured to excite his pity, but in vain. The bystanders, too, were bold enough to plead for her, but the stubborn chief was not to be moved. The hapless young woman was led out and beaten to death with knobkerries, and, as was the custom to do with those who wronged the king, her body was cast outside the town to be devoured by vultures.

On another occasion—and here the missionary was himself a witness—some young Kafirs and Kafir girls, who had joined in a dance, were falsely reported to the king, by some of their enemies, to have been guilty of immorality. Now, the only punishment for immorality was death. Lobengula summoned to his presence at Buluwayo all the young men who had taken part in the dance, found twenty of them guilty, sentenced sixteen to death, and ordered the ears and noses of the remaining four to be cut off.

Another event that only too clearly manifested the vicious character of the Matabele monarch was the murder of his brother. Perceiving how wealthy the latter was becoming, Lobengula feigned to be suffering from gout, and ascribed the cause of it to witchery on his brother's part. Immediately thereupon it was resolved to slay the supposed offender, and the resolution was carried out without delay. When those enjoined to do the cruel deed came to the innocent man and informed him of their orders, he said:

"This is only what I have long expected. My possessions are many, and I know who covets them; well, here I am—kill me! But save my body from the vultures!"

They brought him out and slew him with their knobkerries. This done, his wife was seized and dealt with similarly. Being of royal blood, Lobengula's brother was put into a grave, but his wife's body was thrown to the birds of prey.

Leaving Vlijfontein, our road took us over a rugged mountain-pass, on the one side of which was a deep precipice. It cost us considerable trouble to get across with our heavily-laden spring waggons, and when we at last reached the foot of the mountain on the other side, we discovered that the pole of one of the waggons had broken. On the suggestion of Mr. Venter, a thorn-tree was cut down, stripped, and tied against the broken pole by means of strong leather straps. This plan answering admirably, and all being in order again, we once more proceeded comfortably on our way.

The next place we halted at was a Kafir location— a large group of straw huts—situated on the Marico River and peopled by Matabele. They spoke Zulu; and Mr. Rhodes, who had spent several years of his earlier life in Natal, and had consequently learnt the language, carried on some conversation with them. He wanted to buy a waggon-pole from them, but there were none in the whole place, except one belonging to an old waggon, the owner of which was not at home. We next asked whether they could obtain any beer for us, and hardly had the request fallen from our lips, when off ran some Kafir girls to their huts, and returned with heavy, hollowed calabashes on their heads, filled with Kafir beer. The day being hot, we enjoyed the drink immensely, and we gave the donors ample reward for it, a kindness they much appreciated.

Our Premier wanted to know from them why they, being Matabele, were living on Transvaal territory. This was explained to him. The chief of the location was a brother of Lobengula, and he used to live in Matabeleland; but when the news of the murder by Lobengula of his other brother reached his ears, he fled during the night, with all his family and followers, into the Transvaal, and settled on this side of the Marico River, where he knew he was beyond the grasp of the envious monarch. Later on he applied to the Government of the South African Republic to be allowed to dwell there undisturbed. This was of course willingly granted, provided he subjected himself to the laws of the State and regularly paid the required annual taxes. This petty chief, like Lobengula, is a son of Moselikatse and a relative of the bloodthirsty Dingaan, whose history in connection with the massacre of Piet Retief and his followers is well known to all of us.

We left the location, and halted next on the bank of the Marico, whence we continued our course up the side of the river, both banks of which were grown with trees, tall grass, and thorny shrubs; but the veld round about looked miserable.

CHAPTER IV.

The banks of the Limpopo—Mr. Rhodes a good shot—Mr. Venter fails to imitate a lion—An unsuccessful wild duck hunt—Arrive at Palla's Camp, and again meet the Governor.

At noon on the 13th of October we arrived at the junction of the Limpopo and Marico rivers. The Limpopo —or Crocodile, as it is called by many—is a magnificent stream, densely grown on both sides with heavy trees of all descriptions. The view up or down the stream, the banks of which are overhung with heavy green boughs, is most romantic, and pleasing to the eye of the traveller.

We were now 1040 miles from Capetown.

In the afternoon Mr. Rhodes and Mr. Venter went out hunting. Clouds soon began to gather in the sky, and they grew heavier every minute. A few heavy raindrops announced the approach of thunder and lightning, and very soon thereafter the storm broke out and raged violently. The two hunters returned to the camp soaked to the skin, but they had not been out in vain. Mr. Rhodes brought with him five pheasants, and Mr. Venter a korhaan. In this way our pots were continually supplied with delicious birds. Mr. Rhodes is a good shot; he seldom returned from a bird-hunt without bringing with him a number of partridges, pheasants or korhaans.

The following day we were fortunate enough to come across, on our way, an abandoned cart, the axle of which was broken. We took the pole out of it and fitted it into our own waggon, and found it to serve its purpose capitally; no waggon-builder could have helped us better.

Early in the afternoon we again outspanned on the river's bank, at a place called Harde Kool Boom— so called from a large thick tree close by, the stem of which had the appearance of burnt coal. We again travelled on, but only at a very slow speed, because Sir Henry Loch, whom we had agreed to meet at Palla's Camp, was still behind.

We went out hunting in the afternoon, Mr. Rhodes and Mr. Venter choosing one direction, Mr. Lange and myself another. Instead of hunting, however, my friend and myself began measuring the sizes of trees and ant-heaps. We found thorn-trees and wild syringas of immense height, some of them measuring round the stem from twenty to twenty-five feet. The ant-heaps we measured were from fifteen to twenty-five feet high. We had been told at Kimberley that at the Crocodile we would meet with ant-heaps of that enormous size and had ridiculed the idea, but now we realised the fact with our own eyes; and though when we were told at Vrijburg that we would meet with trees, through the trunks of which a path could be cut wide enough for a cart and pair of horses to be driven, we smiled incredulously, yet now we measured such with our own hands.

Returning to our waggons we suddenly heard a faint roar. My companion knew where it came from; I did not. He stood still for a minute, and I was rather anxious to know what it was. I suggested, however, that we had better walk on.

"No," replied Mr. Lange, "let us go and see what it is!" But the difficulty he had to refrain from laughing was so obvious that I soon discovered the roaring was a sham. Just then Mr. Venter made his appearance from behind a thicket, bursting out into laughter as he did so. He intended to frighten me by imitating a lion, and he might have been successful in the attempt had Mr. Lange's eyes not discovered the would-be wild animal and thus betrayed the practical joke, for who would have expected a man to roar amongst the bushes of that wild and solitary place?

The following morning, at ten o'clock, we outspanned at a "pan" (lakelet), where hundreds of wild duck were to be seen. I took my gun and quietly crept towards the water, soon reaching a spot from which I could easily have shot some of the birds. Instead of firing at once, I foolishly first wished to make certain whether they were really wild duck. So I stood up and stared at them for a little, when away flew the whole lot of them! They made their way towards the Limpopo, where I pursued them; and then they returned to the "pan." Hoping to be compensated for my trouble and loss of time, I again followed them. But how disappointed was I when, just as I was at the point of firing, Mr. Venter sent a bullet amongst them from a great distance, killing only one and causing the rest to fly away, whilst I stood there with one of those old-fashioned muzzle-loaders charged heavily with water-fowl shot, with which I could easily have felled a dozen birds, if I had approached them a little nearer! I felt greatly annoyed, but what could I do?

Mr. Rhodes had meanwhile shot seven snipe—a dainty tit-bit in the dish.

From there we started for Palla's Camp. On our way thither we passed a small straw house, occupied by a white man, an Australian, whose acquaintance we afterwards made. Some distance on this side of the Camp we found a monstrous dead crocodile suspended to a beam. The animal, which had evidently been killed a couple of days before, was nailed through the mouth on to the wood, on which was written, "Welcome Sir Henry Loch!"

At one o'clock on Wednesday, the 16th, we arrived at Palla's Camp, situated on the Crocodile in Khama's country, and about 1070 miles distant from Capetown and 430 from Kimberley. Here were stationed the British Bechuanaland Police and a number also of the Chartered Company. We waited there for the Governor, who arrived the following day with all his officers, hussars, spiders, carts, waggons, etc. "The more the merrier" the saying goes, but it certainly could not have been applied in this case. To travel with so large a company was rather a nuisance than a pleasure; for, henceforward not only would all game in front of us be shot away—at least, *chased* away—but we would have to travel in a ploughed and dusty road.

At Palla's Camp, where there was a telegraph and a

post office, we all had the pleasure of getting news from home, a privilege we had not enjoyed for eight days. We amply availed ourselves of the opportunity of sending away letters and telegrams. The offices there belong to the Chartered Company. Amongst the messages I sent home there was one to my youngest child, a boy of seven, that on my return home I would have a lot of tales to tell him about lions and crocodiles; but little did I then know the tidings I was to receive the following day.

CHAPTER V.

Hunting in clay—A visit to a Transvaal shopkeeper, and a look at a boa constrictor—How Grobbelaar met his death—Major Sapte's compass not so useful as horses' hoofs—I receive very sad news from home—Pietje upsets Mr. Venter.

NEXT morning Mr. Rhodes, Mr. Venter, Major Sapte, and I went out hunting on horseback. We first rode to the little house of an Australian, who had promised to accompany us on our hunt and direct us to the game. The soil was loose and clayey, and was in consequence a source of great annoyance to us, as it stuck to our boots in clods whenever we dismounted our horses and walked. The party, on the whole, remained, however, in high spirits, and were determined to make the best of the chase. But I, individually, was of a different mind. Stepping in clay four inches deep was not much of an enjoyment to me, and, knowing what good shots the rest of the party were, and what little chance I therefore stood of killing anything, I decided to turn back to the camp.

In the afternoon Mr. Lange and myself had our cart inspanned, and rode for an hour and a quarter to the other side of the Limpopo, on Transvaal soil, to a shop belonging to a Mr. Chapman. There we purchased some provisions and some Cape brandy, for which latter we were charged at the modest rate of twenty-one shillings per gallon! The shopkeeper showed us a boa constrictor which he had dug out on the banks of the river two days before. It was twelve feet in length, and looked rather pretty and very clean, as it had just cast its slough.

Mr. Chapman gave us a detailed account of how Grobbelaar had come to his end. Mr. Chapman himself had been a witness of the collision between Grobbelaar and Khama's Kafirs. He was perfectly certain, in spite of Sir Sidney Shippard's denial of the fact, that a Bamangwato Kafir had shot him. Mr. Grobbelaar received the bullet in the ankle, and, if medical attendance had been rendered in time, his wound would very probably have healed; but, as it was, a surgeon was not called for until inflammation had set in, which soon afterwards ended in the death of the farmer.

On our way back to the camp we shot three pheasants, having now five in all. Arrived at the station, we found the hunters busy at their dinner, of which they partook rather eagerly, for they had had nothing to eat since the morning. Mr. Rhodes gave us an account of the hunt. All along the Crocodile there is a dense growth of trees and bushes, and there is much resemblance between one part and another. The Australian evidently knew but little of the place, for he had not been living there long, and had never gone far away from his house. Consequently the hunters soon deviated a considerable distance from the road, and when they wanted to return to it they were in a puzzle whether to go to the right or to the left. Most perplexed of all was the Australian "guide," who knew as little as the rest which way to turn. They alternately walked and rode now in this direction, then in that, in the forest, but could not discover where they were. Major Sapte, who had as strong faith in his compass as the Philistines in Dagon, repeatedly threw it down; it showed north, south, east, west, but was of as little use as a mouse. The sun was meanwhile fast sinking in the west. Mr. Venter, an expert in following footmarks, at last suggested that the party should turn back on the horses' footprints until they reached the road. This course was adopted, and the road at length discovered to the joy of all. They returned without having shot so much as a fly, and it was confessed on all hands that I had acted wisely in leaving them.

A little later in the evening sad news reached the camp and put an end to the cheerful spirit of the party. At seven Mr. Rhodes informed Mr. Venter that he had just received a telegram from the Hon. J. H. Hofmeijr to the effect that Stavie, my little son, was seriously ill. On being told the news, a cold shiver ran through me.

"How can that be?" I said; "only yesterday both Mr. Sauer and Mr. de Kock wired to me that my family were all well.—No! an accident must have happened, and my Stavie is dead!"

Immediately I wired to my wife, to Mr. Hofmeijr, and to our doctor, to telegraph in detail what had happened to the child, and to conceal nothing from me, whether he was alive or dead. The Governor, who deeply sympathised with me, kindly telegraphed to the authorities at Capetown to keep the wire open until my telegrams had been answered. Mr. Rhodes directed that the same should be done on his line; and at eight the latter placed into my hand the telegram that told me of Stavie's death and the particulars connected with it. The boy had, along with a little cousin of his, of his own age (a daughter of the Rev. W. A. Joubert), been pushed along in a hand-cart in childish play by his sister, a little older than himself. The declivity of the road being great, the cart soon began to run with a force the little girl could not control, till one of the wheels struck against a projecting stone on the side of the road, causing the vehicle to fly out of her weak hands and completely capsize. Little Rijkie Joubert arose, only having received a fright, but Stavie, with still a smile on his lips, lay a corpse. He had met with instantaneous death, his neck having evidently been broken by the fall. The shock this news gave me can only be imagined by a father in similar circumstances.

We left Palla's Camp in the morning of the 18th. In the afternoon Sir Henry tapped the telegraph wire and several telegrams were again received: I myself got four, all relating to my son's fatal accident and stating the arrangements that had been made for his burial. To think of going home would, of course, have been madness on my part; for, to do so, I should have been obliged to wait nine days at Palla's Camp for the earliest postcart, and to spend another twelve on an ox-waggon on the way to Mafeking.

As night approached we again outspanned on a bank of the Limpopo, and in the beautifully transparent water running over the clear drift sand we enjoyed a bath. The view from there over the endless woods and verdure was a sight most picturesque.

Thousands of sheep, goats and cattle from near and far came to drink water. The cattle looked particularly well, and one could hardly believe that scarcely any rain had fallen there during the previous eight months. The sheep, too, looked well; they must make a pretty picture in the rainy season when grass is at its best. The veld was dry, but vastly better than that along the Marico River in the Transvaal. No wonder, therefore, that Transvaalers always have had such an envious eye on Khama's country. Judging from the numerous herds of cattle and sheep that we continually met with on the borders of the Limpopo, Khama must be exceedingly rich. It is indeed to be regretted that whites cannot obtain farms there.

We passed the night at Brakpan—1150 miles from Capetown—and travelled the following day through dense forests. We were now some distance ahead of the Governor's party. On our way we noticed at a distance two koodoos grazing—a bull and a cow. Mr. Venter, who was the first to catch sight of them, seized his rifle, mounted his grey horse, and, followed by Pietje, our valet, rode towards the animals at a gallop. Having approached them sufficiently closely, he sprang from his horse and was about to fire, when Pietje, who had come on at full speed behind, rode over him. The horse trod upon Mr. Venter, knocked the gun out of his hand, and slightly bruised his shoulder.

The startled koodoos ran away at a short gallop and passed our carts at a distance of some 150 yards. Not wishing to spoil Mr. Venter's chance, I would not at first shoot at them from the cart, but Mr. Rhodes shouted, "Shoot at them! Shoot at them!" so I fired, the bullet striking the ground under the belly of one of them. Had I known that Mr. Venter had been ridden over by Pietje, I might have taken my time—might have got down from the cart, lain in ambush for the animals, and taken proper aim. Anyhow, I confess I should have made a better shot, and I feel ashamed of myself to think that I completely missed an animal as large as a mule at so short a range. Mr. Venter after the accident again pursued the koodoos for some distance, but had soon to give up the chase owing to the density of growth round about the spot. He was fairly out of humour on his return and felt strongly inclined to give Pietje a flogging, but the latter appeared in such a state of terror that he was let off with a scolding.

CHAPTER VI.

We arrive at Sofala—Journeying through a kloof—Too large a company has its drawbacks—Mr. Rhodes shows the strength of his resolution and gets drenched—The meeting with Khama—The chief's differences with the farmers—Khama's wife—Reflections on the country.

AT half-past seven we arrived at a place called Sofala, one of the prettiest places we had yet come to. The fig, the syringa and various other trees grew there luxuriantly: prettier trees one could hardly see. Densely covered with a grand foliage of a peculiar kind, those broad, lofty trees present a stately aspect. Sofala lies on the slope of a mountain from the one side of which there runs from a spring a stream of water large enough to supply a great city. The water issues from underneath a rock and with such force that it could easily set a large mill in rapid motion. But, as it is, it is allowed to run waste into a marshy vale, the surface of which is of a very spongy character. We observed that many Kafirs and Kafir women from the neighbourhood fetched their water from there. Close to the fountain itself, however, no one is allowed to dwell, for Khama reserves the place for his cattle. I was surprised that the chief did not construct a dam there, nor does it seem to have struck his subjects to do so. I am positive that ere long a village will be laid out there by white people.

From Sofala we journeyed through a long kloof with high hills on each side, the soil of which appeared capitally suited for agriculture. Thousands of bags of corn might be produced there annually. Here and there we noticed a Kafir woman on the hill-slopes digging in the soil to plant mealies. At noon we outspanned under a few thorn trees. The day was hot, and there was no water for our horses and mules. At half-past three we again inspanned, and at six we reached Mahapi, a large pan, green and pretty, but containing hardly any water—so little, that when we had satisfied ourselves we could barely quench the thirst of our horses and mules, and the poor animals of the Governor had to drink mud. It is on such occasions that the disadvantages attendant on travelling in large parties are most plainly evident.

We left Mahapi at five o'clock the following morning, and had to travel on a road both sandy and heavy. Mr. Rhodes, Mr. Lange and myself at first sat upon the cart, but the poor horses had to exert so much strength in pulling the vehicle along that the Premier and I got down and walked. It was a pretty forest we were going through, and amongst the trees we passed there were some literally decked in yellow flowers which yielded a sweet perfume much like that of the common garden violet. As the road afterwards became easier for the animals, Mr. Rhodes and I again got into the cart. The next place we stopped at was Malalola (or, the Vley, as some called it), a nice green spot over which a stream of clear water was running as strong almost as that at Sofala. The water ran into large pools, out of which our draught animals eagerly satisfied their thirst. The grassy valley abounded in different kinds of water birds, amongst them the snipe. Having all taken a bath in the cold water, which we extremely enjoyed, Mr. Rhodes began snipe hunting. He killed two; but how did he look when his sport was over? His suit was soaked with water from top to bottom, and besmeared with mud; but this was only another minor manifestation of that conspicuous characteristic of his of carrying out what he has set his mind upon, no matter at what cost.

At noon Khama, with a retinue of a hundred men on horseback, came out to meet us. The Premier, on noticing the approach of the chief, went to the telegraph where it had been tapped, and engaged himself in despatching wires. Meanwhile the High Commissioner received the black ruler with all honour and respect. At half-past one the horses were saddled and the Governor and his train rode with Khama to his town. We followed. The road thither was not one to boast of; it was full of stones, stumps and other obstacles, but at last we crossed a small *nek* and the great Kafir town of Palapye lay before us. It consisted of thousands of straw huts, but the trees in the town were so high that they concealed most of the dwellings from our view, and gave the place the aspect of a wilderness. In the centre there was a large open square. We could hardly at first sight believe that we were beholding a city of between 25,000 and 30,000 inhabitants. I was indeed surprised on closer inspection to see so many thousands of well-built huts together. These have all been erected within the previous eighteen months, their present occupants having formerly lived at Shoshong, which they abandoned owing, they say, to want of water and salubrity. Palapye, by virtue of its elevation, is a much healthier place than Shoshong, and it has its own running water, whilst at the latter place water had to be dug for. However, it may pretty safely be asserted that Khama would never have undertaken the *trek* to Palapye were it not that Palapye lay within the sphere of influence of the Chartered Company, and, consequently, under British protection. Before the Chartered Company had a hold on the land, Khama did not dare to move one mile nearer to Lobengula than he was; but now, under the shelter of the white man, he has been enabled to shorten the distance between Lobengula's capital and his own by seventy miles. He is, therefore, under obligation to the British, and particularly so to Mr. Rhodes.

We regretted to learn that, a few days previous to our coming, Khama had prohibited some Transvaal farmers, who had arrived there with waggons heavily loaded with corn, mealies, oatsheaves, etc., from selling to the British South African Company, and had ordered them immediately to quit his town under penalty of forfeiture of their produce. Khama had furthermore commanded Mr. Gifford not to buy anything from the farmers. If he did so, Khama would seize the purchased articles and drive the Company out of his land. No course was open but to obey, and the farmers with their full waggons and their thin oxen (for it was very dry just then) had to return whence they came. Mr. Rhodes, who was very annoyed on hearing this, asked Mr. Gifford the cause of Khama's attitude towards the farmers and the Company. Mr. Gifford ascribed it to the chief's hatred of the Boers, the reason assigned by Khama for which being that the farmers were in the habit of stealing a number of his cattle on their way home from his town—a tale which, of course, neither Mr. Rhodes nor Mr. Gifford would credit.

We could not get in the whole of Palapye sufficient forage to satisfy the wants of our comparatively few draught animals. The little there was had to be carefully and sparingly divided between Sir Henry's and our own well-deserving beasts—hence the reason why we so soon departed from the town. Sorely to be pitied must have been the cattle that visited Palapye shortly after our departure from it!

Indignant at Khama's conduct towards the farmers and dissatisfied with the meagre food our horses had received, I prophesied as we left the town that as sure as Khama lived his day of reckoning would come: only a little time more and his powers would be crippled, if not destroyed. Mr. Gifford repeated to the High Commissioner what he had told the Premier. What weight His Excellency attached to it I cannot tell; but this I know, the Prime Minister's intercourse with Khama was as conspicuously little as the Governor's was the contrary.

My personal estimation of the strength of the Bamangwato chief is that, as sure as twice two are four, two hundred and fifty Boers would be able to capture his stronghold, and clear every living soul out of it within the space of twenty-four hours. The Bamangwatos appeared to us a weak, miserable lot. One Boer would put a hundred of them to flight.

Palapye lies about 4500 feet above the level of the sea, and has therefore a pleasant climate. Khama dwells in a neat Kafir house, and has a passably decent, but uncomfortably fat, woman for a wife. He has a tall, slender, well-dressed and not bad-looking—as far as features go—son of twenty-one, who appears however not to be worth much; he looks a feeble good-for-nothing. Almost all Khama's people wear clothes.

At Palapye, where there is a telegraph and a post-office, I received about half-a-dozen telegrams from home. The offices are built after Kafir style, for Khama objects to having square houses on his land.

Palapye is 1185 miles from Capetown.

We left the Kafir city at a quarter to seven, Khama and his son conducting Sir Henry out of the town with a train of riders. The way wound over hills and dales, and was exceedingly stony and stumpy. After an hour's journey over the roots and rocks Khama ceremoniously bade the Governor, lords, majors, captains, colonels and lieutenants farewell. The comedy was then over, and we travelled comfortably on along an extensive and verdant valley on which we here and there observed a Kafir woman planting mealies. Through the middle of the valley runs the Lotsani River, on the bank of which we outspanned after having covered fifteen miles from Palapye. After breakfast we continued our travel up the side of the river until we reached Tjopong, a place situated on the slope of a mountain and rich in verdure. It resembled Sofala to some extent, and, like Sofala, was an admirable site for a village. From there we had an extensive view far over the picturesque Lotsani valley, a valley some twenty-five miles long and six broad. Its soil being as fertile as soil can be, thousands of people should be able to gain their living out of it. Of the excellence of the veld on every side of the valley the condition of the cattle that grazed upon it afforded ample proof. It is indeed a pity that land which might yearly produce thousands of bags of grain, potatoes, beans, mealies and various fruits should lie uncultivated. But I hope and expect that that tract of land, which is now the habitation of the riet-buck and the red-buck, the guinea-fowl, the water-fowl and the bittern, will in time—and in time not far distant—be occupied and tilled by the white sons of South Africa.

CHAPTER VII.

Leave Tjopong—We outspan and I go a-fishing—A man saved from drowning—A talk with Sir Henry Loch.

WE left Tjopong the following morning, and after crossing some hills, again outspanned on the banks of the Lotsani. The Premier's party was the first to arrive at the spot, and we selected our outspan place beneath the sheltering boughs of three large wild fig-trees near to which there was a very large natural pool of water abounding in various fish, if not also in crocodiles. The weather was rather oppressive, and so at half-past ten, while Tonie was getting our breakfast ready, we went to refresh ourselves in the pool close by; but, as we were wont to do in such strange waters, we were very careful not to go in too deep. After breakfast we began fishing, and the first fish I drew up was a barber, a creature as large as the "geelbek" (Cape salmon). Meanwhile the Governor had arrived with his party and outspanned not far from us. His reckless hussars very soon dashed into the water, and swam and dived without any regard to the probable presence of crocodiles there. I went on fishing. Dark clouds meanwhile gathered above my head and sent down some intermittent big drops. These were followed by a strange crashing noise in the air; I ran to our waggons, and Mr. Venter advised me to immediately get into one of them, for the noise I heard was the signal of the approach of a hailstorm. I obeyed, and hardly was I in the waggon when down came the hailstones, some as large as pigeon eggs. Fortunately it was only a small portion of the shower that passed over us, the main part falling some miles off.

When the bad weather was over I returned to the pool and found all my fish there still except the barber. I inquired after it, and discovered to my vexation that, after the barber had lain there for more than an hour, Pietje had taken it and repeatedly dipped its head in the water, with the consequence that it revived in strength and escaped from his hands into the pond. My fingers itched to box the fellow's ears, which I certainly would have done had he not outstripped me in the race that followed. I resumed fishing, but the air had been so chilled that the fish became too lazy to bite. Whilst still at my post, lamenting my loss, half-a-dozen hussars made their appearance at the pool, and, at the other end of it, jumped into the water. These men had arrived after the rest of the company, having been left in charge of the crippled and sore-backed horses.

Our boys were now busy inspanning the mules, and a fish was meanwhile cautiously biting at my hook. Mr. Lange had already called me twice, but I was determined to haul up the tantalising creature before I left. Some noise from the other end of the pond reached my ears, but I was too interested in my fishing to pay much heed to it, until I plainly heard that it was a cry for help. I ran up to the place where the hussars had been bathing and, as I approached it, perceived a man's hand stretched out of the water whilst his comrades on shore appeared in great consternation. In a moment I threw off my jacket, waistcoat and boots, and without further undressing myself, leaped into the water. The drowning man had then already sunk, but I swam to the spot where I had last caught sight of him, dived to the bottom, and chanced to strike his body. I grasped him by the arm and brought him up. As soon as I had his head up a large quantity of water belched from his mouth, but his colour was blue, his head as well as his arms hung slack, and, as he did not make the faintest motion, I naturally believed the man was dead. Holding him up by the left arm, I managed to keep his head above water, and so swam shorewards with him. Mr. Rhodes, Mr. Lange and Mr. Venter, who had suspected danger when they noticed me run to the spot where they knew the hussars had been bathing, now appeared on the scene. Mr. Venter threw his boots off and came to my assistance; and, together, we succeeded in bringing the man to the shore. I was then very fatigued, but felt pleased at having done my duty. The poor hussar revived in the hands of his comrades, recovered his senses, and soon was able to rise and walk away with the others, who all were now very quiet, and whose looks were mingled with joy and shyness.

Returning to the waggons, Mr. Rhodes made me take some whisky and soda to strengthen and refresh me.

The Premier, who had been afraid that the drowning man in his distress would seize hold of my arms and drown me along with himself, praised my conduct, but at the same time warned me to be very careful on such occasions. I should not, said he, in any case have entered the water with clothes on; for, had the distressed hussar in his terror caught hold of my braces or anything else that I had on, it could only have had one result—the drowning of both of us.

"But," said I, "I had no time to consider all this; and had I lingered a few seconds longer the fellow would have perished." Yet, I must confess that there is much truth in what Mr. Rhodes said, and it was a fortunate thing for me that I had not sooner become aware of the man's critical position than I did, when, as above stated, he had already by exertion become completely exhausted.

At two in the afternoon we started from there, and ended our day's journey in the evening at Brak River No. 1, where the water was bad and scarce, but sufficient for our horses. As for ourselves, we had no need to drink it, for we had brought with us from the Lotsani a plentiful supply in kegs and canvas bags.

The Governor, his aide-de-camp Captain Bower, and the military officers now came to me to express their appreciation at my manly conduct, as they called it, for having rescued the life of the hussar.

I asked them not to thank me. "I can swim," I said, "so it would have been cowardly conduct on my part to see a man struggling in the water for his life without going to his assistance. I have only done my duty."

CHAPTER VIII.

An adventure with a lion—The weather not what we expected—Mr. Rhodes reminds me of my grandfather—Sunday in the camp—Sir Henry goes out hunting, and Mr. Venter and I spend the morning tree measuring—We lose our way and meet some game which we fail to secure—The Premier the best sportsman.

CONTINUING our journey the following morning in chilly weather, we arrived and outspanned at Brak River No. 2. The river contains numerous deep pools, on the sides of which pretty shells were to be found. We met a handsome young Matabele there with a broad scar upon his back. The Prime Minister, who has a fluent command of the Zulu language, asked him how he had received that mark, and "Lion" was his answer. He then proceeded to relate his encounter with the king of animals. While hunting once with some of his comrades they met a lion, and, to overpower the animal, they surrounded it. Finding itself locked in on all sides, it rushed upon the Zulu (our informant) and with its paw tore a deep gash in his back. Fortunately for him, one of his fellow-sportsmen just then drove an assegai into the enraged animal, which thereupon abandoned the Zulu without using its teeth and fled; but they had not seen the last of it: the proud beast, to avenge its wound, returned with renewed fury and again attacked them. A long and desperate fight ensued between the young adventurous Kafirs and the animal-king, ending in the latter succumbing to exhaustion and the umerous assegai-wounds inflicted upon it—not, however, before it had torn to pieces some of the best dogs of the hunters and had injured several of the latter, among whom our informant came off worst.

From there we journeyed on to Mequeche, a pretty watering-place, where fine, fat, bastard sheep were to be seen grazing on the healthy veld.

The night was chilly and the sky covered with clouds, whilst a bitterly cold wind was furiously blowing. We expected heavy rains, but Mr. Venter, a clever weather-prophet, assured us that not a drop would fall, for the wind was too strong and cold, and his prediction proved correct. The Hon. J. H. Hofmeijr (M.L.A.) had told us before we left Capetown that we should prepare ourselves to meet with excessively hot weather in the region through which we were now travelling. He would have been more correct if he had warned us to do the contrary. We had now to walk in overcoats. I must add, however, that we were assured by the natives of the place that the low temperature we were meeting with was exceptional for the season of the year.

Our course next morning was through a rather dense wood and in a path full of stumps of hewn-down trees, a source of considerable inconvenience to us, our cart suffering repeated shocks. We were now far in advance of Sir Henry. At half-past nine we outspanned on the grassy border of the little Parkwe River, kindled a large fire, and seated ourselves around it. I was forcibly reminded, in the picture Mr. Rhodes presented sitting on his little chair by the fireside, of my departed grandfather, who was wont in the winter evenings to sit before his hearth and warm his hands over the fire.

The Parkwe valley has a very rich soil. The low-lying plains round about are pretty densely inhabited and the hills beautifully adorned with trees. There is a small station at Parkwe. We outspanned not far from it, and close also to some large crematart trees. We measured the trunks of three by means of a tape-line given us by Sir Sidney Shippard. They measured respectively 45, 46, and 47 feet in circumference, and Lord Elphinstone was so much taken up with their appearance that he took a sketch of them.

It was Sunday and all was quiet in the camp. As evening approached a pile of wood was collected for the making of a "bonfire"—as the hussars called it—when darkness set in. At half-past eight the fire was made, and all the camp was lit up by it. The delightful warmth it afforded us was exceedingly appreciated, for the weather was very cold. All seated themselves around the fire—some on chairs, some on footstools, some on benches, and others on the bare ground. The singing of sacred hymns followed, and it was glorious music to listen to in that lonesome wild, 1286 miles from Capetown. That grand psalm, "Psalm 100," especially, sung by the attendants of the waggons and by those of us who understood Dutch, could not but touch our feelings—mine in particular, for my lost sweet child, who had then just been a week in his grave, was constantly present in my mind.

The following day brought no change in the temperature. Heavy clouds still overhung the sky, this making the third successive day that the sun had been hidden from our view.

Sir Henry Loch and all his party went out hunting. So also did Mr. Rhodes shortly afterwards, but in a different direction. Mr. Venter, Mr. Lange and I remained at the camp. Sir Henry's action did not altogether please us. The weather was fine for travelling; we had a long journey still before us; and here we were detained for the pleasure of His Excellency, who, of course, would again shoot as little game as he did at Palla's Camp and at the Lotsani. At the latter place his hunt lasted half a day, and at the former a whole one. Anyway, we had to be content, for without the Governor we could not proceed; and, if we could, we would have been obliged to wait for him at Macloutsie.

After breakfast Mr. Venter and I, having nothing else to do, also decided to go out hunting. We walked through the river and came out upon a plain as level as a table and thickly grown with large trees, under which numerous footprints of various kinds of bucks were to be seen. We walked on till we came to a high elevation which we mounted, and from there we had a distinct view of our camp. At the foot of the hill stood some huge baobab or crematart trees, and beyond, as far as our eyes carried us, there was nothing but one vast, endless forest. We descended the hill and went to take the measure of the baobabs.

The circumference of the trunk of one of them was fifty-three feet, and that of another (six feet from the ground) sixty-five. These were the largest trees we had thus far met with. Fancy a trunk with a diameter of twenty-two feet!

Some distance farther we met the two special reporters for the *Cape Argus*, along with the heliograph signalman. One of the three had clambered up a baobab tree to pick some of its fruit, but found the difficulty of making his way down greater than he had foreseen. It was amusing to watch the anxiety the poor fellow was in. The four of us beneath the tree stood ready to catch him should he tumble—a thing that appeared very probable. However, he landed safely on the ground. We each took some of the fruit with us, the reporters and their associate returning to the heliograph hill. Mr. Venter and I again made for the camp, but, after having walked about two hours without reaching the banks of the Parkwe, we discovered to our dismay that we had lost our way. We turned back to another hill, and from the top of it we could see our waggons at a distance, as also a large herd of oxen and goats near us making their way towards the river. We descended the hill, entered the footpaths of these animals, and followed their direction. On the way we met the tutor of Sir Henry's son, who, like ourselves, had missed his way. We also came across three red-bucks of the size of donkeys, but, the growth there being rather dense, they disappeared from our sight before we could fire at them. At length, warm and weary, after having wandered about in the forest fully six hours, to our great relief we reached the camp, and spent the rest of the afternoon resting in a waggon.

Towards sunset the Governor and his party returned from their hunt. Sir Frederick Carrington had shot a steenbuck, and that was the only game the party was able to bring home with them. Sir Henry Loch and his son, I was told, had fired several shots at koodoos (antelopes of the size of young cows), and kwaggas (striped animals resembling the zebra), but all without success.

It became late, and Mr. Rhodes and his two companions were still out. We felt rather uneasy about them and resolved to kindle a large fire when it grew darker, on a hill close by; but before there was any necessity for it the three turned up, bringing with them eight pheasants and two korhaans. Tonie had meanwhile prepared an excellent dinner, and the hungry Prime Minister and his tired companions had no scant share of it.

We did not see the Governor that evening, either because (I suppose) he felt fatigued and was lying on his couch, or because he was out of sorts at not having shot anything that day, and did not feel in the humour for company.

CHAPTER IX.

"The place of death"—Macloutsie—Though man proposes, God disposes—A review of the British Bechuana police—Telegraph facilities—A separation which Sir Henry Loch disapproves—Mr. Rhodes wishes to see Mashonaland, and we go forward.

LEAVING Parkwe on the morning of the 28th of the month, we again passed over veld of a good kind well grown with trees, and the next place we stopped at was the Marapong River. "Marapong" signifies "the place of death." This name was given to the river owing to the terrible fevers that once upon a time used to rage there and the many lives they carried off. The river is broad and deep and must be very strong when full.

At half-past ten we came to Macloutsie, a large camp, where three hundred of the British Bechuanaland police and one hundred of the British South Africa Company were stationed. By these men we were well received, and were provided with everything we needed except drink. It surprised me to find so well built a camp in that wild part of the world, considering that the station was then only half a year old. It had a neat hospital under a galvanised roof, and amongst the few patients in it was a son of Lord Elphinstone, who had come along with Sir Henry. I need not say that the father was exceedingly happy to see his son, as also the son his father. The young man had been sent to that dark corner of the globe some months before to serve in the Army, to gather knowledge of the region, to gain distinction—in short, with much the same objects as induced the widow of Napoleon III. to send her son, the Prince Imperial, to Zululand in 1879, namely, of acquiring reputation and then to return with honour to his mother country. It had been expected that war would arise with the Matabele, and that the young son of Lord Elphinstone would thus have an opportunity of distinguishing himself, and I fully agree with those aristocrats who think it better to make their children useful for the world than let them be idle; but then, "Though man proposes, God disposes." And, just as the youthful Prince Napoleon had found his grave in the wilds of South Africa, so I feared it would fare with the nobleman's son. However, the young man appeared rapidly to regain his strength after our arrival, and the "sisters" who nursed him cherished the expectation of his speedy recovery.

There was plenty of water at the camp both for man and beast, the Macloutsie River flowing not far from here.

The following day the Governor and the Premier held a review of the troops, who were in excellent form. Young, healthy, vigorous men all of them were. In fact, they made such a good impression on me that I thought it would be a pity if they were not given a chance to measure their strength with the Matabele-

After the review His Excellency delivered an eloquent speech, which every listener heartily applauded.

I was surprised to see so many Africanders amongst the troops of the Chartered Company—there were as many, I think, as British—and it gave me pleasure to find them all cheerful and in the best of spirits. True, there had been a few rare cases of fever at Macloutsie, but hitherto no deaths owing to that disease.

After the delivery of Sir Henry's address we visited the fort, a strong solid piece of work defended on all sides by Gatling guns, from which a thousand shots could be fired within the space of thirty minutes. Macloutsie also enjoyed the privilege of a post and telegraph office.

Young Elphinstone was much better the following morning, and the delighted father began making arrangements to take him to the Cape, and thence to England.

The distance between Macloutsie and Capetown is 1,302 miles. Up to there the telegraph wire had followed us, and a telegram could be sent from either terminus to the other end and be answered all within half-an-hour. Who will still dare say that Southern Africa does not advance with rapid strides? The Macloutsie Camp stands about 2,300 feet above the sea-level, and, therefore, more than a thousand feet lower than Palapye. However, the spot is healthy and has been well chosen.

Up to Macloutsie, the disputed boundary between Khama's and Lobengula's countries, the parties of the Governor and the Premier had been travelling together, but they were now going to separate; the latter wished to extend his trip northwards, whilst the former was going to turn. Sir Henry expressed great dissatisfaction at Mr. Rhodes's resolve, but ultimately assented to his proceeding up to Tuli Camp—about another seventy miles—but not a yard farther.

The reason of this reluctance of the High Commissioner lay in the fact that he had received earnest warnings from Buluwayo, Lobengula's capital, from Mr. Moffat and others, to the effect that the young blood of the Matabele yearned for war, would no longer be controlled by their king, and would certainly capture the "Kozi Mali" (man of money) if they got the opportunity; and that, therefore, it was extremely inadvisable for the Premier to penetrate into the Matabele country. Besides, it would be an insult to His Black Majesty if Mr. Rhodes travelled through his land without visiting his capital. On the other hand, should he visit that town, the chances were ten to one that Lobengula would take him prisoner merely to please his people, if for no other reason. The Governor added that, should Mr. Rhodes be captured, he, as High Commissioner for the colony of which Mr. Rhodes was Prime Minister, would be bound to come to the rescue; and what unpleasantness, which might easily have been avoided, would be created! War would be the probable outcome, and it might cost millions to carry it out. "Remember," Sir Henry reminded him, "you are not Mr. Rhodes alone, but also the Prime Minister of the Cape Colony." Sir Frederick Carrington, Sir Sidney Shippard and Captain Bower endorsed the Governor's words.

Mr. Rhodes courteously replied that the object of his journey was not to see Bechuanaland and Khama's land, but Mashonaland; he was standing on the border, he said, of the British Protectorate, but wanted to cross over to his own protectorate; and his fellow-travellers, he added, had come for the same purpose as himself. He therefore hoped it would not be taken amiss if he did not return then and there with the Governor's party. Having done with Mr. Rhodes, Sir Henry sent for Mr. Venter and myself. With us, too, as he had done also at Palapye, he spoke long and seriously on the situation, earnestly requesting us to consider and alter our plans, laying before us the several dangers we would otherwise incur, and asking us to use our influence in inducing the Premier to abandon his project of carrying his journey farther than Tuli Camp.

"You would run the risk," said he, "of being made the prisoners of Lobengula and locked up in Buluwayo; of being attacked and murdered at Mount Hampden; and of being detained by swollen rivers, which would give the Matabele ample opportunity of disposing of you at their will."

These words carried some weight with them, but we remained firm in our resolve, for it would indeed have been folly on our part to turn back after having nearly reached the border of the country we had come to see.

"But," said we, "if your Excellency is of opinion, and Mr. Rhodes agrees with it, that it is better for Mr. Rhodes not to prolong his tour, let him halt and turn at Tuli, while we take a waggon and some of the stronger mules and enter Mashonaland."

"Yes," replied Sir Henry; "but that is not what Mr. Rhodes would like to see. If you extend the journey, he will not stay behind."

But the Governor's endeavours to persuade us to change our mind were exercised in vain, and with some degree of mutual dissatisfaction the meeting ended.

We thought that the sooner we left the camp the better; so we had our waggons inspanned towards evening, and a little after sunset we drove off, leaving the Premier, who promised to follow us the next morning, behind.

CHAPTER X.

A dark night, and a recalcitrant driver—We find we have an invalid in the company—We go on and pass through a country deserted through fear of Lobengula—A letter of warning from the Governor.

THE road leading from the camp was in a deplorable condition, and, as darkness was setting in, we could only move forward slowly and cautiously. It soon became so dark that we could hardly see the way. Mr. Venter and I mounted our horses and rode in front of the waggons, two of the Chartered Company's police directing us. The waggons and their inmates had no pleasant time of it, as they had to endure shock after shock through the brokenness of the road. With Mr. Lange's approval, we outspanned sooner than we had at first intended, for our patience at such travelling was beginning to give way.

On rising next morning we found that we had outspanned in front of some dangerous ditches, and that we had thus been fortunate in halting where we did. To return to the previous night: shortly after we had unteamed the animals, we noticed that George, one of the drivers, was more talkative than usual, so much so that no further indication of his being under the influence of Bacchus was necessary; he must have been drinking at Macloutsie. Mr. Lange advised him to hold his tongue, but that only made him worse; he became impertinent and threatened to leave the party.

"Well, go if you like!" said Mr. Lange.

George took his bag and all he had and made his way back to Macloutsie. Arrived there, he complained to Mr. Rhodes that Mr. Lange had ill-treated him. The Premier, however, paid no attention to his tale, and George thought it best to forget the matter and return to the waggons in Mr. Rhodes' cart. But the poor fellow had to discover to his regret that he had cheated himself, for the Premier next morning refused him a seat in the cart, and there was no other means by which he could again overtake the waggons —and this was the last we heard of George. He probably returned to Palapye, where he had a wife (a native of Genadendal), who had been brought up by Mr. Moffat at Buluwayo.

During the night Mr. Venter complained of somewhat serious indisposition, so we decided next morning to send for the doctor at Macloutsie before we again proceeded on our journey. We despatched Hackwell, one of the police, for the purpose, and not long afterwards the military doctor arrived in company with Mr. Rhodes. The patient was carefully examined, but nothing was found wrong with him except that his stomach was a little disordered, and that was quickly remedied by a few pills.

Mr. Rhodes returned with the physician to Macloutsie, and we shortly afterwards crossed the Macloutsie River, the banks of which were adorned with the palm and the wild date. Twelve miles further we rested at the Lotsani River, and there awaited Mr. Rhodes.

The latter had met Colonel Pennyfather (who had come from Mount Hampden) at Macloutsie the night we left it, and the Premier had much to communicate to his friend and some business to transact with him—hence the delay. He promised to leave Macloutsie at night time with the rise of the moon, and overtake us.

During the day we went out hunting and shot some pheasants and partridges, but we took care not to go too far from the waggons, for fear of losing our way. During the hunt we came across some desolate Kafir kraals, abandoned probably on account of their dangerous situation. All about these places shells of wild dates and seeds of various fruits were to be seen on the ground. Amongst the animals inhabiting that part of the country are the lion, the wolf, the ape, the koodoo, the kwagga, and the wild dog. But though we saw the traces of most of these animals, we did not leave our waggons sufficiently far to chase any of them.

We were now travelling on the disputed territory between Macloutsie and Tuli, a beautiful piece of country with many streams flowing through it. No one owns it and very few live in it. It is the country where Lobengula so unexpectedly once fell upon Khama's Kafirs, slew the men, and carried off their wives and children. No wonder, therefore, that we passed so many kraals destitute of people.

As intended, Mr. Rhodes left Macloutsie at half-past twelve at night, as the moon lifted its head above the horizon. But before he started he had to suffer some annoyance at the hands of Anthony, the coachman, who was not at his post when the cart had to be inspanned, notwithstanding the repeated injunctions he had received the previous evening. Anthony had evidently been making some friends at Macloutsie, with whom he enjoyed himself longer than his duty allowed. Mr. Rhodes, however, did not take much trouble to find him, and filled his place by one of the police of the Company, Malherbe by name—whose parents, by the way, lived near Capetown—and in the morning early he and Colonel Pennyfather arrived at the waggons. Shortly afterwards we again moved on.

The Prime Minister and the Colonel were tired and sleepy, and so laid themselves down in a waggon for a nap; but, before doing so, Mr. Rhodes handed Mr. Venter and myself a letter he had received from Sir Henry Loch, which he wanted us to peruse and consider. Its contents were a repetition of the warnings given us by the Governor before we left him. Mr. Venter and I read the letter and read it again, with all due deliberation; and we agreed to propose to Mr. Rhodes, at the next halting-place, that the party should resolve nothing until they arrived at Tuli, and there make their final decision, but that we—Mr. Venter and myself—should be at all events allowed to continue the journey if we should choose to do so.

Our next outspan-place was at a lovely stream. By that time both the Premier and the Colonel had waked from their morning sleep, and the first thing the former asked for was the conclusion to which we had come about the letter. We told him our mind, and he accepted the suggestion.

Our course again wended through veld rich in grass, wood and water.

CHAPTER XI.

We arrive at the Tuli River—Other tourists there besides ourselves—Our ideas considered impracticable—Mr. Rhodes gives up his project with regret—The story of a brave lion-hunter.

On Saturday morning, the 1st of November, we found ourselves close to the picturesque Tuli or Shashi River. Not many days previously the river had been so dry that it contained only small pools of standing water here and there; but now, due to the rain that had fallen two days before, it was converted into a roaring current. We could hardly believe our eyes when we saw so strong a stream in so comparatively dry a country. Not far from the river stands the Tuli Camp, situated on a hill about 2000 feet above the sea-level, and therefore lower than the camp at Macloutsie. It is a pretty and well-fortified camp, plentifully supplied with cannon and ammunition. The police, numbering about two hundred, were in as good a condition, as strong and healthy, as might have been desired.

We were now on the northern border of the disputed territory and 1370 miles from Capetown. The fort was provided, on a small scale, with shops, smithies, and a church.

We made the acquaintance there of Captain Turner, a very amiable and good-natured gentleman.

We took a bath in the Tuli and enjoyed it immensely. The water was as clear as crystal. The banks of the river were covered with beautiful trees, the wild fig being the most prominent; some of them measured round the trunk between 45 and 50 feet. From shore to shore the Tuli has a width of from 600 to 700 yards, but during the rainy season it frequently happened that the river overflowed, and then it was half-a-dozen times as wide—in fact, there have been times when the river in some parts has had a breadth of three miles.

Not far from us some Boer waggons were outspanned. Mr. Venter and I went to them and made the acquaintance of the people; they were farmers from the Zoutspansberg District who had come to sell their produce at the camp, for which, they said, they always received good value, and the members of the camp always treated them with courtesy and kindness. On this occasion, for instance, they told us, Captain Turner had been so pleased to see the waggons approaching that he immediately sent a team of eight oxen to the assistance of each waggon, for he was afraid that the tired oxen of the farmers would be unable to draw the waggons through the stream. At this action of the Captain the farmers were as much pleased as surprised, the more so because they had nothing to pay for it. They spoke very highly in praise of all the Englishmen at the camp, avowing they had never in their lives met kinder people.

They had received a cheque from Captain Turner payable at the Standard Bank, Pietersburg, but, not being used to paper money, they asked whether that mode of payment was all right. We assured them it was, and told them it was better to have their money paid in cheques than in coin, for the former could be more safely and conveniently carried; at Pietersburg they would receive every penny of the sum stated on the cheque. They thanked us for the assurance. Some of them, I may mention — of whom Messrs. Visser, Du Preez, and Van Aarde were the ones we most conversed with — belonged to the *voortrekkers* (i.e. earliest emigrants) to Zoutpansberg, where they earned their living chiefly by hunting and by dealing in ivory, feathers, hides, etc. They also were well acquainted with Mashonaland, for they had spent much of their life there in hunting. They supplied us with detailed information on the nature of the country and its separate divisions, and, hearing their account of the fertility and the grandeur of the land, we could not but feel inclined to become Mashonalanders ourselves. Our informants were extremely desirous to fix their permanent abode in that land, but for fear of the Matabele shrank from doing so.

"How is it then that you are not afraid to hunt there?" we asked.

"Because," was the reply, "Lobengula gave us the permission. We may shoot any game except hippopotami, for these are looked upon by the Matabele as sacred animals; but live in the country we dare not. But if Mr. Rhodes conquers the Matabele and makes them subservient to the white man, we will all move to that land." It was to be lamented, they said, that so savage a race should have the almost exclusive enjoyment of so beautiful a land: God certainly could not have intended that region for those barbarians.

They wished a quarrel would break out between Mr. Rhodes and Lobengula, and were prepared to stand by the former.

"But then," one of us interrupted, "what is to become of Lobengula and his tribe in the event of his defeat?"

"Become the white man's subjects. Or, Lobengula can take his tribe across the Zambesi, and possess land there, whilst we take in Matabeleland. This should have been done long ago!"

"And what do you think," we asked, changing the topic, "of our travelling on to Mount Hampden? Shall we be able to return before the rivers get full?"

"Oh no, never!" they unanimously replied, somewhat astonished at the question. They thought it folly on our part to think of doing such a thing, as the Lundi was already swelling, and was too high for waggons to pass through it; but even if we were able to cross it now, it would be wholly impassable by the time we wanted to return, and we would be obliged to stop at the river for months. They told us of a farmer who, on his way home from Mashonaland, arrived at the Lundi and found it too high to cross over, so he had to wait there from December till May, when at last the river became passable. Beside the Lundi there were other rivers which we would not be able to get across during the rainy season; for example, there was the Tukwi and Lotsani.

F

"So you think," asked Mr. Venter, "it is utterly impossible for us to proceed to Mount Hampden and be back by the end of November?"

They laughed. "If you say 'end of March,'" replied one of them, "there is some possibility of your achieving it, but 'end of November'!—that's quite out' of the question. And, you must bear in mind, that if you stop long on the banks of a swollen river you will certainly catch fever. No! don't think of going deeper inland! Make this your turning-point and avail yourselves of your spare time in hunting, and see whether you can achieve the honour of shooting some of those fierce lions round about here!"

We invited the farmers to our waggons, and there we drank to each other's health, after which they returned to their waggons. Mr. Venter and I after some deliberation determined to follow the counsel received from the Boers and to inform Mr. Rhodes of it. It proved a blessing—as events will show—that we had met those men.

After supper, as Mr. Rhodes was quietly enjoying a cigarette and the rest of the party their pipes, my friend and I submitted to the Premier the final decision to which we had come. Mr. Rhodes, after listening with keen interest to what we told him, expressed his appreciation of the information and advice the Boers had given us, and thanked us for having consulted them. He fully agreed with us, and added that he had received similar warning from the men in the fort. Colonel Pennyfather also, though he disliked interfering with our programme, expressed his conviction that if we travelled farther inland our road back would be blocked by both the Lundi and the Tuli, perhaps also by the Macloutsie, Lotsani and other smaller rivers. In the face of such information, the Premier acknowledged that it would be an act of wanton folly on our part to shut our ears to the advice given us.

"It is true," said he with a sigh, "our horses and mules are fat and strong; we, healthy and in sound spirits; our provisions more than enough,—and it is most disappointing, after having travelled nearly fourteen hundred miles and reached a spot within four hundred miles of our destination" (eight days' further journey), "to be compelled to turn back; but no other course is open to us than to do as we have been advised by Sir Henry Loch, Sir Frederick Carrington, Colonel Pennyfather and the experienced Boers. Thus, good friends, I am decidedly at one with you. We turn here, we cross the Shashi and the Crocodile, we travel down the Transvaal *viâ* the Blauwbergen and Zoutpansbergen, pay Oom Paul a visit, and return to Capetown."

So said, so done. The hope of seeing Fort Salisbury and the Zimbabe ruins was abandoned. We left Fort Tuli on the 2nd of November, crossed the magnificent Shashi, and travelled through an extensive, picturesque and most fertile valley abounding with the palm, the date and the wild fig, and forming part of the disputed territory between Khama and Lobengula. We crossed the Tuli once more; here it was some thousands of yards in breadth, and its shores were densely covered with trees and shrubs of various sizes and descriptions, which indicated the presence of wild animals.

We were now near to the spot where, a month previously, an old gentleman, a Mr. Vivier—called by some Bebeyee—was killed by a lion. The veteran adventurer had met three lions. Two of them he succeeded in shooting dead; the third he mortally wounded, but before he could again mount his horse the infuriated injured animal was upon him, threw him to the ground, and revenged itself as much as its dying condition allowed it. Its strength exhausted from loss of blood, the fierce animal fainted and died. The well-known huntsman rose, but his limbs were so mangled that he could not get upon his horse again. He was lifted on it by some fellow-hunters who had arrived at the scene, and was brought home and attended to, but the following day he died. Thus the expert sportsman, who had lived to see his seventieth year, fell a victim to one of those ferocious animals of which he had killed dozens, and of which he had always been considered a particularly skilful hunter. The skin and teeth of that lion are kept in the camp at Tuli.

Towards evening we outspanned on the southern border of the Tuli. We thought of bathing in the river, but its bank was so rough and craggy, and so many footprints of wild animals were to be noticed on the soil, that we gave up our intention.

CHAPTER XII.

A bad night—Solomon fears he is going to die—Traces of hyænas and snakes—We come to an African paradise!—Mr. Venter and I go in search of milk, and are nearly torn to pieces—We cross the Crocodile, and have an interview with Mr. Greeff—A proposed big hunt.

I DID not spend a pleasant time in the dell in which we slept that night. All seemed to suffer restlessness, and Solomon, one of our rein-holders, groaned loudly. He had before complained of pains in his chest and other parts of his body, and had subsequently neglected to take the necessary precautions: he had, for instance, more than once gone to swim in the cold waters of the Tuli when he should have kept his body warm. The result of this was that he caught a severe cold. Having pity on the fellow, I got up, went to him and felt his pulse, which beat rapidly. His forehead, too, throbbed badly, and he complained piteously of backache and pains throughout his body. It touched my feelings when the poor fellow, a very decent and truly obedient boy, and one for whom I always had a great liking, looked with an expression of anguish into my eyes and said, in a broken tone:

"Dear master, must I die in this wild land?"

Deeply did I sympathise with him, but I told him

not to feel melancholy and fret about his illness, else he would certainly die, but that he should keep up his spirits. Mr. Venter, who had also meanwhile left his couch, brought the patient some medicine; and we rolled him tightly in blankets so that he might perspire well. Nevertheless, we were much afraid that we would lose Solomon, and we could ill afford that, not only because he had always proved a faithful and competent servant, but because we had already lost two of our boys, Anthony and George. The following morning, however, Solomon felt better, though still far from right. We placed him in waggon No. 3, and again covered him up well.

But Solomon's sickness was not the only anxiety we had to suffer that night. Our dog was continually barking, and the cause of it we found out in the morning to have been the presence of hyænas near our waggons; their freshly-made footprints indicated it. We also discovered that we had outspanned in a narrow basin-shaped dell surrounded by high, dry hills (hence the depressing heat during the night), and one which during summer must be exceedingly marshy, judging from the black mud-soil with its deep cracks, in which doubtless hundreds of snakes had their abode. All of us felt somewhat indisposed that morning, a proof of the unwholesomeness of the close air in the vale. And were it not particularly dry just then, I have no doubt more than one of us would have caught fever. One must be very careful when travelling in that country as to the places he selects to sleep at; it is always safest to choose the open veld.

Continuing the journey, we passed through a truly

lovely tract of country. The fine rivers and valleys we had to cross; the trees and shrubs on each side, with the birds singing behind their leafy screens, and with the pheasants on the ground under them; the exquisite beauty of the scenery around us—these, combined with the glorious weather we were enjoying that morning, rendered the country a paradise. We met several troops of birds on the wing, of which Mr. Rhodes shot a few and I one. Water was plentiful. Now and then we passed a straw hut occupied by the most savage Kafirs. Perhaps, however, we misjudged them—perhaps it was only temporary terror caused by our presence that made them appear so savage, for the reader must remember that we were still travelling in lawless " No-man's-land," the disputed territory.

At evening we outspanned on the side of a small stream, where Captain Turner overtook us; he was to accompany us to the Limpopo, where we intended to have a big hunt.

At five the following morning we set out again, our way carrying us through valleys covered with tall grass, and with such trees as the palm, the wild cocoa-nut, etc. We could not help admiring the land and regretting that, through dread of Lobengula, it should be uninhabited. During the whole of the day we saw only one hut; and that hut, to be concealed from view, was built under the cover of some large trees. It was a big and neatly-built straw house, and in front of it there stood a strongly fenced kraal with a number of oxen and milch-cows in it. Mr. Venter and I went to the hut to ask for milk, but no sooner had we arrived there when, as if at a given signal, a troop of dogs rushed out towards us, and we had to take to our heels and run as if a demon were behind us.

Mr. Rhodes had meanwhile been shooting pheasants. When he returned he asked us for some of the milk we had gone to fetch.

"What—milk!" I said. "Rather congratulate us on still being alive! Upon my word, if we had not run as though seven evil spirits were at our heels, torn to pieces we certainly would have been by that dog regiment!" Mr. Rhodes did not ask us for milk again.

Leaving the dog fort, we crossed the majestic Crocodile at seven, and outspanned on the other side of it—*i.e.*, on the Transvaal side. The river there presents a peculiarly romantic picture, is about three hundred yards wide, and runs very deep. Its banks are covered with stately trees and jungle extending about a mile in width. Clear white drift-sand covers the bottom of the pure, transparent water: and the branches of the bordering trees overhang the river's banks with such symmetry of form as to make it difficult for the eye-witness to imagine that man's hand had not there come to nature's assistance.

Judging from the marks in the sand on the river's sides, thousands of animals must have their home in the adjoining woods, lions not excluded, for their footprints also were to be observed. Large birds resembling young ostriches were also to be seen there.

Not long after our arrival on the Boer border, Captain Turner visited the waggons of Mr. Greeff and Mr. Leah, which had been outspanned a short distance from our own, and shortly afterwards he returned with the above-mentioned gentlemen, both of whom made a good impression on us. They had considerable knowledge of both Mashonaland and Matabeleland: Mr. Greeff had spent fifteen years of his life in the neighbourhood of Buluwayo. He asserted that the veld stretching for more than two hundred miles towards the Zambesi, from the Matabele capital, was beautifully adapted for cattle and sheep. Mashonaland he described in a word as grand; he was burning with the desire to live there, and he said to Mr. Rhodes in my presence:

"Take my word! if you want men to-morrow to clear that land of the pest that now governs it, my son-in-law and myself will be at your service, and we shall get another hundred of our Boers to join us; and, believe me, those Doppers who live in Zoutpansberg, Blauwberg and Waterberg, never miss a shot: three of them are a match for three hundred Kafirs. All that we desire of you is to grant us farms and not to stop us when we fight with the natives. If you agree to that, Lobengula's glory will soon be past."

Mr. Greeff spoke so earnestly and so dramatically, that our Premier could not keep from laughing.

"Yes, Mr. Greeff," answered Mr. Rhodes, "I shall certainly some day be pressed to do as you want me to do, but you must remember that I have only the right to dig gold in that land; so long, therefore, as the Matabele do not molest my people, I cannot declare war against them and deprive them of their country, but as soon as they interfere with our rights I shall end their game; I shall then ask your aid, and be very glad to get it, and when all is over I shall grant farms to those who assisted me."

"Yes, that is right," replied the Boer with a nod.

"But," added the representative of the Chartered Company, "nothing prevents you to trek into the land *now*. If you wish it, I will give you a permit to dig for gold there and to choose a farm for yourself to live upon, cultivate and keep stock upon. And your farm will always remain yours, whether the Matabele fight or not, and it is sure to become more and more valuable as the white population in the land increases."

At this announcement the two visitors appeared exceedingly pleased. Mr. Greeff terminated the discourse on that subject—

"Well, Mr. Rhodes, you may depend upon it, next March, when the rainy season will be over, I will trek to that country with all I have, and I will get many others to go with me."

We next busied ourselves in discussing the arrangements to be made for the "big hunt" we had so long been looking forward to. Mr. Greeff, after attentively listening to the conversation, remarked that our programme was not a bad one, but that he could suggest a better. He said that his son-in-law and he had decided to go out hunting the day after for three days. They intended to take with them an open cart drawn by oxen for carrying the necessary provisions and the game to be shot. In addition to that, they would take with them four Kafirs, with as many mules, to convey the meat which could not go on the cart. The course they would take would be down by the side of the Crocodile until they reached certain large but shallow pools, in which they were sure to find hippopotami as well as crocodiles. He was certain also that they would meet on their way such animals as lions, tigers, leopards, kwaggas, koodoos, blesbucks, elks, striped-bucks, etc. "Come with us!" he concluded, "and you will spend a most enjoyable time."

"Yes," said I, "your proposal is good, but suppose, whilst we are out on the hunt one of our horses fails—say mine fails or lags behind and causes me to lose sight of you—a thing not at all unlikely—for my pony is but a lazy beast—what then?"

"Ah, well," responded Mr. Greeff, "you will have to wait at the spot where you last lost sight of us till we return on the footmarks of our animals and find you."

"No! old friend," said I, "that will never do."

"Well," he said, "if you don't wait where you are when you lose sight of us, you will lose your way altogether, and, as true as the sun shines, no trace of you will ever be seen again."

We looked into each other's eyes with a smile and felt all but inspired with zeal for our enthusiastic friend's proposed three days' hunt. We did not at once refuse the invitation, but promised to consider it; and we decided, at the same time, to join in a short chase in the afternoon.

CHAPTER XIII.

We divide our forces—The prospect of a delicious supper—I meet with some curious wild animals—An interview with crocodiles—The return of our hunters—An adventure with a tiger—Mr. Greeff tells an exciting story.

WHEN the time arrived the company divided itself into two parts; Mr. Venter, Mr. Leah and myself forming the one, and Mr. Rhodes, Colonel Pennyfeather and Captain Turner the other, the former to hunt bucks and other of the larger game, the latter to shoot birds and such of the smaller game as they should come across. A third party, consisting of Messrs. du Preez, Visser, van Aarde and Joubert, who had also outspanned not far from us, went out hunting. Each party chose a different direction.

We had not left our waggons long when koodoos came within sight. We now began to ride with greater speed; but Blauwbok, Mr. Venter's horse, became crippled and could not keep pace with the rest. I gave my disappointed friend my own horse and took his. At a slow pace I then followed the rest of the party. Shot upon shot was soon to be heard, and I thought in pleased anticipation of the delicious meal I was going to eat in the evening. Dimly I could also hear the shots fired by the other parties. But I now began to find that the longer my sickly jade carried me the farther it lagged behind. The prospect of getting lost in the woods was not a very pleasant one, and so, without much hesitation, I resolved to turn back. Following on the traces of our horses in the direction from which they had come, I reached, after spending some time and trouble, the faint little footpath out of which we had deviated. I now felt at ease, and continued in the path through the woods up the side of the stream. On my way, at a distance of about a hundred yards from me, my eyes fell upon some strange wild animals standing as still as mice; their large ears stood erect to catch the faintest noise I made, whilst their eyes were fixed on me. I could not make out what kind of animal they were. Without dismounting I fired a shot at them, but without effect, the bullet striking the dust in front of them. The creatures did not move. Again I fired, but again I missed—and away ran the wild hogs into the woods! A little farther on I met a troop of small apes. The inquisitive little creatures could not take their eyes off me. They scanned me from top to toe with an expression of "What *can* it be?" I felt inclined to shoot one of them, but I had not the heart to do it, for they looked too much like human beings; in fact, I could not see much difference between them and Bushmen. I therefore left them unmolested.

Arrived at the waggons, I got Mr. Lange to join me in a swim in the river. He warned me not to go deep into the water, but I paid no attention to what he said, for I did not think that there was any danger to fear;

but no sooner had I thrown myself flat to swim when there was a loud splash in the water not far from me; it was caused by two crocodiles that had leaped in from the shore. A cold thrill ran through my body. I swam back with all my might and ran to Mr. Lange. The reptiles had certainly startled me more than I them. However, they were not large animals—about four feet in length, I should say. Mr. Venter the next day saw some crocodiles at the same place.

At sunset our two hunting parties returned. They had met with kwaggas, elks and koodoos, they said, but all were so wild that none were shot. Mr. Rhodes, however, did not come home empty-handed. He brought with him some partridges and pheasants.

After taking a bath in the river we gathered round our table and took our evening meal, Mr. Greeff and Mr. Leah joining in with us. We had hardly begun, when Messrs. Joubert, van Aarde and du Preez passed us by with their sleeves rolled up and their hands red with blood. These gentlemen had been more successful than our parties, for they had shot two koodoos and had come into possession in a very curious manner of a large red-buck. A young Kafir, whom they had left some distance behind, heard the screaming of a buck. Thinking that one of his masters had wounded it, he ran towards the spot whence the sound came. Arrived at the scene, he was startled to behold a tiger with its paws upon the breast of the dying buck. The negro hesitated for a few seconds whether he would flee from or attack the animal. Then, thinking that it would be a disgrace on his part to allow the tiger to eat what his master had shot, he threw his *kieri* (stick) at the tiger; whereupon the latter, instead of rushing on its assailant, cowardly glided away with its tail between its legs. Shortly afterwards the hunters, on the shouting of the Kafir, came to the spot. We can imagine how surprised they were at what they found. The buck, a large, healthy one, was dead when secured; but, save that its neck was bitten through, no part of its body was destroyed. The story seemed almost incredible to us, but it was proved to be true.

Events of that kind are not of rare occurrence in that part of the world. Only two days previously Mr. Greeff and Mr. Leah had an adventure with a lion. Mr. Greeff told us his Kafir ran up to him and told him that he had just seen a lion on the other side of the stream eating something. The Kafir explained to him and Mr. Leah where he had seen it, and the two gentlemen took their guns and made for the place. As they neared the spot the lion roared.

"I trembled in my boots," so proceeded Mr. Greeff, "but would not think of turning back before I had at least made an attempt to overcome the animal. 'Hendrik,' I whispered to my son-in-law (Leah), 'be ready to shoot him when he comes.' Hendrik shivered no less than I. We now saw the lion and the lion us, and so loud a growl it gave that the earth seemed to tremble beneath my feet. I took good aim and fired and—good heavens!—the lion came! and all that I had time to say to Hendrik was, 'Run, man, run!' And, believe me, my friends, never did I know that old Greeff could run as fast as he did. Upon my word, I ran so hard that fire issued from my eyes."

At this we all burst out laughing.

"Yes," said Mr. Greeff, "it is all very well to laugh when you sit round the table, comfortable and safe; but if to-morrow in a hunt you meet the lion, I should like to see who would laugh then."

Mr. Greeff was in earnest, but we could not stop laughing at his over-graphic account of the event.

After a short interval, however, when we were again prepared to give him a quiet audience, and when his excitement had cooled down a bit, he continued the story.

"Hendrik and I at last stood still and listened, but heard nothing. I must have wounded the lion severely. As it was beginning to get dark we would not return to see what had become of our enemy; but the following morning—that is yesterday—we again went to the place where we had seen it last, expecting to find it either dead or wounded. But we saw nothing except a few blood patches, which show that the lion must have been badly wounded."

"Why did you not go in search of him again?" queried Mr. Venter; "whether dead or alive, you certainly would have found him!"

"I dare say we would, if we had tried," replied Mr. Greeff. "My dog barked in some bushes yesterday; probably we might have met the lion there, but I am never over-anxious to meet a wounded lion, especially when amongst woods. Believe me, there is nothing more dangerous than a lion hurt. When it comes down upon you, all that remains for you is to kill it or die. And I was not going to risk my life, nor was Hendrik his. But, to-morrow, we might find the lion on our hunt, perhaps also its mate, for the one is seldom without the other. We will have some fun then!"

We next reverted to the topic of the hunt we intended to have the following day. Mr. Greeff was again chief speaker.

"Inspan your waggons early to-morrow morning, drive them down to ours, and leave them there. We shall mount our horses, have ourselves followed by an ox-waggon with a plentiful supply of ammunition and provisions, and go out hunting three or four days; we shall seek the lion I have injured and make it ours; we shall visit the homes of the hippopotami on the river's side and kill at least one of those huge river-horses—which means supplying ourselves with 1200 or 1500 lbs. of meat; thence we make a general chase on large game, and return to our waggons. If you follow my advice," added Mr. Greeff, "I am sure you will enjoy the hunt more than ever you did any before."

"Why will two days not suffice?" we asked.

"Because," answered Mr. Greeff, rather annoyed at our aversion to his proposals, "it will take nearly a whole day to ride to the hippopotamus pools and back again; it will take us about half a day to hunt up the lion, and how much time have we left then? No, if we don't make up our minds to stay at least three or four days, we need not think of going out hunting at all, for it would not be worth the trouble."

"In that case we had better give up the hunt altogether," remarked Mr. Venter.

"I think so too," said Mr. Rhodes.

"And so do I," followed Mr. Lange.

A long and lively debate ensued, and in vain Mr.

Greeff again endeavoured to persuade the party to adopt his proposals. Even I, who had so ardently looked forward to the lion and hippopotamus hunt, could not but shake my head at Mr. Greeff's desires, especially as I pictured to myself the situation in which any of us would find himself when his horse should fail or he should lose his way; he must wait, Mr. Greeff had said, till the party returned to him, or else run the ugly risk of never being seen by man again.

The end of it all was, that we decided to take up the journey the following day. Captain Turner, however, was determined not to lose the hunt, so he stayed behind with Mr. Greeff and Mr. Leah to spend four days on the chase. After supper Mr. Greeff and his son-in-law bade us "Good-bye," once more expressing their disappointment at our decision. The parting was mutually regretted, for we had by that time won each other's sincere friendship.

We sent one of the police along with the two gentlemen to fetch us a sheep. We expected him to return soon again, but he did not turn up at all that night. This cost us some anxiety, for the night was dark, and the place strange, and hence it was not improbable that he had lost his way. However, he appeared the next morning with a fat sheep from Mr. Greeff, and a tin of fresh butter as a present from the latter's wife. Mr. Greeff would accept no payment for the sheep from our deputy, remarking, "A tin of butter and a sheep are little enough to give to such kind people." We, on the other hand, could not but speak in the highest praise of that gentleman, as well as of his son-in-law.

CHAPTER XIV.

Mr. van Aarde's farm—Too tired to run after koodoos—A difference about our journey, and Mr. Lange has to give way—Crematart River and the trees there.

We left the majestic river at half-past five on the morning of the 5th of November. Our road—one that I would recommend to those who wish to break their necks—wended over hills and through *kloofs*. We passed the farm of Mr. van Aarde (the father of the young van Aarde we had met at the Limpopo) and entered and outspanned upon an extensive and monotonous-looking plain. There being no water for our animals, our stoppage was very short.

As we proceeded, some koodoos crossed the road some distance in front of us. We lazily fired at them a shot or two from where we were, but missed, and we felt too tired and low-spirited to pursue them. At length, much to our relief, we reached the other end of the unvarying plain and ascended a hill, on the slope of which we were fortunate enough to procure sufficient water for ourselves and our beasts. At sunset we found ourselves on the top of a high elevation, and there we stopped to spend the night. Both Mr. Venter and Mr. Lange, however, were dissatisfied with the site as outspan-place; they wanted the party to proceed to Crematart River before closing the day's journey, because at that river there was plenty of water for our animals, whereas on the hill there was none. Mr. Rhodes was opposed to this; he saw no necessity in our going farther, inasmuch as we found ourselves on a safe, comfortable and healthy spot, and as our animals had already more than quenched their thirst during the afternoon, and we for ourselves had more water with us than we needed. I agreed with the Premier, though it was to be admitted that another five miles would be no small gain to our horses as well as to ourselves. The otherwise submissive Eppie Lange was particularly out of humour on this occasion—not so much, I believe, because he was anxious to bring the horses to the stream, as because he wanted to be there himself; for he was longing for a bath. Anyhow, the decision had been made, the discontents had to bow to it, and we passed the night upon the hill.

The following morning we drove to Crematart River and there outspanned. After breakfast Mr. Visser took us to a gigantic baobab, the circumference of the trunk of which measured no less than 97 feet. The tree was therefore wide enough to have a way cut out of it of sufficient breadth to allow four oxwaggons, side by side, to be driven through it. I am afraid that the reader who has not himself witnessed such an enormous tree will find it difficult to realise the sight. Imagine a tree with a trunk as wide as a broad street and with branches as thick as the thickest of trunks we see in the Cape Colony.

We continued our journey from there through the

woods of Mapani, and met on our way a huge wild pig. Mr. Venter fired a shot at it, but missed; it was amusing then to see the heavy animal run. Our road gradually grew less distinct as we ascended the richly-wooded Blauwberg, and it was not without keen observation that we kept in it. Mr. Visser carefully directed us how to travel and where next to outspan (a spot where there was water), but, somehow or other, we missed the place. Luckily, however, we met a Kafir on the way, who, on my offering him half-a-crown, was willing to show us where to find water. He led Colonel Pennyfather and myself a long way through the woods until we reached a green valley at the foot of the mount, where there was water, fresh, sweet, and as clear as crystal. We brought our horses thither and, as the quantity of fodder we had with us was rather scant, we drove them into the grassy valley to graze there all night.

We had now outspanned at a very pretty place, but it was rather warm and marshy. At the lower end of the valley, some distance from us, there stood a cluster of reeds, towards which clouds of bush-finches were seen to fly. The sight attracted me. I walked down to the thicket, the circumference of which I found to be hardly greater than that of the baobab we had seen at Mr. Visser's, and found to my astonishment that all those thousands of birds—aye, tens of thousands—found shelter in it. I watched them for a while, enjoying to listen to their incessant chirping and chattering and twittering, and thought as I stood there, "Ah, little finches, judging by the blue mountains in front of me, by the fruitful valleys yonder, by the streams of water close by, by the luxuriant veld around me, and by the Kafir towns in the neighbourhood, the time is nigh when the white population at the foot of this mount will outrival you in number!"

We did not sleep so well that night as we did the night before, for the air was somewhat depressing and not very healthy, owing to the swampiness of the valley.

CHAPTER XV.

Fascinating scenery—The River Nile, so called—We make another effort to buy milk—The Kafir women as bad as the dogs—A delusive hill—The Premier is dissatisfied, but the oxen are not—A born hunter and his family—Salt waggons from Zoutpansbergen.

THE following day our road took us through a long kloof. It was not a road that of itself would allure a traveller, it being so stony and broken that every one of us preferred walking to riding, for no one cared to share the violent shocks the carts and waggons had to put up with. The fascinating scenery, however, that the opposite side of the mountain presented, compensated for the inconvenience the road afforded. Extensive plains, too, at a distance, with here and there a Kafir town upon them, now appeared to our view, whilst at the same time we spied the dim blue tops of the Zoutpansbergen. Passing several Kafir kraals, we reached the " River Nile "—so called by the Dutch *voortrekkers*, who believed it to be the source of the great Nile. Some rain having rendered the soil soft, the Kafirs were engaged in ploughing mealies when we arrived there. Judging by the cultivation carried on, the Kafirs in the neighbourhood of the Little Nile are far more industrious than any of those we had hitherto met.

Mr. Lange, Mr. Venter and myself drove in our cart to a little town to get some milk where we had observed some cattle-kraals. Several native women, both old and young, were just busy milking the cows when we came there, but when they saw us they all, as if at a sudden alarm, jumped up and ran as swiftly as they could to their huts, from where they peeped at us as if we were a triplet of the basest vagabonds. We stood still for a minute or two calling "Milk, milk!" and "*Mali, mali!*" (*i.e.*, money), but the frightened women only turned a deaf ear to us. "Well, go to the dickens!" we thought and drove away.

The waggons had taken a different road from our cart, but we had agreed to meet each other again at a watery place called Witteklip. The cart was ahead of the waggons, and was going at a fair speed, the road being level and good, but Witteklip was still far from being reached. At length, having driven without stopping for four-and-a-half hours, we caught sight of a small white hill—our apparent destination—which seemed to be only a short distance off. We continued the drive another half-hour, but owing to the surrounding tall trees, of which the syringa was the most prominent, we soon again lost sight of the hill. I became impatient, jumped from the cart, and climbed like a cat to the top of one of the larger trees, from where it appeared to me that we were still as far away from the white hill as we had been an hour before.

I suggested that we should outspan, for our horses had already made a longer run without stopping than usual, but Mr. Venter would not hear of it. It was folly, he said, to stop within so short a distance from a place where there was plenty of water; but, being in the minority, he did not have his way, and we unharnessed the horses. At this action of ours, our stubborn friend was so displeased that he sulkily walked away to Witteklip. Two hours later Colonel Pennyfather arrived with the waggons. The Premier did not speak a word, but we could read upon his face —what we had only expected—dissatisfaction at our having kept the horses in harness so long. When, however, his eye fell on the beautiful pasture around him his features changed again. Our animals enjoyed an hour's grazing before they were again inspanned, and another three-quarters of an hour brought us to Witteklip.

The klip itself was a huge rock, a few hundred feet in height, situated on an elevation. At the foot of it there was a fountain, the clear cold water of which we much enjoyed; and a little farther on there was a large dam, where our animals satisfied their thirst. We climbed up the rock, and from there had an extensive view over the Zoutpansbergen and Blauwbergen.

Before leaving Witteklip we made the acquaintance of a hunter who had outspanned his waggon there. He had with him his wife, his children, his dogs, his fowls, and what not—all that he possessed. Hunting was his occupation and his *only* occupation; he had lived by it for years, and hoped to live by it till his death. Only the previous day he had shot two bucks. He had made up his mind to trek to Mashonaland as soon as the winter was past. I may mention that almost all white men to be met with in that northern region of South Africa are huntsmen.

Leaving Witteklip we travelled through fine grassy fields, on which numerous partridges and korhaans were to be met with. Mr. Rhodes again shot some. Towards evening we unteamed our animals close to a large *pan* containing water. Some heavy rains having fallen there some days before, the veld looked well, and we allowed our horses to graze on it all night.

The following morning we passed the Zoutpansbergen on our left, and saw a number of Kafir towns and thousands of cattle. In spite of the undulating character of the country the veld was open, and we could see far in every direction. At a distance of about 150 yards from the road we passed a vulture ("lamb-catcher") sitting on a tree. Mr. Rhodes fired a shot at it from the cart and felled it. It was really piteous to see the poor bird shrink and fall. Since the Kafirs in that part of the country reared no sheep, lamb-catchers there could do no mischief. Farther on our way we met three waggons coming from Zoutpansberg loaded with salt. We had a short chat with the Boers on them, and inquired from them where the old Mr. Barend Vorster was living. It chanced that one of them was a son-in-law of that gentleman, and he kindly directed us to Mr. Vorster's farm, which happened to be the place also to which the salt-laden waggons were going, though at a less speed than that at which we were travelling. Meeting, however, with so many roads leading to Kafir towns, we very soon turned into a wrong one; but the mistake was quickly discovered. Noticing some men fishing in a stream flowing not far from where we were driving, I got down from the cart, went to them, and said "Good morning." The greeting was returned, though in a rather gruff manner, by all except one, who cast a look at me savage enough to frighten me. I courteously asked them to show me which way to take for Mr. Vorster's, and they were good enough to do so. I then returned to the cart; we got into the correct road again, reached the top of a hill, and from there we looked down upon the farm of Commandant Barend Vorster. Not little was our joy to see it, for it was the first farm we had seen since we left Mr. Taylor's.

CHAPTER XVI.

A carriage and four horses—Mr. Barend Vorster—Mr. Adendorff and his concession—A tiresome invitation which has to be accepted—We reach Pietersburg, and read sad tidings in the newspapers—We do not enjoy our quarters and decide to leave—Expensive hospitality—We hear more than we desire of the concession.

WE outspanned near to a dwelling-house, and next to a clear stream whose sides were sheltered by some pretty willows. In the garden close by, surrounded by a wall, we noticed a number of haystacks, and so we knew where to get food for our animals. After taking a bath in a deep pool close to the house, we purchased for our horses a quantity of fodder at a cheap rate, but for ourselves we could obtain neither poultry nor any other meat, so we had to have recourse again to our tinned food. Whilst still at our meal, we saw a showy carriage drawn by four smart horses coming in our direction. This gaudy sight made it difficult for me to realise that I was sitting in a corner of rude Zoutpansberg. The vehicle stopped at our waggons, and out sprang Mr. Barend Vorster, junior, member of the Volksraad, with his pair of crutches. He at once invited us to his father's house, but was sorry to tell us that his father was not at home, being out on state duty in his capacity of commandant. We accepted the invitation, and a little afterwards found ourselves seated in the sitting-room of Mr. Vorster's house. The good old house-lady and her daughters treated us with great courtesy and kindness. We met at the house Mr. Adendorff, and others, amongst whom I recognised the man who had given me that wild glance earlier in the day. With cake and filled-up wine-glasses in front of us, and with cigars or pipes in our mouths, we could not feel more comfortable than we did.

After some preliminary casual remarks on this and that, we were soon engaged in earnest conversation. Mr. Barend Vorster, the Raadslid, fell into an interesting discourse with the Premier, and Mr. Adendorff talked with me.

"What do you think of the interior?" asked Mr. Adendorff. "Do you expect war there?"

"As to the interior," I replied, "I have a very high opinion of it; and as to war—well, I don't expect it. Lobengula is not so stupid as not to know that to fight against the white man is to bring about the destruction of his own power, for he is aware of how it fared with his ancestors, with his relatives, and with all those tribes who took up their weapons against the European. But, if he wants to fight, he may—we are not afraid of him; we know the war can only have one result, namely, that Lobengula will be deprived of both his power and his country."

"By whom?" asked Mr. Adendorff with a gentle sneer.

"By our people," I answered, rather astonished at his question.

"By your people!" he sarcastically returned; "and who may they be?"

"Burghers from the Cape Colony, the Transvaal and the Orange Free State. Already no less than five hundred South African burghers are employed by the Chartered Company, and what is it to us to add fifteen hundred to that number? It will be a work of a few days, especially if we promise to distribute farms, each thousands of acres large, amongst those who assist our Premier."

Mr. Adendorff smiled. "Yes," he replied, "but we have also a concession there."

"Indeed! and where may that be?"

"In Banyailand," was the challenging answer.

"And from whom did you get it?"

"From Chibe," he replied.

"From Chibe—so! And who are the 'we' who obtained that concession from Chibe?"

"Mr. Vorster and myself."

"But excuse me if I remind you, Mr. Adendorff, that Chibe is only a captain of small significance who pays taxes to Lobengula and lives in Lobengula's land. What right has he to make concessions of land not belonging to himself and already conceded by Lobengula to Mr. Rhodes?"

"Anyhow," was the response, "he has done it."

"Well, then your concession is of no value," I rejoined, "for Chibe is a subject of Lobengula's, and has consequently no right whatever to make concessions of territory to anybody."

The more my opponent argued in support of his claim the more manifest became its invalidity.

"But," he remarked, "there is no obstacle in your way; Mr. Rhodes can buy our concession."

"Why then," I asked, "don't you show him your concession? If it is legitimate, he is sure to buy it."

But the whole talk went to show that the so-called concession was worth very little, if anything at all. We dropped the topic and spoke on other matters.

Many Kafirs were to be seen about the place. Indeed, one meets with swarms of them and their cattle all over the Zoutpansberg district.

At three o'clock in the afternoon Messrs. Vorster and Adendorff took leave of us. They warmly invited the Premier to get into their landau and drive with them to Pietersburg, but the honourable gentleman had no inclination to do so. However, he was not let off before he had given his word that he would visit Thorncastle, the residence of Mr. Vorster, junior, the following Monday, and pass the night there. The fishermen whom I had met at the rivulet had already left when the gay four-wheeler with its spirited steeds started for Thorncastle, a distance of forty miles from there, which had still to be covered before night. We next said good-bye to the hospitable Mrs. Vorster and her children, who gave us a small bag filled with cake to eat on our way, and then we left.

Our road now passed alongside a verdant valley in which some gardens had been laid out, and there were also some small shops kept by Jews, who seemed to carry on a thriving business. Their customers are Kafirs for the greater part—and the Kafirs of that district were not poor, as many of them had been labourers at the gold or diamond mines. I learnt from good authority that the amount they contributed as annual taxes to the Transvaal treasury was very considerable.

On our way we passed hundreds of bush-doves that were enjoying themselves on the patches of cultivated land, the harvests of which had just been mown. The Premier and the colonel each shot a number of them. We halted in front of one of the Jewish shops and bought some necessaries—oatsheaves and mealies for our horses, and a piece of mutton for ourselves; and the generous shop-keeper presented us with a bucket of potatoes into the bargain.

Towards the close of the day we outspanned next to a stream running between two Kafir towns. As the sun had not yet set, we began target-shooting as a pastime at antheaps on the other side of the valley, at distances roughly estimated by us to range from 500 to 1000 yards. We had not been firing long when an amusing incident, but one which might have been serious, took place. A Kafir, who had apparently taken no notice of our shooting, came striding along through our target area as if he were monarch of all he surveyed; but didn't he startle and run when just a little in front of him a bullet sent up dust! His legs could never have carried him off faster than they did then.

Continuing our journey from there the following day, we passed through several Kafir towns, in and round about which thousands of cows and oxen were to be seen; but, owing to the dryness of the veld and to the immense number of cattle that had to live on it, they were far from fat.

At half-past twelve we outspanned within four miles

of Pietersburg. As it was Sunday, we did not think it proper to enter the little town at that hour and disturb its tranquillity. One of our mules had become ill, so we left it in the hands of a farmer.

Towards evening we entered Pietersburg, but, on account of the troublesome flies in the village, we immediately again left it and outspanned a little outside of it. We much preferred sleeping in the waggons to sleeping in the village hotel; our food and drink, however, we got at the latter.

Between Tuli Camp and Pietersburg it is 184 miles.

We obtained a large number of the latest South African newspapers in the village, and learnt from them that the son of Lord Elphinstone had died at Palla's Camp on the return of the Governor's party to that place. Little did Lord Elphinstone know, when he was condoling with me at Palla's Camp on the loss of my son, that at that same place he was to lament the death of his own a fortnight afterwards. As I had expected, so it had happened—the ambitious young nobleman who had come to seek fame in the wilds of South Africa had found there, as had been the case with the French Prince Imperial, his death instead. He died in his twenty-first year.

Pietersburg is a pretty place. It has some very neat buildings and is well supplied with water. We left it on Monday afternoon (November 10th) at half-past two, and an hour later we arrived at Thorncastle, the well-known property of Mr. Barend Vorster, junior. Our journey thither lost us a day, and if all had been of my mind, we would never have made it; but since the Premier had promised to touch at that place, it was only his duty to keep his word. Besides, Mr. Vorster is not a man of insignificance; he is looked upon as the leading man in Zoutpansberg and, as I have already stated, represents that district in the Volksraad. Two days previously he invited us so warmly to his place that we thought we would greatly disappoint him if we did not accept the invitation, and when we observed on our arrival at Thorncastle a very large gathering to meet us, we naturally expected that there was grand entertainment awaiting us; but when the day was over and we crept into our waggons at ten at night, we saw that all the fuss that had been made was a mere farce, and that our going to Thorncastle was only waste of time.

Early the next morning we inspanned and left. The inmates of the house were all still sound asleep. Not knowing whether our Thorncastle host would accept money or not for the forage our horses and mules had consumed at his place, we left Bandmaster behind with a horse to wait until that gentleman was up and then to ask him what our expenses were. We promised the boy that we would wait for him at Smitsdorp, one and a half hour's ride from Thorncastle. Shortly after our departure Mr. Vorster got out of bed, and Bandmaster did as he had been bidden—asked what he had to pay.

"One pound for mealies," was the answer, "and one shilling for every oatsheaf."

Bandmaster paid the money, mounted his horse and rode away. Before he did so, however, Mr. Vorster remarked to him;

"I will follow you later, for I should like to see Mr. Rhodes about something."

We had only been three-quarters of an hour on the way when Bandmaster overtook us and informed us what he had been made to pay. We were shocked at hearing the charges, for, since we had entered Zoutpansberg we never had to pay more than 17s. for a bag of corn; in fact, we had more than once only paid 13s; and the price of oatsheaves never exceeded 9d. the piece; we had sometimes only paid 6d. The other piece of news that Bandmaster brought with him, namely, that it was Mr. Vorster's intention to overtake us again, was not received with any greater pleasure —so little, in fact, that we immediately ordered the drivers to drive faster. They obeyed, and we now went at a rate of six miles an hour on a level road. We had more than one reason for being eager to get away. In the first place, we had already grown very tired of Messrs. Vorster and Adendorff's persistent pleading that Mr. Rhodes should purchase their so-called Banyailand Concession, and we longed for an end to it. Secondly, disappointed in the entertainment we had received at Thorncastle, and regretting the loss of time consequent on the visit, the farther we were away from that place the happier we felt; and, thirdly, we had been asked by Mr. Kirsten to take breakfast with him at Smitsdorp that morning, and we were anxious to conform to the request.

We passed through Marabastad without stopping in it longer than a few minutes. It is a new village situated on the roadway, and is furnished with a very decent hotel. As we were approaching Marabastad, we caught sight in the distance of a vehicle following our track. At once we suspected that it was the landau of Mr. Vorster, and we were not wrong. Notwithstanding the accelerated speed at which we were travelling, the showy carriage soon overtook us. Messrs. Vorster and Adendorff were again its occupants, and they immediately upon reaching us invited Mr. Rhodes and myself to take seats in their carriage. Although already sick of hearing of their supposed concession which they so pressingly besought Mr. Rhodes to purchase, for politeness' sake we complied with the request.

CHAPTER XVII.

The concession again—A sumptuous lunch—Makapaan's Poort—
 The cave of the Kafirs—A fearful death—We reach Potgieter's
 Rust—Kafirs on the way to the goldfields—The advantages
 of Kafir labour.

AT Smitsdorp we outspanned and took breakfast at Mr. Kirsten's, the Gold Commissioner. The two gentlemen from Thorncastle of course partook of the breakfast which had been intended for us alone. However, there was more than enough for all, and we enjoyed our excellently prepared morning meal immensely.

After breakfast Mr. Reed took us to the Waterfall Gold Mines. On our way thither Mr. Vorster again began entreating the Chartered Company's representative to buy his untenable claim on Banyailand: But, of course, our Premier was not fool enough to waste money on so worthless a thing.

With the Waterfall Mines we were much taken up. The machinery used, as well as the quartz itself, looked well; and we felt convinced that the mine, if the company owning it had sufficient funds to work it properly, would become one of the best paying in the country.

On our return to Smitsdorp Mr. Vorster intimated to me that he had ultimately succeeded in getting Mr. Rhodes to promise that, on his submitting to

Mr. Rhodes's examination the papers he had received from the Banyai chief relating to the concession, the Premier would, if he found the concession in any way valid, pay its value to the concessionaires. With this promise Mr. Vorster appeared satisfied.

We had our waggons inspanned and were on the point of starting again when the kind Mrs. Kirsten—who, by the way, is a daughter of Mr. Albert Biccard of Koeberg—asked us to wait a little and have lunch there before leaving. The request was gladly accepted, and to our surprise we found that not a lunch, but a big dinner, had been prepared for us in true South African style. The well-roasted fat ducks and the pure Cape wine were much enjoyed; it was the second time that day we ate a meal better than we had enjoyed for many days before.

At two o'clock in the afternoon we bade our kind host and hostess farewell, as also Mr. Vorster and his companion, and left Smitsdorp. Our road now ran over a pretty tract of country—water copious and the veld green. But the graminivorous animals to be seen there were all in a poor condition owing to the grass being sour and of an inferior quality.

At sunset we arrived at Makapaan's Poort (*i.e.*, gate of Makapaan), a place lying about thirty miles from Smitsdorp, and of considerable historical interest, many a tough fight having been fought there between the Makapaan Kafirs and the Boers under Potgieter. Thousands of Kafirs were here to be met with, and we could descry numerous towns of theirs in the immediate neighbourhood. Not far from the Poort there is to be seen a large deep cave, into which, during the war against the Boers, thousands of Kafirs fled to save their lives; but this their white enemy discovered, who thereupon placed a body of men at the mouth of the cavern to prevent any of those inside from escaping. The thus imprisoned natives preferred death to surrender, probably because they thought that surrender only meant death (having little reason to hope for mercy after having in cold blood butchered so many Boer families), and that it would be more heroic to voluntarily perish by starvation than die directly by the hands of their foes. As it was, every one inside the cave died of hunger, and the bones of those unfortunate creatures are still on view there.

We left Makapaan's Poort the following morning, and after unteaming our horses for a short while on the way, we went on till we had climbed up an elevation. On the top of it we outspanned and spent the night. Next morning we journeyed to Klein Nijlstroom, where there was the station of a Hernhutter missionary. He had a fine orange orchard, which, however, was of no use to us, for oranges were then out of season.

The next place we halted at was the "Groot Nijl." Upon the waters of that river myriads of waterfowl were to be seen, whilst in the grass upon its shores a number of owls sat looking on. Towards night we outspanned in the open veld and slept there. The following day we drove through Potgieter's Rust, in the Waterberg district, a newly marked-off township with wide borders, but consisting at present of only a few buildings. The village gets its water supply from the Transvaal Nile. The soil is fertile, but the grass is unwholesome for cattle. Fruit trees thrive there when spared by hail and frost. There was a time when the population of the place was far larger than at present, but owing to frequent outbreaks of fever many of the residents abandoned it. Now, however, the number of its inhabitants is again on the increase. A church has been built, and the congregation support their own clergyman. But it is my opinion that the people now living there will, as soon as they may safely do so, trek to Mashonaland. Old pomegranate and other hedges, as well as some large syringas and similar trees, remained as relics of the earlier village, but those who had planted them had almost all either died of fever or trekked to healthier places.

Continuing our course, we arrived towards evening, after crossing some hills and valleys, at the farm of Messrs. Nadab and Thompson, a place that for many years had been held in the possession of Boers, and which only recently fell into the hands of the above-mentioned *Uitlander* gentlemen. The old Boer dwelling-house, with its thick solid walls, stands there still, but some new buildings, one of which serves as a shop, have been added. These houses, together with the various kinds of trees surrounding them, present a pretty picture. We passed the night there, as did also a large number of Kafirs who were *en route* to the goldfields. These men kept themselves remarkably quiet that night: they sat around the fires they had kindled not far from our waggons, and, though there were about a hundred of them, they hardly made themselves as much as heard. Early the following morning they again took up their march. We followed a little later and soon overtook them. It was a pretty sight to see them march—all in faultless step and every one dressed in white cloth. They were young, tall, strong Matabele, with beautifully shaped bodies. As we passed them each one politely saluted us. Again I thought, "What excellent labourers these men would make for the white man!" If Kafirs only knew the advantages of serving under white masters, they would gain more civilisation in one year than they do from missionaries in fifty; selling wives as slaves would cease, polygamy would die out, and they would have a fair opportunity of hearing the Word of God, for wherever the white man is, there also are churches and preachers. As it is, there is now a general scarcity of labourers: Kafirs can live so cheaply and earn their living so easily that they decline to be dependent on the European. They are, however, beginning to recognise their degraded position, and some of them already know the privileges to be enjoyed by being servants to the white man. We may hope that the day will soon dawn when not a single farmer will need to complain of being short of hands. When that time comes the productions of our land will become double of what they are at present, even though its population should not increase; and there will be general content and progress.

CHAPTER XVIII.

No hurry to reach Pretoria—An officer meets us with an invitation—We enter in procession, and sleep, after two months' travelling, under a roof—Nelmapius gives me a headache in Pretoria—The gold mines of Johannesburg—I am treated discourteously by a post-office clerk at Kimberley—Home at Capetown once more.

WE arrived towards evening at a large river—the name of which has escaped my memory—and after crossing a bridge we outspanned on the other side of the stream. It was quite a treat to meet there with such a mass of water in so dry a season. Owing to heavy rains that had fallen the previous day, the river had come down in a tremendous torrent and filled up every nook in its bed that had been empty and dry before.

The next day we had to drive through a heavy, muddy road that made our poor animals spend no small amount of energy. But, slowly though they dragged the vehicles along, they did so steadily; and the Premier rather liked this tardy travelling, because he was by no means eager to reach Pretoria before late in the evening or early the next morning. He wished to escape any of that formal ado that men in his position might reasonably expect on arriving in such a town. At ten in the morning, however, we were met by a military officer on horseback who rode up to our front waggon (the one in which Mr. Rhodes happened to sit), requested the driver to stop, and asked:

"Are these the waggons of President Rhodes?"

"Yes," replied the driver.

"And where is the President?"

"Well," answered the Premier, "I am Rhodes—is there anything I can do for you?"

The officer drew a sealed letter from his pocket and handed it to the Cape "President." It contained an invitation to him and his company to be the guests of the Transvaal Government during their stay at Pretoria, and stated also that the necessary arrangements for the reception of the party had been made at the Fountain Hotel. The officer also wished to know at what time Mr. Rhodes expected to enter Pretoria, for the President intended to meet him on the way.

"About six o'clock," replied the Premier.

"Good-bye!" said the officer, and off he rode as hard as he could. Other riders with fresh horses were placed on the road between us and Pretoria to relieve each other and so bring the news to President Kruger as soon as possible.

We outspanned next on the borders of a pretty stream, took a bath in the refreshing water, and trimmed ourselves up a bit, in anticipation of our entrance soon into the capital of the Transvaal.

At five o'clock the State carriages, containing the Honourable Messrs. Bok, Wolmarans, and Dr. Krause (members of the Government), followed by a number of other vehicles carrying many of the leading ladies and gentlemen of Pretoria, came to bid us welcome near Wonderboom, about half an hour's drive from the city. Having greeted each other, we took seats, at the request of the Government members, in their carriages.

At half-past five we arrived at our hotel, in front of which a large crowd of people had assembled, who, as the Cape Premier alighted from his carriage, hailed him with three loud and hearty cheers. Capital accommodation was furnished us; our horses, too, were well provided for, and in every respect we had good reason to be pleased with the hospitality which we received at the hands of the executive. We would now, for the first time in nearly two months, sleep inside a house.

We received visitors from all quarters that night. Amongst others there was Mr. Hennie Hofmeijr (son of Mr. S. V. Hofmeijr of Capetown), with whom I had a long and very pleasant chat. Little did I then think that only a month later I would learn of his death. That fatal fever that had carried off so many of my young friends, among others Judge Jorrison, Dr. Davis and Dr. Wessels, also bore away the kind, gentle Hennie Hofmeijr at the age of twenty-five.

We learnt at Pretoria that two days after we had crossed the Limpopo the river came down in a powerful stream, and that it was still quite impassable by waggons, and daily growing higher. We could therefore congratulate ourselves on having hearkened to the counsel we had received from the Boers at Tuli; had we acted contrary to their advice we would have been compelled to wait at least three months at the Limpopo —if not at another river *before* we came to the Limpopo—ere we could cross it.

I arose the following morning with a shocking headache which I ascribed to my having drunk the night before what was supposed to be "Scotch whisky," but was nothing but Nelmapius, I am pretty sure. Mr. Venter attended the Reformed Church in the morning, but I stayed at home, for I could hardly lift my head. In the afternoon, however, when I felt better, I accompanied Mr. Rhodes for a ride.

The following morning we drank coffee with the President, with whom we had an interesting conversation, the meeting breaking up with mutual expressions by President and Premier of their pleasure at having met each other. At three in the afternoon we departed from Pretoria and were accompanied to Six-Mile-Spruit by the state-ministers Bok, Krause and Wolmarans, escorted by an artillery regiment. At the Spruit we overtook our waggons, which had left Pretoria in the morning; and there, after drinking to each other's health, we parted with our entertainers.

At the approach of evening we outspanned within a few miles from Johannesburg, upon an elevation called Wijnberg, close to an hotel. As usual we slept in our waggons, but a stormy west wind blew so bitterly cold throughout the night that, in spite of our rolling ourselves in double *karosses*, our feet felt frozen, and it was in vain that we tried to sleep. It was the most unpleasant night we had had on all our journey, and, indeed, the coldest I can recollect having spent in all my life. Of course, we regretted that we had not gone to sleep in the hotel, but the regret only came when it was too late. We had not thought that the temperature there could sink to so low a degree in the middle of November.

We hailed the dawn of day with delight, and the clock had hardly struck six when we arrived in Johannesburg. Mr. Rhodes had been expected there the previous night, but had purposely delayed his entering into the town in order to escape a public demonstration. Everyone was still indoors and all was quiet when we rode into the Golden City. We made direct for the buildings of the "Gold Fields of South Africa Company," where we took up our quarters.

The distance between Pietersburg and Johannesburg is 211 miles.

After visiting the gold mines, we left Johannesburg per coach for Kimberley on the 20th of November, and had as travelling companions the Rev. Mr. Postma of Pretoria and Mr. Hofmann, the Raad-member for Bloemhof. Both were men very pleasant to associate with, and in their company our long coach-journey to the Diamond City appeared a great deal shorter than it really was. We arrived at Kimberley in two days. The Premier there gave us a parting dinner, as we had now practically come to the end of our journey, and the evening was spent in a very pleasant manner. At a quarter to nine Mr. Venter and the Rev. Mr. Postma bade us farewell and left Kimberley by train at nine o'clock.

The next morning (Sunday) I went to the post-office —only open from eight till nine on the Sabbath—to inquire for letters, for before leaving Fort Tuli I directed the post officials there to forward to Kimberley all letters and papers which should arrive for me. Mr. Jan Lange, M.L.A., had advised me to see that I was at the post-office exactly at eight o'clock, because there was generally such a crush that those who came there later had frequently to turn back empty-handed, without even having had an opportunity of asking for their letters. I therefore took care to be early at the office-door. Soon a large crowd had assembled on the step. Exactly at eight the door flew open and the big Irishman, O'Leary, pressed his heavy body past me and was immediately handed his letters. I then asked for mine, but the post official made me no reply—in fact, took no notice at all of me. The whole room was soon crammed with people, and one after another was served; but I, who was the second to be there, had only to look on. I became impatient. In the first place, I could not afford to lose so much time, for every minute that morning was valuable to me; and, in the second place, my heart was burning to have tidings from home. I asked the clerk why he would not attend to me, but the young fellow again pretended not to hear. Again I asked him the reason for his conduct, and inquired whether he wanted my name.

"Yes," he gruffly answered.

I gave him my full name and address, but it availed me nothing. Hitherto, I had kept calm, for I felt rather despondent that morning, but after I had waited half-an-hour, and had seen a number of niggers served before me, I approached the uncivil twenty-two-year-old official, and sternly addressed him:

"Postmaster, *why* don't you attend to me? From the outset I have been standing here, and I've seen you serve scores of niggers, but me, a stranger, you entirely ignore, and treat as you would not treat a Hottentot. Tell me, what do you mean?"

No answer.

"Clerk, will you serve me or not?" I asked for the last time.

"No!" he hurled at me.

"Good!" I uttered. I jumped into a cab and rode off to the Kimberley Club to find someone to get my letters for me. Luckily I met Mr. Rhodes there, to whom I communicated my disappointment. He immediately got into the cab with me, and together we rode to the post-office. Very courteously the Premier asked the clerk whether there were any letters for me.

No reply.

Again Mr. Rhodes put the question, but all the answer he received was a contemptuous look.

"Clerk!" said the Premier sternly, "I am *Rhodes!* Will you answer me immediately?"

"Yes, sir!" the unmannerly clerk replied, greatly scared. He then fidgeted about from one corner of the room to another, but could find no letter for me. I turned back fairly out of humour, for I knew there *must* be letters for me, having had a telegram to that effect. Not contented, I went to Mr. Jan Lange, and he and I, after breakfast, went to the general-postmaster, to whom my friend communicated the whole affair. The kind postmaster immediately went to the office to make inquiry, and on his return was able to inform us that all letters addressed to me had been forwarded to Dr. Harris at the office of the B. S. A. Company.

"Well," said I, "if your clerk had only told us that, all would have been right; but, instead of doing so, he wasted about three-quarters of an hour of time that I cannot afford to lose."

"I am sorry," he replied, "that such has been the case, but I shall certainly investigate further into the matter."

I went to the house of Dr. Harris, and there found a number of papers and letters for me. All was right now, but the impolite young post-clerk I shall not soon forget. Officials of his stamp are a curse to the public, and should be dismissed without hesitation.

I left for Capetown in the evening by the nine o'clock train, and arrived at my home on Wednesday, the 25th of November. Nearly two months had I spent on my tour, and during that period I had travelled over 2,800 miles. Much had taken place during that short time—much that shall never quit my memory.

END OF PART I.

D. C. De Waal, M.L.A.

PART II.

OUR SECOND TRIP.

CHAPTER I.

Introduction—We leave Cape Town for Port Elizabeth—The Premier shuns a public demonstration—The mosquito in Durban—On board ship—Beetles as company—Mr. Rhodes does not mind them, but I do, and crack my crown in consequence.

LAST year I related in the *Zuid Afrikaansche Tydschrift* the journey Mr. Rhodes, Mr. Venter and myself had made into the interior towards the latter end of the previous year (1890). Encouraged by the numerous readers, and the satisfactory amount of appreciation the account received, I now propose describing briefly the trip we have just made to Mashonaland, *viâ* the East Coast, and trust that the description will not prove uninteresting.

To our regret, Mr. M. M. Venter, our fellow-traveller on our previous trip, could not accompany us this time.

Mr. Rhodes, Major Johnson and I left Capetown

by train for Port Elizabeth on the 14th of September, 1891, and reached it the following evening. Desirous of bidding the Premier welcome in their midst, the Port-Elizabethans had prepared to raise a great to-do on his coming; but Mr. Rhodes, who never cherished any liking for ceremonials (much as he may have appreciated the honour the Bay-people were willing to show him), immediately after his arrival at the port made for the wharf, where he got into a boat and rowed to the *Drummond Castle*, which was waiting for us in the bay. I, however, remained behind, waiting for Tonie, who had been left in charge of the luggage, and without whom, therefore, we could not proceed. He soon turned up, and together we left by tug for the *Drummond*. All was now ready for the voyage, and, as twilight set in, we said farewell to the bay.

The following morning we found ourselves in the haven at East London. We sailed up the Buffalo River, and much enjoyed the pretty scenery on its banks. At one o'clock we had lunch in the courtroom. Some speeches were there delivered, and a not unpleasant afternoon was spent.

Towards evening we left for Durban, Natal, where we arrived the following evening. Our horses, carts, and all our luggage had here to be transhipped to the *Norseman*, with which boat we were, two days afterwards, to continue our northward voyage.

We spent the night at the Durban Club. The room allotted to me was a large, well-furnished one, but the bed was very uncomfortable, and the mosquitoes tormented me so mercilessly throughout the night that I felt more inclined to cry than to sleep. But if that had been the only night I was annoyed by vexatious insects, I would not have much reason to complain; it was, however, but the first of a series of nights that I was to endure that provocation.

The following morning Mr. Rhodes and I left for Pietermaritzburg, and there we had dinner in the evening with Sir Charles Mitchell, the Natal Governor. We put up for the night in the Imperial Hotel, where I had hoped to make up for the loss of sleep I had suffered the night before; but it so happened that a dinner was being given that same night, in the same hotel, in honour of a certain Plymouth gentleman, who had been visiting South African sea-ports, to induce the people to sign petitions in favour of our mail steamers henceforth landing the "homeward" mails at Plymouth instead of at Southampton as at present.* The merry banqueters kicked up such a noise in the dining-room that it was absolutely impossible for one to sleep. Every speech made was followed by deafening applause, and it was not till two in the morning that the jovial party broke up.

We left Maritzburg at eight o'clock in the morning,

* The mails are now landed at Plymouth—often to the inconvenience of Cape Merchants—as frequently letters would be much sooner in London if sent *viâ* Southampton. For example, a steamer arriving at Plymouth at midnight on Sunday lands the mails, which are sent off on the Monday morning, and (on account of the *long* railway journey) delivered in London about the time City men are closing for the day. Had the steamer gone direct to Southampton, the letters would have been sent from there early on Monday morning, and (because of the *short* railway journey) delivered about eleven o'clock in London.—*Translator.*

returning to Durban, where we embarked in the *Norseman* in the afternoon. At half-past five, in weather clear and cool and on a sea beautifully calm, our vessel steamed out of the Durban harbour. Small though the *Norseman* is, she is a very comfortable boat, and our horses as well as ourselves were very well accommodated. We had on board five ponies and a Cape-cart transported from Cape Town, a number of cart-horses bought in Natal, and some pretty dogs, which Major Johnson had managed to secure at Durban.

It was not till ten o'clock that I entered my cabin. Lighting my candle, I was struck with horror at the sight of a host of blackbeetles creeping on my bed and up and down the iron wall. For the moment I sadly regretted that I had undertaken the journey. "Goodness!" I said to myself, as I stood there shivering at what I was seeing, "what if these disgusting insects run up my nose to-night, or my ears, or my mouth!" And it was ten to one that they would, I thought. "No!" I said to myself, "this will never do!" And off to the steward I went.

"My dear man," I said to him, "in that cabin of mine it is impossible to sleep; it swarms with all kinds of dirty little insects. I want to sleep on deck!"

"No, sir," replied the steward, "you cannot do that, because the deck will have to be scrubbed at four to-morrow morning. Besides, sir, why should you be afraid of those harmless little beetles? They won't disturb your rest—I'm sure they won't."

Nothing was left but to subject myself to his advice and betake myself again to the beetle-infested cabin. It was with great reluctance, however, that I did so. But when once I threw my tired body on my couch I sank so fast asleep that I forgot all about the unclean creatures that surrounded me until I awoke in the morning, having, after all, enjoyed a very pleasant repose.

The views of the Zululand coast we had next day from our vessel were very beautiful, and by means of our telescopes we could every now and then distinctly observe naked natives on the shore, as well as several little fires.

We passed St. Lucia Bay, a pretty inlet a little to the south of St. Lucia Lake. Two fairly large rivers, which unite some ten miles from their mouth, empty themselves into it. The combined rivers are about half a mile in width. St. Lucia Lake is forty-two miles long and ten broad. I was told that thousands of water-fowl dwell upon it, and that these birds are seldom disturbed by the gun, for very few white men have as yet visited that part of South Africa.

At noon we passed the coast of Amatongaland, one of the very few countries in South Africa hitherto unclaimed by the European,* and its inhabitants are the only native tribe in South Africa, excepting Majaatje's people in the Zoutpansbergen, who are governed by a queen. This queen (Sambele) entered into an agreement with Natal in 1888 that, if ever by force of circumstances she should be compelled to deliver up her country, she would give it to that colony. It was from this treaty (drawn up by Mr. Moffat) that Sir

* Amatongaland has recently (1895) been proclaimed British territory.—*Translator.*

D. C. DE WAAL, M.L.A.

PART II.

OUR SECOND TRIP.

CHAPTER I.

Introduction—We leave Cape Town for Port Elizabeth—The Premier shuns a public demonstration—The mosquito in Durban—On board ship—Beetles as company—Mr. Rhodes does not mind them, but I do, and crack my crown in consequence.

LAST year I related in the *Zuid Afrikaansche Tydschrift* the journey Mr. Rhodes, Mr. Venter and myself had made into the interior towards the latter end of the previous year (1890). Encouraged by the numerous readers, and the satisfactory amount of appreciation the account received, I now propose describing briefly the trip we have just made to Mashonaland, *viâ* the East Coast, and trust that the description will not prove uninteresting.

To our regret, Mr. M. M. Venter, our fellow-traveller on our previous trip, could not accompany us this time.

Mr. Rhodes, Major Johnson and I left Capetown

He came on deck and took over the command of the vessel, whilst his two black assistants remained in the little boat and connected it by a rope to the stern of the ship with evident joy, because this would save them the trouble of rowing their boat back to the land. They lit their pipes, seated themselves, and seemed to have everything to their heart's content. But hardly had the *Norseman* begun to move on when the boat behind began to pitch and toss most dreadfully over the foaming waves. The amusing sight was greeted by roars of laughter from our deck. Up went the boat to the top of a billow, then splash—down again! The niggers had an awful time of it. All they could do was to bale out the water with the one hand and cling to the boat with the other. But their position grew every moment more perilous; the boat began to leak, the inflow of the water was twice as great as the outpour, and the boatmen were as wet as fish. Greatly alarmed, they now began shouting at the top of their voices for their skipper (our pilot) to come to their assistance. The latter, on hearing the cry of his boys, immediately ran to the stern, and, seeing the plight they were in, threw a butcher's knife into the boat. At once the Kafirs cut the rope they had tied to the vessel, and were relieved from their awkward predicament. Soon the sails were set, and the boat was steered to Pig Island. The *Norseman* meanwhile passed both Pig and Rat, two densely-wooded, picturesque little islands with a few Kafir huts on them.

Inhambane Bay is about thirteen miles broad and nineteen and a half long.

At eleven o'clock we threw out our anchor, and soon afterwards a small boat carried us to the shore, a very short distance from the ship. The first thing that struck us when we entered the little Portuguese town was the deteriorated stage—generally speaking—to which its inhabitants had sunk. The Portuguese section of the population reside in the central part of the town; they are supposed to be the whites of the place, but are, in fact, not white at all, their colour corresponding with that of the coloured people of Capetown; the latter, however, are more civilized. Not only are those Portuguese ugly, thin, weak and narrow-shouldered, but, judging from the little I saw of them, they have fallen to such a low grade of animal life, that I would be ashamed to describe their mode of living.

The natives dwell in the outskirts of the town and in the neighbourhood in huts shaded by the branches of the fig, the palm, the date, and other subtropical fruit-trees, some of which are very tall; the cocoanut-palm, for instance, measuring from eighty to ninety feet in height. In order to climb the tree to pick its fruit, steps, about two feet apart, are cut into the stem. The tree is thin below, thick in the middle, and, like the ordinary palm, has a crown at the top, whilst between the crown and the ground it is perfectly naked. We had some dozens of cocoa-nuts picked for us, it being fortunately just then the season for them. One does not know what a delicious flavour that fruit has until he has tasted it fresh from the tree.

To see the police and the military in the town

is enough to make one laugh his tears out of his eyes. They are, indeed, a miserable-looking lot! And yet they have their own Governor, and, what is more, their own music-band; and we had the honour of hearing that band play. Didn't it amuse us!

At Delagoa Bay we had been told that Inhambane, as far as the landscape was concerned, was a lovely place, but I had no idea that it was such a grandly picturesque spot as I now found it. The blue, calm bay, the wild-tree gardens stretching inland from its shores, the charming scenery around—all combine to form a picture which no human eye can fail to admire. The bay itself, like that of Delagoa, contains a magnificent natural harbour. The country round about the little town excellently suits fruit-trees of various kinds. One has only to cultivate it—something the Portuguese will be the last to do. Lack of energy, lack of ambition, not to mention lack of cleanliness, are characteristic defects of the Portuguese, taken on the whole, on the East Coast. No wonder their forefathers, after whom they take, sailed past such places as Capetown, Port Elizabeth, East London and Durban—these places needed toil and money if they were to be turned into decent landings—and steered up the east coast to Inhambane, Chiluan, Sofala (Pungwe), Zambezi and Quilimane, where hardly a penny had to be spent on harbours, and where fruit could be abundantly picked without previously planting the trees. We may thank Providence that our southern shores did not offer sufficient inducement to the Portuguese to be retained by them, but that they fell into the hands of the Dutch, who began to lay out pretty villages and towns, and turned the Cape into a very useful country for the white man; whilst, since 1486, the East Coast has practically undergone no alteration whatever, or, if it has, the change has been for the worse. There is, however, this difference between the Portuguese of 1486 and those of the present day: the former deserved to be called decent Europeans, whereas most of the latter are a disgrace to the white man. It is indeed much to be regretted that these harbours did not fall into the hands of van Riebeek, van der Stel, or van Talbagh—active and energetic men who would have turned those naturally beautiful spots into delightful pleasure-resorts, in which the Cape would have had a splendid market for its wines and other products.

The population of Inhambane numbers between 5000 and 6000, of whom only about 300 are Portuguese. There are 700 Indians, and the rest are, with a few exceptions, natives. To the same extent that the Portuguese are abnormally thin, pale and sickly, the Kafirs are fat, strong and healthy, the latter living almost exclusively on mealies, rice, nuts and other fruits. The Indians, who seem to like the place and with whom the climate appears to agree, earn their living solely by trading; they purchase from the natives mealies, cocoa-nuts, ground-nuts, hides of various kinds, ivory, ostrich feathers, etc., and export them to Europe.

At Inhambane Mr. Rhodes wanted to pick out some Kafirs to take with him to Mashonaland. Some sixty were prepared to follow him, but he selected only fifteen out of the number—all fine, strong, vigorous young men. One of them, Matokwa, was the cook of an English Agent there who, thinking that his wife (a Portuguese woman) could ill afford to lose the services of the boy, refused to let him go. On the lady being consulted, however, she consented to the boy leaving her. He joined the rest, and very cheerfully the fifteen went on board.

But, to our annoyance, when we were about to leave the bay, a young haughty Portuguese officer brought our Premier a letter from the Governor of the place, forbidding him to take the Kafirs with him, unless, before doing so, the boys satisfied him (the Governor) that it was with their own free will that they were leaving for Mashonaland, and demanding the immediate return of the boys to the shore. We at once took counsel as to whether we would submit to the Governor's demand or not. Mr. Rhodes had already advanced each Kafir a few sovereigns, besides having provided them with shirts and blankets. To permit them now to go ashore would simply have been to allow them to run away with what they had received, and this they could do very easily, as it was now dark. Besides, they had already lawfully entered our service and taken their quarters with us, and they were as willing to go with us as we were to take them—a fact which their merry singing and whistling proved as clearly as did their free statements. Having fully discussed the question, we could not come to any other conclusion but that the Governor's demand was intended to baffle our plans; we therefore decided to refuse to yield to it. The letter-bearer was meanwhile waiting for our answer.

The Premier went up to him and courteously said to him—

"Tell your Governor that neither the English Agent nor the Dutch Agent, nor any other person that lives here, has told us that it is illegal to hire the natives of Inhambane. And, if you wish to make certain whether it is with their own free will that the boys intend to follow us, you may go and speak to them. If I had only *consented*, fifty more would have followed me. I cannot let them go on shore now—it is too dark and late for that!"

"My order is," replied the young Portuguese with apparent determination, "that the Kafirs return with me."

"And my reply is," retorted the Premier, who was getting warm, "that that shall not happen! Here they shall remain! Now, not a word more from you—go and do your message!"

Immediately upon the departure of the messenger, Mr. Rhodes turned to the Captain of the *Norseman* and told him that if he was ready for departure he had better not delay.

No further message did Mr. Rhodes get from the Governor, but two Portuguese gentlemen with big black moustaches came on board.

CHAPTER III.

We depart from Inhambane—The pilot proves an unsuccessful acrobat—We reach Beira Bay—In trouble once more about our Kafirs—Captain Pipon to the rescue—The Governor outwitted.

At eleven o'clock we left Inhambane. It was a dark night—so dark that it became dangerous for our ship to continue its course. Consequently, after having sailed a few miles up the bay, we cast anchor again. All the sky, as far as we could see it, was overhung with dense clouds, and the rain soon came down in heavy showers.

The following morning the weather was beautifully clear again, and it was pretty to watch the multitude of little Kafir-boats that lay fishing in the quiet bay. The natives build their own boats, and they do it very skilfully. It is surprising to see how swiftly these little vessels can be rowed over the water.

At six o'clock the anchor was heaved, and the pilot we had had the previous day was again on board our ship with his two Kafir assistants. The awful time the latter had undergone the day before, as a result of connecting their boat by rope to the *Norseman's* stern, had made them wiser; this time they came on board and hoisted their boat on deck. With remarkable dexterity the black pilot now steered the vessel. At eight o'clock the anchor was again lowered and the pilot's boat loosened. But here an amusing accident took place. As the boat was about to be let down with the two Kafir boys in it, the ship-boy, to whom the duty of lowering it had been entrusted, through careless management, instead of letting it down slowly, let it drop into the water with a splash. The consequence was that the boat's unfortunate occupants lay sardine-like on its bottom. Though it was with awe that we beheld the boat go down, the result was the signal for a roar of laughter from the deck. The poor fellows might be thankful that the boat had not capsized. Neither of them was hurt, but both were greatly startled, and they looked exceedingly embarrassed when they saw us so much amused at their expense.

This, however, was not the last comical accident we were to be entertained with that morning. The gallant pilot now arrived on the scene. His boys immediately informed him how "those Englishmen" had nearly drowned them. He put on an air of dissatisfaction at our conduct and told us in a fatherly manner that we might have cracked his boat. The captain begged his pardon for what had happened, and the pilot, a very big man in his own estimation, shook hands with the captain and some others. Very pleased with himself, he pompously stepped down the ladder on the side of the ship where his boat lay. Reaching the lowest step, he tried to jump in; but, having miscalculated the distance, his foot only touched the rim of the boat, and head over heels the heavy pilot tumbled in the water. Fortunately, one of the other Kafirs quickly seized his master's foot, held it, and, with the aid of his companion, dragged the pilot into the boat. Not an inch of his dress was dry. His watch hung out of his pocket; he opened it, examined it, blew into it, put it to his ear,—the poor thing was as wet as its master. And so was the telescope that was hanging from his arm. Who could refrain from laughing? The pilot's ludicrous mishap did not, however, in the least affect his self-esteem; he uttered not a word, and, as we stood there shaking with laughter, he looked up at us with a most sedate expression on his face as if nothing at all had happened, and seemed to be wondering what was entertaining us.

We resumed our voyage, and, sailing opposite the Hlengaland coast, we could see on it trees of immense size, but of what kind they were we could not discern. During the night following we passed the mouth of the Sabi, a large river of which the Lundi is a tributary; and a little higher up we passed Chiluan Bay—a bay, I am told, almost as pretty as that at Inhambane. Chiluan is, like most of the harbours on the East Coast, a very fruitful place. The next large river-mouth we passed was that of the Shashi, twenty-two miles south of the Pungwe. The mouths of these rivers present magnificent views, and birds and wild animals are there to be met with in great abundance. In course of time, I dare say, the rivers will prove to be of much use and convenience to trading vessels, for many of them are navigable far inland, some from forty to fifty miles.

On Saturday (26th Sept.) the *Norseman* — with

the mouth of the Pungwe on the right, and the mouth of the Busi on the left, the former of which is by far the larger of the two—steamed into the beautiful Beira Bay, the end of our voyage in that boat—1610 miles from Capetown—and at a quarter past two she cast anchor.

Beira Bay is undoubtedly a very fine bay, but its shores are not so richly wooded as those of Inhambane and Chiluan. Beira, the port, contains some fifty or sixty houses and some stores, almost all of which are built of galvanised iron.

There were lying at anchor in the Bay one English and one Portuguese man-o'-war and ten small ships, exclusive of the *Norseman*.

On our way from Inhambane to Beira we had discovered that the two Portuguese who had embarked on our vessel at the former place were not men of insignificance: one was a high official under the Governor, and the other a judge.

We had intended to convey our Kafirs, horses and luggage from the *Norseman* to the *Agnes* immediately on our arrival at Beira and to proceed up the Pungwe without delay, but the Beira Governor (or the Chief Commander, as the Portuguese called him) destroyed our programme. We received an order from him that the Kafirs we had taken on board at Inhambane should all be brought before him so that they might personally declare to him whether or not they had voluntarily joined us. Meanwhile, some Portuguese officials came on board to see whether we had brought with us any articles to smuggle into the country! Mr. Rhodes, accompanied by Mr. Dennis Doyle and

Major Johnson, went ashore to the customs office, taking his fifteen Kafirs with him. Under the charge of Mr. Doyle the boys were sent to the Governor, but his Honour did not think it worth his while to come and speak to them that day. After letting them wait at his door the whole afternoon, he coolly made his messenger tell Mr. Doyle that he could not see him that day, but would meet him the following morning at nine.

Darkness had already set in when Mr. Rhodes, Major Johnson and Mr. Doyle returned to the *Norseman* with the Kafirs, having accomplished nothing. The hope we had cherished of spending a nice quiet Sunday (which was the following day) on the *Agnes* had now to be abandoned. It was not difficult to guess the meaning of the Portuguese Commander's conduct. He evidently wished to show us some of his red tape, and he did so under the cover of being "Oh, such a humane man! Such a saviour of those poor innocent natives whom that Englishman of a Rhodes had apparently deceived!"

No, but we knew better. The cool treatment we were receiving at his hands was as little occasioned by his anxiety to protect the natives as to protect the man in the moon; it was simply to defy and tease the great Chartered-Company man, whom the Portuguese both envy and hate.

We at once resolved to have recourse to Captain Pipon, the captain of the British man-o'-war lying in the bay, who was also British Consul at Beira, and to lay our grievance before him. He received us with the greatest courtesy, and the Premier informed him how he was being treated by the Portuguese. The captain thereupon sent the Governor a message, stating that Mr. Rhodes was anxious to depart from Beira at the flood of the tide early the following morning, and that it was a matter of urgency for the Prime Minister to get away from there as soon as possible. Having waited a couple of hours for the reply, a message was brought us that the Kafirs could come to the Chief Commander's house at seven the following morning instead of nine. This was pleasant news, of course, but we still felt greatly annoyed at the unpleasant delay and the fuss about nothing.

We left the man-o'-war at eleven o'clock at night and returned to the *Norseman*, being much obliged to Captain Pipon. Early the next morning Mr. Doyle, Major Johnson and I went on shore with the Kafirs. We found good Captain Pipon waiting for us there, and he went with us at once to the Governor's house. We knocked at the front door and a boy opened it and invited us to come in. We went in, Captain Pipon leading the way, and presently we stood before the so-called Governor. There he sat, a yellow, undignified-looking Portuguese, with nothing of the ruler about him. His interpreter, who was to speak English to us, did not look much better. I shook my head. "Indeed," thought I, "are *you* the men who are thus detaining us? What next, I wonder!"

The old yellow Commander now began to question us through his interpreter, but the latter spoke English so miserably that we had the greatest difficulty in understanding him; in fact, we could not understand him at all.

"*Pardon, Mynheer!*" I said to him at last, "*spreekt u Hollandsch?*"

"*Non,*" replied he.

"*Sprechen Sie deutsch?*" I next tried.

"*Non,*" repeated he.

"*Parlez-vous français?*" Captain Pipon put in.

"*Oui, Monsieur*" was the answer, and the obstacle was overcome. Captain Pipon then made clear to the Governor all that was necessary, but the great Beira lord tried to raise every possible objection to our retaining the Kafirs, and wound up by saying that he would decide nothing until he had personally examined the boys. Accordingly, the latter were immediately called in. To our surprise, both the Governor and his interpreter addressed the Kafirs in their own (the Kafirs') language. I thought that we were now beaten out of the field, but Mr. Doyle, who had grown up in Natal, understood every word that was uttered. All sorts of ridiculous questions were put to the Kafirs, and they were reminded of the awful journey before them, its many dangers, etc. Then Mr. Doyle stepped forward and took up the cudgels for us; he spoke in Kafir, and with such fluency that it was with astonishment and admiration that the Portuguese gentlemen listened to his words.

To make a long story short, the Governor at last asked the Kafirs whether they did not think that twenty-five shillings a month were too little, adding that they should each get at least forty shillings. They answered that they expected forty shillings. The Governor now turned to Mr. Doyle and said to him,—

"Ah, you see they have been misled!"

"No wonder," answered Mr. Doyle, "that such *seems* to be the case after you have put the words into their mouths."

Anyhow, we were not going to waste any more time there. "Good-bye, sir!" Mr. Doyle said to the Commander. "I cannot say I much esteem your conduct towards us. As for these boys, you may keep them if you like."

When we came outside Mr. Doyle said to the Kafirs, "Now do as you choose—either you return with me to Mr. Rhodes, or you return the money he has given you and stay here! At once you must decide, for we are ready to depart!"

For a few minutes the Kafirs discussed the question among themselves, and unanimously decided to follow us. After buying some provisions, we left by boat for the *Norseman*; Captain Pipon returning to his man-of-war, the *Magicienne*. To that kind captain we were much indebted: without his assistance we would certainly have been delayed another day or would have had to leave without the Kafirs.

Major Johnson now discovered that two of the cases of our provisions had gone astray, probably at Durban, where they were transhipped from the *Mexican* to the *Norseman*. This naturally to some degree troubled his mind, and he again went on shore to endeavour to recover the lost cases, but could find no trace of them.

At half-past eleven we left Beira in the *Agnes*, a fine, comfortable, flat-bottomed vessel built after the style of those boats one meets with on European lakes. She is the property of Messrs. Johnson and Co. Sailing up the river for half-an-hour, we passed a beautiful little island densely wooded with the mangrove, a useful tree for building purposes—for boats as well as houses. Some desolate huts are still to be noticed on the island.

On the shores of both the Pungwe and the Busi there are to be seen numberless beautifully straight and tall trees. When Beira becomes the great seaport town for Mashonaland—as I expect it ere long will be—there will certainly be no scarcity of excellent building material as far as wood is concerned.

At a quarter-past two we passed another islet, resembling the one we had seen at noon, both in its woods and in its size. We were now ten miles up the river, and yet its width was one-and-a-half miles, and of a fair depth.

CHAPTER IV.

Our first sight of hippopotami—Native canoes—A lovely night—
We row to the shore and have a water-buck hunt—Major
Johnson the "man of the day"—We reach Naves Ferreira—
Notes on the Portuguese inhabitants and the native Kafirs.

A QUARTER of an hour later we passed a third islet, on which we observed a number of large huts. It is safer for the natives to live on the island than on the mainland, especially in time of war. The Gazaland Kafirs often make plundering expeditions to that part of the country, and at such times the natives on the borders of the Pungwe flee to their canoes and make for the land surrounded by water, where they know the enemy would not take the trouble to pursue them. The man they most dread is the notorious marauder, Gungunhana. The huts on the island are not built, as elsewhere, upon the ground, but up in the trees. The reason for this is obvious. It is not an uncommon thing for the Pungwe to flood the island, leaving only the trees above the water; a hut, therefore, built upon the ground would be swept away during such an overflow and its inmates drowned—as has been the case more than once in earlier days.

At half-past two we saw the first hippopotami. There were four. It was interesting to watch them splashing in the water. Numerous tracts of theirs, the paths they used at night when out grazing, we could distinctly discern on the river's banks.

At four o'clock we were thirty miles from Beira, and here the river was still very broad. We passed another "river-horse," and, shortly afterwards, two more, the latter swimming very close to our vessel.

We passed a fourth island, a very small one, but also densely grown with trees with many a native hut amongst them. As we sailed past this islet, two pirogues, each with a crew of four Kafirs, passed us. Most of the canoes possessed by the natives along the Pungwe are very old and have been handed down from generation to generation. They are exceedingly strong and have been the means of saving the lives of hundreds during the pillaging excursions of the Gazas. These canoes are made out of the trunks of trees, and the instruments used for the purpose are tools manufactured by the Kafirs themselves.

Towards evening we passed close by a group of six hippopotami. Some shots were fired at them from our moving ship, but without success. Just then another pirogue passed us. It was in one of these canoes that Messrs. Vosloo, Jan Eksteen and Adriaan de Waal came down the river from Mapandas to Beira a fortnight before.

Lions, I am told, are frequently to be seen on the banks of the river from the vessels sailing in the stream. We, however, noticed none.

The sun having set, it was rapidly growing dark, and the captain of the *Agnes* thought it advisable to cast the anchor, as sailing in the black night in that winding stream might result in a stranding. Our boat was now lying thirty-five miles from Beira. It was a quiet evening and the water was so calm that it did not appear to move. We sat on deck. All around us solemn silence reigned. The weather was glorious, the sky cloudless; and as we sat there with the gloomy stream around us, the black forests yonder on our right and left, and the starry heaven above us— a picture that the ablest artist could not reproduce— our feelings could not but be affected and our thoughts carried into the mystic land.

At eight o'clock we betook ourselves to our little saloon and had supper. At nine we were again on deck. We could now hear the howling of hyænas, and not long afterwards the roaring of lions. Hearing hyænas howl was nothing strange to me—I had heard that scores of times during our previous travel to the interior—but I had never before heard a lion growl, at least, not in the open country.

As it got later the dew began to fall, a thin mist formed over the water, and we were advised by the captain to go to our cabins, for such was the sort of weather, he said, that so often caused fever. Major Johnson confirmed his words, and soon we were all in bed.

The next morning the weather was again delightful, and on every side of us we enjoyed majestic scenery. At five the anchor was weighed, but our ship had hardly been an hour in motion when she struck sand and had to lie still once more—an inconvenience for which we had to thank the Beira Governor, who had detained us so long.

To avail ourselves of our leisure, we resolved to lower

one of the boats we had on deck, row to the shore and have a water-buck hunt. The Premier, the Major, and myself comprised the hunting party, and we were attended by four of our Kafirs. We pulled straight for the shore, got out there, and clambered up the slippery bank. Scarcely had we reached level ground when we caught sight of a herd of hundreds of water-bucks, or witgatbokken, as some call them. Perceiving us, and startled by the shots we fired, the animals ran bewildered into grass two and a half feet high and very moist with dew. Nothing daunted, however, we pursued them there, though it was a picture for *Punch* that we presented as we struggled through the wet grass. After an hour's chase Mr. Rhodes and I gave up the pursuit in disgust. Major Johnson, however, was determined to shoot something before he returned, so we left him behind with two Kafirs, while we returned to the ship with our nether garments as wet as the grass that had made them so. We changed our clothes and had breakfast. An hour afterwards Major Johnson arrived, his two Kafirs together carrying half a buck. He had shot two, a male and a female. We sent eight Kafirs to fetch the buck and a half that had been left behind, and within an hour the boys returned with their heavy load. We were thus well supplied with meat, the he-buck alone weighing 250 lbs. The animals were soon flayed, and it was surprising to see how greedily the Kafirs ate the raw liver and lungs. I had witnessed some of them on the *Norseman* cram themselves with the raw stomach of an ox, and I thought that singular, but never did I expect to see them gluttonize over raw lung, pancreas and liver.

At lunch we drank the health of "the man of the day," Major Johnson. The game he had shot was particularly welcome, since the meat we had brought with us was all consumed. Not only we but our Kafirs were now amply provided for.

At twenty past two in the afternoon the rising tide set the *Agnes* afloat again. As we proceeded, we saw a Kafir kraal near the river's bank, some of the huts of which were built on the ground and some in trees. During the dry season those on the ground are inhabited; during the rainy those in the trees are resorted to.

A little higher up the stream we sailed very close to two hippopotami; but, owing to the motions of the vessel, we failed to shoot them.

The *Agnes* now passed round the corner of land where Major Johnson the year before lost a purse containing £75, whilst he and Dr. Jameson were reconnoitring a route for the Chartered Company. Early the next morning the *Agnes* reached her destination; she had now carried us as far up the river as its depth allowed—sixty miles from Beira.

While we were landing at six o'clock, 120 natives sat upon the shore with folded arms and legs, inquisitively staring at us as if we were supernatural creatures; more like a troupe of big baboons human beings could not look.

There was a Portuguese military outpost there, called Naves Ferreira. The fruitfulness of the place arrested my attention. Tropical vegetation—such as rice, coffee, cotton, the sugar-cane and the banana—luxuriate there. But, suitable as the place is for these plants and fruits, it is very unhealthy for the European. With the aborigine, however, the climate seems to agree very well. The Portuguese soldiers stationed there look simply miserable. I firmly believe that that place, together with the adjoining country, would, if it were cultivated, thereby having its insalubrity lessened if not altogether taken away, develop into no insignificant a source of supply to the world for coffee, rice, sugar, etc. As regards its summer temperature, it is no warmer than that at Durban, Natal.

The Portuguese there, like the natives, dwell in huts; and there is no difference between the hut of the Portuguese and that of the Kafirs, and not much distinction between the two races. The Portuguese wear clothes, the Kafirs do not; the Portuguese are yellow, the Kafirs black; the Portuguese are physically weak, the Kafirs strong—these are the only striking differences; for the rest they are one. They mix with each other, take each other around the waist, and talk one language when together—Kafir. *This* is certain though: the natives are more cleanly in their habits than their yellow masters. The latter are as thin as dried fish, and they die like rats.

CHAPTER V.

Unloading under difficulties—Pikenin astonishes us with an acrobatic feat—" Crocodile Nest"—Supper at Mapandas—A novel way of destroying rats—A wild-goose chase—Outspan at Muda—Our night's rest disturbed by lions.

IT cost us some time and trouble to remove our goods from the *Agnes*. One by one, by the help of pulleys, our horses in their boxes were lifted from the boat to the shore. Four of them were in this way safely landed, but, as the fifth was being swung over, the rope snapped, and down came the cage with horse and all. The box broke, and the startled horse escaped unhurt. But Pikenin, the boy of seventeen whom I had selected at Beira to be my attendant, had been hanging to the rope with which the horse in its cage had been hauled up; and so, when the rope snapped beneath him, the pole to which it was attached was swung back with great force and the boy along with it. I trembled at the sight, expecting a serious accident. But, to the amazement of us all, Pikenin still firmly clung to the rope, and there hung high in the air over the water like a fish hooked to a line. How to free himself from this awkward position he did not know. To throw himself down into the river, among the crocodiles, was dangerous; to remain clinging to the rope was impossible. What was he to do? The only course open to him was to risk the fall, and that course he adopted. I shuddered to see him go down. Head and heels he went under the water; but up again he came, and, amid loud cheers from his fellow-Kafirs as well as from ourselves, swam like a fish to the ship.

"Bravo, my boy!" I hailed him. "Few would do what you have done to-day."

Had he been a white man much would have been said of the surprising feat he had performed; but, being a negro, his gallant performance was to be appreciated only so long as it lasted. Pikenin, of whom I was now more proud than ever, appeared to know nothing of what had happened. Without paying the slightest regard to the praises he received, he quietly sat down for a rest, and soon afterwards was again hard at work. I watched him all the while and could not but admire his conduct.

At half-past three all was landed. Our cart, packed with as much as could go on it, was inspanned, and we were ready to start on our land journey. Every horse, too, had to carry something.

In the forenoon, as Major Johnson was having considerable difficulty in landing the horses, I went to his assistance and instructed some of the boys how to act, but this action of mine seemed to please neither the Premier nor the Major, and the former smilingly said to me—

"Do you know, my friend, that too many cooks spoil the broth?"

I answered not a word, but felt inwardly indignant. "All right," I thought; "see how you get along!" I stepped into the boat and rowed to the ship. As a shower of rain was just then coming down, I was, after all, rather glad that my assistance had been rejected. Not long afterwards Mr. Rhodes also came on board.

Now, in the afternoon, when Major Johnson, who had the cart and horses under his charge, was to leave for Mapandas, an hour's journey from Naves Ferreira, it was in vain that he endeavoured to get the wretched Montevideo horses, which he had purchased at Durban, to move from the spot. The dampness of the harness and the strangeness of the country strengthened the horses in their obstinacy. First a breast-plate burst, next the harness was entangled, then something else went wrong—and so it went on. I looked on quietly from the ship. By and by Mr. Rhodes came to me and said,—

"Well, what do you think of this?"

"It certainly is not very promising," I answered. "Those Montevideo horses are stubborn old post-cart jades, whose previous owners were only too glad to get rid of them; and Major Johnson understands as much about handling them as a crow does about baking cakes."

"Well," he asked, "why don't you go on shore and help him? They are making no progress whatever, and I fear they won't get away at all."

"I would have been on shore long ago," I answered, "were I not afraid of getting another unpleasant look from Johnson; besides, don't you know 'too many cooks spoil the broth'?"

"Nonsense!" said the Premier, with a guilty smile. 'Go on shore and help them."

I jumped into a boat, rowed to the bank, and at once ordered the two most unruly of the six horses to be outspanned. I shortened the breast-belts and some strings, put the harness right, placed six Kafirs at the wheels, made one take the rope in front, took the whip myself, and commanded as I struck the horses—

"Now, boys—push!"

And off went the cart. It had not gone far, however, when, in a little valley, the horses again stopped. I went thither, again made the Kafirs put their shoulders to the wheels, gave the horses another drubbing, and again they started.

Major Johnson, attended by the Kafirs, followed the cart on horseback. I returned to Mr. Rhodes, who was waiting for me at the river to leave by boat for Mapandas, where we were to meet the cart. The journey thither by river would be about eight or nine miles. It was half-past four when we entered the boat with two Kafirs, who were to be the rowers. We soon sailed round a corner of the Medinkidinki Island, a piece of land about forty miles long and twenty broad, around both sides of which the Pungwe flows. It is the abode, I am told, of many kinds of wild beast; bears abound there, and the place is so noted for its reptiles that it is known by many as "Crocodile Nest," and no native would venture to live near the river. Yet, upon that same "island" Major Johnson and Dr. Jameson spent a night last year, not, however, a very comfortable one. They only became aware of the sort of place they had chosen to sleep in when their rest was disturbed by the presence of hippopotami and the roars of lions.

The sun set and we were still far from Mapandas, and we now became afraid that we would not reach the place before night, so Mr. Rhodes promised the boatmen each an *extra* sovereign if they succeeded in bringing us to our destination ere dark. With increased energy the boat was now rowed, the Kafirs singing merrily all the while a most monotonous tune, which still seems to ring in my ears. At seven o'clock we reached Mapandas. Mr. Rhodes and I each mounted a Kafir's back, and with great difficulty were carried on land, the ground being very slippery.

Mapandas is a Portuguese station, lying about seventy miles from Beira, and provided with a couple of small shops. It is a damp, and, consequently, unhealthy place.

Major Johnson had already arrived with the cart when we came there. We put up at the Messrs. Cowhan, who treated us very hospitably. They gave us a well-furnished, comfortable room, with fine beds. We changed our wet clothes, and thereafter partook of an enjoyable supper. As we sat at table, rats were running to and fro along the beams and rafters, whilst little Kafir boys were busily engaged shooting at them with small arrows. But rats are not the only creatures that annoy the inhabitants of Mapandas. Mosquitoes are worse. I did not have a bad night there, however, for I had a curtain round my bedstead to keep the insects out; besides, I was too tired to trouble myself about mosquitoes.

The following morning we were disappointed to find

the drizzling rain, that had begun to fall the day before, continue.

Mr. Rhodes bought a cart and an oval-shaped tent from a Mr. Fraser at Mapandas. How we were to get away from there with *two* carts by horses that the day before would hardly pull *one*, time must show.

The weather began to clear up in the afternoon and we made ourselves ready to depart from the damp mosquito-camp. At ten o'clock the two carts were inspanned, each with four horses; and three ponies were saddled for Mr. Rhodes, Major Johnson and me. We had a great deal of trouble with these almost ungovernable — perhaps also untrained — animals. Horses were repeatedly changed, and ultimately all three ponies we had chosen to ride upon were in harness. Mr. Rhodes, Major Johnson and I sat on one cart; William and Tonie on the other; whilst the outspanned horses carrying the pack-saddles were being led by the Kafirs.

We had not left Mapandas far behind when we came across a group of bucks and, a little further, a herd of Lichtenstein hartebeests; but we failed to shoot any. Many strange animals ran about from one bush to another every time a shot was fired; amongst these I noticed wild pigs looking like lions from a distance. The Lichtenstein hartebeest is a pretty animal and is found only on the East Coast of Africa.

Just before sunset we crossed a spruit (*i.e.* a tributary of some river), and, as we did so, we caught sight of some large wild geese walking on the side of a pool about half a mile from our cart. My two friends pressed me to go and shoot them. Well, an opportunity to shoot wild geese—dainties in the dish—is not offered me every day, but I had no inclination to make use of the present one.

"Why won't you go?" asked both the Premier and the Major.

"Because," I answered, "this is a wild, unknown world to me. I feel anything but desirous to creep in that tall grass with a gun loaded only with partridge-shot. Suppose I come upon a lion! What then? You know as well as I do that this part of the country is noted as an abode of lions!"

"Nonsense!" was the reply. "There is nothing to fear—you may safely go."

Just to please them, I took my gun and went. In order not to frighten the geese, the nearer I approached them the less of my body did I allow to appear above the grass. At first I walked erect, then I stooped, and at last I crept; but I had not crept far when I entered into a little path winding through grass taller than myself, and noticed in it the footmarks of various animals, amongst others those of the lion. No, thought I, this will never do. I stood erect, and, as I did so, away flew the geese, and I was not sorry, for I was anxious to turn back at once. I straightway returned to the carts, and when I reached them Major Johnson asked me with a derisive smile whether it was fear that had made me rise up at such a distance from the geese.

"Certainly it was," I emphatically answered—"not because I am a coward—I will not flee from any man in the world—but because creeping in the pathway of lions, so poorly armed as I am, was foolishly risking my life. Of what earthly use would my shot-gun have been to me if a lion had plunged upon me?"

Shortly afterwards Major Johnson fired at some Lichtenstein hartebeests, but missed. Next we met a lot of bastard hartebeests. Zebras, too, we saw in numbers, whilst now and then we also sighted a wild dog, an animal that frequently preys upon the young of zebras. Towards evening we passed groups of three or four kinds of bucks, which appeared as tame as oxen, but we did not take the trouble to shoot any as we had neither the inclination nor the time to do so; the sun being already low in the west and we had not yet reached a spot suitable to outspan at.

Mr. Rhodes, Major Johnson and I drove some distance in advance of the cart which we had left in Tonie's care. But William soon came running up to us to tell us that the wheels of Tonie's cart had sunk in the mud at a marshy place, that the horses were unable to draw them out, and that, owing to all the jerking, one of the swingle-bars had broken. We returned to the cart, made a sort of swingle out of a piece of wood, and set the cart in its course again.

A little past sunset we outspanned at Muda River, some miles from Mapandas. There we pitched the tent that Mr. Rhodes had bought from Mr. Fraser, and spread out his stretcher—a very handy article that Mr. Fraser had presented him with. Both the tent and the stretcher proved of great use and convenience during our journey.

Being aware that lions abounded about the Muda, we took precaution to render our little camp as safe as possible. Having tied our horses, we at seven o'clock sat down to supper, the silence of the evening being repeatedly broken by the howling of hyænas, which was followed shortly afterwards by the roaring of lions.

"Well, my friends," Major Johnson observed, "we may prepare ourselves for a stormy night"; and, as he was an experienced traveller in Africa, having been the leader of the Pioneers to Mashonaland, his warning carried weight. We ordered our boys to see that the horses were well tied, and to collect a large quantity of wood. The darker it grew, the louder became the noise of the lions from all sides.

Between ten and eleven we went to sleep—the Premier in his stretcher in the middle of the tent, the Major and myself on the ground at his side. Small though the tent was, it comfortably accommodated the three of us. The fierce growling of the lions was still growing worse. My two companions were soon fast asleep, but I, feeling anxious about the safety of the horses, could not close my eyes. I knew that we could not dispense with a single horse. If the lions entered the camp and killed our draught animals, the whole programme of our journey would be set at nought, and no other course would be open to us but to turn back. Judging by the noise, some five or six lions were strolling in close proximity to our camp.

At two o'clock in the night one of our horses—probably through a start—got loose. I called William, and ordered him at once to tie the horse again; for I knew that if it ran out of the camp it was sure to fall a prey to the lions. William was afraid to get up; but, on my threatening to punish him if he disobeyed, he crept out of his bed, though very reluctantly, and with the assistance of some of the Kafirs, and not without considerable difficulty, he secured the horse again.

The Inhambane Kafirs, in order to keep away the wild animals from the camp, kept a large fire alive all night. Towards morning the wild noises gradually grew less, till at last nothing at all was to be heard. It was only then that I could fall asleep, and I enjoyed an hour's sweet repose. "Dear me," I thought, as I arose, "if the first night pass like this, I wonder what the rest will be like?"

CHAPTER VI.

Vexatious trouble with the horses—Buffaloes—A natural zoological garden—A dash in a crocodile-pool—Lions dangerously close—Rest at last—Mr. Rhodes shoots a zebra—A wild rush—The Premier chased by a "lion."

At half-past six the carts were inspanned, and the horses, with which Major Johnson had so thoroughly been swindled, again gave us no little trouble. And —what vexed me more—my two companions coolly had their horses saddled and rode away, leaving me alone with the Kafirs to struggle with the restive animals. It cost us at least two hours to get the beasts to start, and that was only with *one* cart, which I now left in the hands of William and Tonie. With the other I, with two Kafirs, was able to follow a little afterwards; but it had hardly been in progress half an hour when it stuck again; I had come to a small furrow, and the horses were determined not to draw the cart through it. But a sound thrashing altered their mind, not, however, before another half hour had been wasted.

As I was helping to push the cart along, Matokwa suddenly stopped and exclaimed,—

"Master! *boho! boho!*"

I looked up and saw the Kafir excitedly point with his finger at two large animals. I at once seized among the crocodiles, was dangerous; to remain clinging to the rope was impossible. What was he to do? The only course open to him was to risk the fall, and that course he adopted. I shuddered to see him go down. Head and heels he went under the water; but up again he came, and, amid loud cheers from his fellow-Kafirs as well as from ourselves, swam like a fish to the ship.

"Bravo, my boy!" I hailed him. "Few would do what you have done to-day."

Had he been a white man much would have been said of the surprising feat he had performed; but, being a negro, his gallant performance was to be appreciated only so long as it lasted. Pikenin, of whom I was now more proud than ever, appeared to know nothing of what had happened. Without paying the slightest regard to the praises he received, he quietly sat down for a rest, and soon afterwards was again hard at work. I watched him all the while and could not but admire his conduct.

At half-past three all was landed. Our cart, packed with as much as could go on it, was inspanned, and we were ready to start on our land journey. Every horse, too, had to carry something.

In the forenoon, as Major Johnson was having considerable difficulty in landing the horses, I went to his assistance and instructed some of the boys how to act, but this action of mine seemed to please neither the Premier nor the Major, and the former smilingly said to me—

"Do you know, my friend, that too many cooks spoil the broth?"

I answered not a word, but felt inwardly indignant. "All right," I thought; "see how you get along!" I stepped into the boat and rowed to the ship. As a shower of rain was just then coming down, I was, after all, rather glad that my assistance had been rejected. Not long afterwards Mr. Rhodes also came on board.

Now, in the afternoon, when Major Johnson, who had the cart and horses under his charge, was to leave for Mapandas, an hour's journey from Naves Ferreira, it was in vain that he endeavoured to get the wretched Montevideo horses, which he had purchased at Durban, to move from the spot. The dampness of the harness and the strangeness of the country strengthened the horses in their obstinacy. First a breast-plate burst, next the harness was entangled, then something else went wrong—and so it went on. I looked on quietly from the ship. By and by Mr. Rhodes came to me and said,—

"Well, what do you think of this?"

"It certainly is not very promising," I answered. "Those Montevideo horses are stubborn old post-cart jades, whose previous owners were only too glad to get rid of them; and Major Johnson understands as much about handling them as a crow does about baking cakes."

"Well," he asked, "why don't you go on shore and help him? They are making no progress whatever, and I fear they won't get away at all."

"I would have been on shore long ago," I answered, "were I not afraid of getting another unpleasant look from Johnson; besides, don't you know 'too many cooks spoil the broth'?"

but, being already supplied with more meat than we needed for the present, we would not shoot at them, for it would have been a cruelty to kill the innocent creatures and leave them lying for the vultures. Besides, Mr. Rhodes had shot half-a-dozen pheasants, and these also required space in the cart, every corner of which was now filled.

At seven o'clock Tonie upset his cart, with the result that the pole broke. It took us half an hour to make another.

At eight we arrived at the Mudichiri River, where we were confronted by an awful piece of road. On the one side of the river we had to descend a slope almost perpendicular to the surface of the shore, and on the other side we had to mount another equally steep. We packed as much of the goods upon the horses as we could, and made the Kafirs carry the rest. We had indeed no easy task before us. Slowly or even at a moderate rate we could not drive down the bank, for that would certainly result in our cart sticking down in the river; on the other hand, if we drove hard, there was the glaring probability of the vehicle being overturned. However, being compelled to adopt either of the two courses, we chose the latter. I took the reins and Major Johnson the whip.

"Pull!" shouted I to William, who held the rope in front, and down the slope we went like the wind. Startled and bewildered, up the opposite bank the horses rushed as if the Evil Spirit was after them, and —thank Heaven!—"cart number one" was through the Mudichiri.

We now returned to fetch the second cart. But it

had to be provided with a better pole before we could venture to deal with it as we had done with the other. Major Johnson, upon whom we could always rely in time of need, hewed down a fairly-straight tree, and, without spending much trouble on it, furnished the cart with a new pole, which we could not trust, however, before we had put it to the test; so we decided to have the cart pulled through the river by the Kafirs. Major Johnson and I each lent a helping hand, and our share in drawing the cart along was more than merely nominal. By means of ropes we tugged the vehicle with all our might, and, at the expense of a little labour and perspiration we succeeded in safely landing it on the opposite bank, When this fatiguing business was over we went to a pool close by to take a wash. Mr. Rhodes warned us to be careful, but we felt so warm and tired and the beautifully clear water was so tempting that nothing could keep us from it. We plunged in and enjoyed a delicious bath.

After the bath we had breakfast, our first meal that day, and Mr. Rhodes and I now seized the opportunity of blessing Major Johnson for having assured us before we started on the journey that we would have a passably fine road all the way between Beira and Umtali. To express it mildly, we did not find it so. Our prospect of making much progress with the cart was indeed a very faint one. Only nineteen miles from Mapandas and already a swingle-bar and a pole broken! It was not very encouraging!

After breakfast Major Johnson and I seated ourselves a little distance from each other in the shade of some trees on the bank of the river. The Major (clothed in little else than a pleasing smile), was engaged mending the trousers he had torn earlier in the morning, while I was taking down notes in my pocket-book.

"De Waal," he suddenly called, "come and see something here!"

I went, and he pointed out to me a huge crocodile basking itself in the rays of the sun on the farther side of the pool in which we had swum.

"Man," I observed, "really we must be more careful with respect to the pools we bathe in, or else as sure as fate these crocodiles will do away with us."

He agreed with me, but added, "You will see, if we swim swiftly, kick hard with our feet, and make as much noise in the water as we can, they will be afraid to tackle us."

At half-past two we left the river, passed through a really beautiful tract of country and halted at half-past four in a valley. Having allowed our draught animals to have a roll on the ground and to quench their thirst, we again put them to the carts, and without further delay—though two of our Kafirs whom we had left in charge of a fine chestnut horse packed with pots and pans, etc., were still behind—proceeded on our way. This, however, was a serious mistake. As it was already late in the afternoon, and we had reached a place where there was water, we should have stopped there. As it was, we travelled on, Tonie and William driving the carts. The road was now level, and we were making steady, though somewhat slow, progress.

Thousands of zebras have their abode in the country

we were now travelling through, and it is chiefly owing to the presence of these animals that so many hyænas, wild dogs, and lions inhabit the place. A lion very easily catches a zebra when it has a foal, as well as the foal itself.

Twilight set in, and hyænas shortly afterwards announced the approach of night. At half-past seven the lions began with their horrible roars. We should by this time have ended the journey for the day, but, as we were still in search of a decent place at which to outspan, a place where there was water, we continued to advance. Major Johnson rode in front, William closely followed him with one cart, and Mr. Rhodes and myself with Tonie and the other cart came on behind. We took care to keep near to the cart in order to protect it from the dangers of the night. The cart in front we knew was safe, being under the Major's care, but we felt very anxious about the party behind us, the two Kafirs with the mare. The later it became the worse became the dreadful roaring around us, and we felt extremely uncomfortable.

Our party, as I have already mentioned, was now broken up into three parts—Major Johnson with William, the Kafirs and one cart leading the way, ourselves with the second cart following at a considerable distance, and the two Kafirs with the mare (our best horse) far behind. And each division was, as it were, surrounded by wild animals, of which their king, the lion, created the greatest noise. We passed through some dark woods, so dark, indeed, that we could hardly distinguish the trees. At eight o'clock Tonie ran the cart into a tree, and it was with great trouble that we got it free again. Meanwhile the lions in the woods appeared to come nearer and nearer to us, and we naturally felt very uneasy. But to outspan where we now found ourselves was in no way advisable, so we slowly continued the course, myself leading the horses by a rope. One lion we heard so close to us that we at any moment expected it to make its appearance, so we had our guns ready for an attack. Step by step our horses slowly moved on, darkness preventing them from going any faster. At length Mr. Rhodes requested us to halt, and asked me whether I did not deem it prudent to outspan. After briefly discussing our position, we thought it better to proceed until we overtook Major Johnson, with whom we were becoming greatly displeased for leaving us in the lurch.

At last—it was not far from nine—we arrived at two Kafir huts, and there we found the offending Major, with his cart already outspanned. Great was our joy. Every drop of water the Kafirs had in their huts we drank up, and we paid them 3s. 6d. to fetch us another two buckets full. The Kafirs who were to fetch them each took a piece of wood in his hand, set one end of it on fire, and thus made it serve two purposes—as a torch in the dark, and as a weapon against the beasts of prey. They returned with water as clear as crystal, and we felt so happy to get it that we soon forgot all the dissatisfaction our friend Johnson had given us that evening. We raised our little tent, made our camp secure and tied the horses, which, to our regret, had to remain without water for the night.

In order to protect themselves from the wild animals, the Kafirs residing there had their huts encircled by piles of wood. It was not a bad plan. We followed it, though on a smaller scale. Hyænas seemed to roam all around our camp. Now and then our Kafir boys would throw a piece of burning wood in the direction from which the noises came, and so caused the disturbers of our peace to retreat for a while.

After taking our evening meal we threw ourselves down to sleep. Never before in my life did I feel so fatigued as I felt then. The previous night I had hardly had any sleep at all, and during the day just past I had twice assisted in making a pole, twice I had helped to load and unload our carts, and several times I had to exert my strength at the cart-wheels—all this had made me yearn for rest. Major Johnson, who was very tired too, fell asleep before he had spread his bed; he lay with his head upon his saddle, and it was in vain that I tried to wake him. I myself had a good couch: I had two cart-cushions as mattress, two pillows for my head, and a rug to cover me. Soon I was sound asleep.

At half-past two in the morning William roused me.

"Sir, sir!" he whispered, "there is a lion in the camp! Please, won't you come and shoot it?"

I called Major Johnson, who was lying next to me, but he was so heavy with sleep that it was in vain I addressed him. I then resorted to shaking him, and he at last opened his eyes for a moment and asked with a faint, drowsy voice,—

"What's the matter?"

"There is a lion about the camp, William says," I replied.

"Shoot him!" he muttered, and he snored on.

I would not trouble him again.

"All right," I said to William, "I am coming."

But hardly had the words been uttered when I was again fast asleep, and knew as little about the lion as did the Major. Meanwhile the Kafirs did all they could to protect the camp.

At break of day, whilst my friend next to me and I were still in dreamland, the Prime Minister got up and walked some distance from the camp, but he had not gone far when he suddenly turned round, and with all the swiftness with which his legs could carry him he made for the camp. Excited and out of breath he wildly rushed into the tent, thereby arousing and startling up the Major and myself.

"What's the matter?" we simultaneously and anxiously inquired.

"A lion has been chasing me!" the Premier replied with emotion, and then he paused to recover his breath. With his pyjamas hanging below his knees and still half breathless, he now began to relate what had befallen him. He had been some distance from the camp, when suddenly he heard a loud roar, and this was immediately followed by the appearance of a lion a short distance from him. He started, and at once took to his heels. He could not tell us how far the lion had followed him, because in his flight he had no time to cast a look behind him. This was a sensational story; but Major Johnson and myself were not bound, much less prepared, to believe it to be exact. In *our* opinion, despite the Premier's avowal that he had *seen* the animal, it was a hyæna that had frightened him, for there were numbers of hyænas strolling about the place; and, as for the roar he heard, it must have been at least a couple of hundred yards away from him. At any rate, the incident afforded us much amusement, and I would gladly pay ten pounds for a photo of our Premier as he looked when he entered the tent with his fallen pyjamas.

Our Kafir-boys assured us that they had not closed their eyes for one minute during the night; a large number of hyænas had strolled in the vicinity of the camp all the time, and more than once some of them disturbed the horses, but were kept from doing mischief by the boys flinging at them pieces of burning wood out of the fire, which was kept alive throughout the night. But what had annoyed and frightened the Kafirs most was the lion that William had wanted me to shoot; it had repeatedly come very near to the camp.

CHAPTER VII.

Sarmento—The apes watch us bathing—We have to abandon one of our carts—Packing and unpacking—Difficulties grow and I am attacked with despondency—We resolve to give up our second cart also—A lion kills one of our horses—Beautiful palms, but bad water.

AT six in the morning we started for Sarmento, and on our way thither we had to descend a kloof with a steep declivity, at the bottom of which there was a small running stream. We managed to make the descent with less trouble than we had expected, though not without breaking the third cart-pole; but now to get up the opposite side! All our endeavours to force the horses to draw the carts up the elevation were in vain. Nothing was left us but to unpack the carts, draw them up ourselves, and return for the unloaded articles. This was done successfully at the expense of some exertion.

We outspanned a short distance from Sarmento, a Portuguese station on the Pungwe. The banks of the beautiful river were here again adorned with the prettiest trees and shrubs that the eye of man could fall upon. Sarmento is charmingly situated, and there, as at Mapandas, the Portuguese dwell in huts. The head officers of the place came to see us, and were exceedingly courteous and friendly. Shortly afterwards we returned their visit. Out of a large demijohn they poured us some of their Portuguese wine, which we enjoyed very much, and though I had a large share of it, it did not affect my head in the least. Before we left them, the Commander-in-Chief of the station asked us whether we could spare him any of our shot-cartridges, which he wanted to use for the hawks that were so often robbing him of his chickens.

"Certainly," said Mr. Rhodes; "we have a couple of thousand, and with pleasure we shall let you have a hundred. We shall soon be passing here with our carts, and then you may select the cartridges you like."

We bade him "So long!" and returned to our carts. On our arrival there we missed some of our horses. Major Johnson and I immediately went in search of them, found them, and brought them back. We then went to the river to bathe, leaving Mr. Rhodes behind at the camp, as he preferred taking a nap in his stretcher. As we were walking down by the side of the river, and passing some beautiful date-palms and other fruit-bearing trees, we suddenly heard a crash in the branches above us. Neither of us could make out what it was.

"There are baboons up in these trees!" I suggested.

"No," replied my companion, "they must be apes!"

"Nonsense!" I responded. "Apes are not heavy enough to cause so loud a crash!"

We turned our eyes to every bough that we could see above us, but neither ape nor baboon could we observe, until a loud scream told us where to look.

An enormous ape sat behind the foliage of a branch above our heads, watching us acutely and evidently wondering what sort of creatures it was he saw beneath him. It was no longer a mystery to us where the strange screaming that we had so repeatedly heard during the morning had come from.

Leaving the animal in peace, we undressed ourselves under some wild fruit-trees, and had a very enjoyable bath in the clear water. On returning for our clothes, we found some inquisitive apes sitting on the branches immediately above us. They did not seem to have the slightest fear for human beings, probably because the Portuguese deemed it waste of ammunition to shoot at them.

After the bath we had dinner, and after dinner we discussed what to do with our poleless cart. It was the cart which Mr. Fraser had sold to Mr. Rhodes for fifty pounds. It had only served us forty-five miles, the distance between Mapandas and Sarmento, and thrice upon the way its pole had broken. Disgusted with the thing, we decided to get rid of it altogether.

At four o'clock in the afternoon we bade the cart good-bye, taking its cushions with us, and rode to Sarmento. There we gave the Portuguese gentlemen the promised cartridges, for which they heartily thanked us. Mr. Rhodes told them they could take the cart he had left behind, but they did not care to have it, since they had neither horses nor oxen; such animals cannot live in that country—the tsetse-fly destroys them.

Leaving Sarmento, our road ran for some distance over a bit of very undulating country. We had to descend so rapid a slope that we were obliged to take every article off the cart and carry it ourselves, and it was not without great difficulty that we brought the cart up to the elevation on the opposite side. Again we packed the things upon it, but they had not been there long when they had to be taken off again, for we were confronted by another ravine with a sharp declivity on the one side and a steep ascent on the other. This up-and-down travelling continued for some distance, with the result that the task of packing and unpacking the cart had to be performed four or five times—a business that fairly exhausted the strength of Major Johnson and myself.

At six o'clock we arrived at a small running stream, and there we ended the day's travel, having completed only two miles from Sarmento, and four altogether the whole day.

I felt unwell in the evening and in low spirits. I saw how our friend Johnson had imposed on us Instead of travelling in a waggon-road, as he had said we would, we were going in a Portuguese footpath; and so wretched was that footpath that in many parts of it a horse could not be ridden—the rider was obliged to dismount and lead the animal. I must, however, acknowledge that, directly, I myself was to blame for the disagreeable time we were now enduring—it was through me that the trip was made by way of the East Coast; Mr. Rhodes had preferred to travel through Bechuanaland, and meet the waggons, which had been specially built for our journey, at Macloutsi, from whence we were to proceed with them. To his plan I would on no account submit; I would rather have stayed at home than take the same route we had taken the year before; and, besides, I knew that if we did that, we would not be able to visit Beira, owing to the fevers that generally prevail there in the month of November.

As it was, our prospects as to the further journey were gloomy and our hearts sinking. Everything seemed to be against us. Our otherwise cheerful Premier was quiet, and that he felt ill at ease could be read upon his face. To add to our adversity, the two Kafirs whom we had left in charge of the mare had not yet turned up, and we were feeling exceedingly anxious about them.

With no great heart we at length sat down to our evening meal, and after some silence we began seriously to discuss the situation.

"Well," said Mr. Rhodes at last, "we are here in a dark, wild world! What will it avail us now to upbraid Major Johnson with having deceived us with the road, or of what use is it now reproaching him for having bought those useless horses? What lies before us is to decide what to do; and if we don't make that decision now, the delay may result in our catching fever. We have only one cart with us, and we can hardly make any progress with it. It seems to me that we shall be compelled to ride on horseback some two hundred miles—and in a scorching heat of between 100 and 120 degrees. Come, speak out your minds, and let us devise a plan by which to make more rapid progress and with less trouble!"

"Well," I replied, "either we must get rid also of the second cart or prepare for fever. As it is, I already feel queer, and, if I should continue working as hard as I have for the last two days, my health is bound to collapse."

"Well, then," said the Premier, "be that decided—to-morrow we shall leave the cart behind!"

We then went to sleep. During the night our rest was again greatly disturbed by the crying of the hyænas round about, but we heard no lions except a few far off.

The following morning—it was the 3rd of October—we packed as much of our luggage as we could upon the horses; and the cart, which up till now had cost us more than £100, we left behind on the veld, as also the harness (for four horses), the cushions, etc. It was indeed a pity to cast away so pretty a vehicle. It was a folding-cart specially made to our order by Mr. King, and was as strong as a thing of its kind could possibly be. Had we known before we left Sarmento that such was to be the fate of the cart, we would certainly not have left (as we unfortunately did) our pack-saddles behind. We now missed them badly.

Before we started that morning an American missionary (whose name, I am sorry to say, has escaped my memory) made his appearance at our camp. He had hardly met us when he asked us whether we had lost a horse with pots, pans, gridirons, etc.

"Yes," we answered excitedly. "We left a mare the night before last in the hands of two of our Kafirs, and since then we have seen no trace of either the horse or them."

"Well," said the missionary, "at a water-pan on

the other side of Sarmento there lie the remains of a horse, which, judging from the footprints in the sand around it, has been killed by lions; and around the animal some kitchen utensils lie strewn."

"It can be no other horse than the one we have lost," said Mr. Rhodes. "What colour is it?"

"How can I tell you that," was the reply, "when all that I saw of the poor creature was its feet and bones?"

"And can you tell us nothing about the two Kafirs?" we anxiously asked.

"No," answered the missionary. "But tell me, from where did they come?"

"From Inhambane."

"Well," said he, "I happen to know a great deal about the natives of Inhambane. What I may assure you is this: either those Kafirs have been killed by lions or, because they were afraid they would perish at your hands for not having guarded the horse against the beasts of prey, they have fled back to Inhambane."

The missionary was on his way to Gazaland, the kingdom of Gugunhana. He told us he had a beautiful station in that country, and that he lived there like a king.

Bidding him farewell, we left at half-past six. It was with a sense of sorrow that I cast a last look at the fine cart, the pretty harness, the useful cushions, and the new blankets, which we now gave over to the mercies of the wilderness. Our travelling was now anything but enjoyable. Now and then a horse's bundle would slide down the animal's back and hang underneath its belly, when we had to halt and put it right again. Our path was now winding through a bamboo-forest, whose growth was so dense that we could scarcely see the sky above us. Thousands of footprints of wild animals were to be noticed in the sand, those of the elephant not excluded. We took care not to leave the road, because the slightest deviation might result in our losing the way and our falling a prey to the beasts of the woods.

At eleven o'clock we halted at the side of a deep little river. Its water was bad, but, as we knew of no better near by, we allowed our horses to drink of it. For our personal use we obtained some water from underneath a rock, but, though it looked purer than the other, it tasted as bad; and, unfortunately, we felt so warm, tired and thirsty that we could not go without it. We drank some brandy with it as an antidote to fever, and we made a free use of the quinine pills we had brought with us.

Every now and then we heard a lion roar, which was something strange to us; we were used to hearing them during the night, but never before had we heard them during daytime.

We next halted under a beautiful palm, an excellent specimen of its kind; it was between sixty and seventy feet in height, very thin at the bottom, thicker in the middle, and wearing a magnificent crest at the top. The fruit of that species of the palm approaches that of the ordinary cocoa-nut in size; it contains a sweet-smelling, nourishing, oily juice, of which Kafirs are very fond. The peculiar large leaves of the tree present a pretty sight, and the faintest breeze sets them in wave-like motion, causing a noise resembling that produced by waves breaking on the sea-shore. The particular tree under which we were now standing was heavily laden with fruit, most of which was ripe and of a dark-brown colour. Though I had already two palm-nuts in my portmanteau, which I had obtained at Sarmento, I was desirous to have some from this large tree, for they were much bigger than any I had seen before; but I could discover no means of getting them, so I had to be content with merely looking at them. The "ornamental palm," as some call it, thrives best near water, and it differs from the date and cocoanut-palms in being far rarer and in not growing together in groups; it was only here and there that we saw one. I took a fancy to them, and I always felt as though I were near a homely friend when I came to one of them.

CHAPTER VIII.

A dreary search for water—Anxious hours in the dark—A happy meeting—The Major challenges me to a rash plunge—We meet Bowden, who appears ill—I lose my dearly-loved pony.

WE were now fifty-nine miles from Mapandas. At half-past four we again proceeded. Mr. Rhodes and I rode in advance, leaving Major Johnson with the Kafirs and horses. We were expecting, according to what we had been told, to arrive, after a ride of two hours from our last stopping-place, at a beautiful stream of water. It was through a forest of wild fruit-trees, bamboos, and bushes that our road now took us, amongst them being the date, the loquat, the orange, the wild fig, the medlar, and the mampas. At last we arrived at a watery place, but it seemed so swampy and unhealthy a spot that we left it without delay. We passed an old deserted waggon, and turned to the right into a little footpath which, though almost invisible, we considered to be the right one to lead us to the water which our dry throats and perspiring bodies were ardently longing for, and at which we should by this time have already arrived. Down a slope our pathway led us—but no water! The sun was meanwhile fast setting. A high elevation we next ascended, but all that we could see from the top of it was one vast continuation of woods. However, we decided to go farther. Down, down, down the hill we rode, and eventually we reached the stream we had so eagerly sought. The water ran in a deep channel, and was on both sides darkened by dense growth. I was more thirsty than I recollect ever having been before, and Mr. Rhodes was not much less so. However, I could now drink to my heart's content—and I drank until I felt I could not drink a thimbleful more. My companion, however, was more temperate.

The intention we had of taking a bath in the river we of course abandoned. Having let our horses drink, we led them back a little distance, and there, at the foot of the declivity, each holding his horse by the bridle with the one hand and his gun with the other, we patiently awaited Major Johnson. We waited and waited, but no Johnson turned up. Imagine our position! It was dark, pitch dark. We stood in a wilderness where only animals reigned. Woods were in front of us, woods behind us, woods above us. The place was damp and most unhealthy. Time drearily passed, and at eight o'clock we heard and saw as little of our friend as we did at seven. We felt very uneasy.

"Will it not be best to return by the way we have come?" Mr. Rhodes at last suggested.

"Impossible!" I replied. "How are we to get up this ascent? It is too steep to ride up, whilst to walk it will cost too much time and trouble. Besides, what chance have we of finding Johnson in the dark? If he has chosen the road by which *we* came, he will meet us here; if he hasn't, our going in search of him will be useless. No, I should think it is best, after all, to wait where we are."

The howling of hyænas in the meantime was worse than ever.

"Have you any matches with you?" I asked, intending to light a fire.

The Premier searched his pockets, and "No!" he answered with surprise. "But, surely," he added, "you don't mean to say that *you* have no matches with you? An Africander *never* travels without matches!"

"Good heavens—no!" I replied.

We felt equally embarrassed and disappointed at the discovery.

In the meantime the water I had drunk was having a very bad effect on me. I felt miserably "sea-sick," a sensation the Premier had also felt, though in a less degree, during the afternoon.

Another half-hour passed, and still we could not hear anything of Major Johnson. It had grown so dark now that we could neither see the sky above us nor the ground upon which we stood. We were indeed in a most uncomfortable position, and we began to dread that we would have to remain in it all the night—*all* the night, that is to say, if nothing worse befell us before the night was over. There was plenty of dry wood around us, but we had nothing with which to light a fire. I would gladly then have given five pounds for a box of matches.

At last, to my joy, I dimly heard a call—

"*Koō-wĕ!*"

"I hear them shout!" I said.

"No, you don't!" replied my friend; "I am sharp of hearing, and I hear nothing."

"*Koō-wĕ!*" again it sounded.

"Yes, I hear it!" said Mr. Rhodes cheerfully.

At the top of my voice I returned the cry, which was again immediately responded to, and at five minutes past nine all the members of our party were again together. Our joy was great. Major Johnson lectured us severely for having ridden so far in advance of him, and he assured us that, if he had not by chance observed the footprints of our horses, he would have chosen a different road from the one we had taken; and what a night would we have spent! We now resolved once for all never again to leave each other towards evening.

The little river at which we now stopped we named "River of Hell," partly on account of its lying in so deep a ravine, and partly because of the very unpleasant hours Mr. Rhodes and I had spent there in the almost opaque darkness. We heard no lions during the night, but since it often happens that the quieter a lion is the more dangerous, we kept ourselves upon our guard.

At six o'clock the following morning we left the river, and after a few miles' ride we unsaddled our horses and allowed them a little grazing. At half-past eleven we arrived at an old camp, fifteen miles from the River of Hell. There were some Kafir huts and a pretty river flowed close by.

It was here that we met Bowden, the well-known cricketer, and a number of other people. Mr. Bowden had with him some thirty Kafirs, who were carrying flour, liquor, and other provisions for his shop at Umtali. The others were *en route* to Beira.

At two o'clock the Major and I took a bath in the river. The water was running over some rocks into a deep pool, on the one side of which stood some large trees, and on the other some rank grass, amongst which a few very beautiful lotus flowers were to be seen. We climbed upon the rocks and there washed ourselves, being rather afraid to get into the deep water; but it looked so tempting under the leafy trees that it was extremely difficult to keep my friend from jumping in.

"Here!" he said to me. "What will you give me if I swim across the pool and pick one of the flowers over there?"

I thought he was joking, for he knew as well as I that crocodiles inhabited the water, and the travellers we had met at the old camp had warned us to be very careful at that pool.

"Well," I answered, "if you do that I shall give you a coffin."

"A coffin!" he repeated with a laugh—"why?"

"Because you won't come out alive—crocodiles won't let you!"

"If I am caught by crocodiles," he retorted, "what do I need a coffin for? Will not their stomachs be my coffin? But, earnestly now, if I bring *you* one of those flowers, will you jump in and fetch *me* one?"

"Yes, I will!"

He leaped into the water, made as much noise in it

with his hands and feet as he could, swam to one of the flowers, picked it, and, holding it with his mouth, returned with it. With anxiety I stood watching him, fearing that at any moment he might disappear for ever. When he arrived on shore he boastingly said—

"Here I am! And see what a pretty flower I have brought with me! It is now *your* turn to fetch another!"

But I had no desire deliberately to cast my life in peril.

"Man," he said teasingly then, "are you such a coward?"

That was enough for me! Before he could speak another word I had plunged into the water. I made for the opposite side of the pool with all possible haste, splashed the water as loudly as I was able, swam farther than the Major had swum, and came back with a prettier flower. As I reached the shore, some Kafirs who had been watching me clapped their hands, and excitedly began to relate some sad accidents that had occurred at that pool. Only recently, they told us, a little Kafir lad, whilst filling a calabash-shell with water, was seized by a crocodile and drawn into the river, never to be seen again.

On our return to the camp we were censured by everyone there for having been so reckless. Our Premier was particularly warm about it. He reprimanded us severely—we deserved to be swallowed by the crocodiles!—"It is now the second time that you have deliberately, and despite all warnings, imperilled your lives; you won't be let free a *third* time!"

We could not very well defend ourselves, and the Major said to me, when we got aside again,—

"Old chap, it is true—we have hazarded much; we ought not to be so foolish again!"

"Well," I replied, "*you* were the cause of it. It was you who challenged me, and who would have thought me a coward if I did not do as you did; but we shall certainly fall into a trap some day if we go on in this way."

"My dear man," said he, "I promise you I shall never do it again!"

Before Mr. Bowden parted with us Mr. Rhodes gave him a bottle of whiskey. At this action of the Premier I felt rather displeased, for we had very little of that liquor left, and I told him so afterwards.

"Well," said Mr. Rhodes, "we have some old brandy still. Bowden complains of feeling poorly and fatigued—his colour testifies to it—and it is only right that I should help him."

"Good and well," I answered; "but *we* need the whiskey as much as *he* does. How will we get through this land of fever if you give away the little medicine we have?"

"Oh," he responded, "we have enough of old brandy left."

"That may be true, but of what use is it to us? I would not give a cent for it; whereas the whiskey is an excellent fever-preventive, and, mark my words, before we are out of this wilderness you will be glad to get a bottle of whiskey for five pounds."

I felt, however, at the same time, some admiration for the Premier's display of unselfish generosity towards a fellow-being; and I would have encouraged him in it had I thought it possible that, taking Bowden's circumstances into consideration, one bottle of whiskey could have saved his life.

At three o'clock we saddled and packed the horses, and at half-past five we arrived at Mandigo, a Kafir location named after its chief. There also stood some huts occupied by Portuguese and serving as a small military outpost.

We had not been there long when the aged Mandigo, accompanied by some of his under-captains, came to see Mr. Rhodes, the white man of whom he had heard so much.

"Is there anything I can offer you?" asked the Chief.

"Yes," replied the Premier, "everything you can."

"What, then?" the Kafirs wished to know.

"Mealies, beans, peas, Kafir-corn, flour, fowls, eggs,—anything!"

The Kafirs retired, and a little afterwards a crowd of Kafir women and children appeared at our camp with everything the Premier had asked, with the addition of pumpkins, sweet potatoes and beer. Of course, we had to pay for everything. We provided ourselves as well as our horses with a big store of food, and we hired four of Mandigo's Kafirs at one pound each to assist our boys in carrying the vegetables to Chimoyo. Some of the boys we had brought with us from Inhambane began to be sore-footed, so we did not wish them to carry much.

At eight in the morning, whilst a drizzling rain was falling, Mr. Bowden overtook us. He complained that his health was rapidly giving way, and that he felt very exhausted. I could see that. But was it a wonder that his health was failing? He had been travelling afoot hundreds of miles to and from Beira in a land where the roads were rough and dangerous, and where fevers were common, to mention nothing of the hundreds of inconveniences the wild state of the country offered. Mr. Rhodes deeply sympathised with the poor man, and I no less.

"How will you reach Umtali afoot, a journey of days, if you already feel as you do?" asked Mr. Rhodes.

Bowden shrugged his shoulders.

"Well," said the Premier, "I shall give you a horse."

I heartily concurred, thinking it was one of the Montevideo horses (all of which were riding as well as draught horses) that Mr. Rhodes intended to present him; but no! the donor must needs overstretch his kindness to the length of granting Mr. Bowden the pony I myself had chosen to ride. It was an animal that I had grown to love, and I therefore felt sorely vexed at the Premier's action. Not to appear disagreeable I did not utter a word, though it was with a feeling of deep regret that I witnessed my dear brown pony leave us, and the animal showed its disinclination to do so by repeatedly neighing as it was being led away. Mr. Rhodes now asked me whether I minded his giving my horse away.

"That," I answered, "you should have asked me *before* you did it."

"But you would have had no objection?"

"Certainly, I would," I replied; "it was my chosen pony. Why could you not have given away one of the Montevideo horses instead?"

"Well," said he, "there are ponies at Umtali and half-a-dozen at Salisbury."

"That may be true, but we are four days from Umtali and fourteen from Salisbury."

CHAPTER IX.

Annoyance at the hands of our boys—We pass a Portuguese Lema; he travels in state—How the natives salute one another—Traces of the tsetse-fly—No pleasure in a bamboo forest—I lose some of my baggage—Chimoyo at last.

THE following morning we had to trot about from one hut to another to find our boys, as also the four Kafirs Mandigo had promised to let us have. The chief assisted us in our search, but it was not before nine o'clock that we succeeded in getting all the rascals together. It had been against our express command that the Inhambanes had left our camp and gone to the huts, and we were very cross about it, the more so because of the subsequent trouble we had in collecting them again. As a lesson for the future, we decided to punish some of them corporally. Accordingly Samsam and Pikenin, the leading offenders, each received a sound drubbing.

When all this bother was over we had our horses saddled and packed, and, in the manner of the Israelites of old, we journeyed forth.

At eleven o'clock we passed a Portuguese Lema, or Governor, with a train of Kafir attendants. The Lema, resting most comfortably in a litter, was being carried by four Kafirs and followed by about fifty others. At regular intervals fresh hands had to take up the litter, whilst the "big Portuguese man," lying upon his back with a book in his hand, troubled himself about nothing; if he wanted anything, he had simply to order and there it was. When the Lema's train of natives saw us they all halted and stared with amazement at us and our horses. Some of them, I dare say, had never before seen a horse, much less a man upon one; for, if I may trust what I was told, no horse had ever before within living memory passed that way. The Kafirs were much taken up with the sight. They placed the Lema down and clapped their hands at us —their usual form of welcome-bidding. The word "Englishman" I heard more than one whisper as they stood beholding what must have been to them an impressive spectacle. The Governor looked very annoyed at the conduct of his servants in putting the litter down until we had passed; I suppose he considered such an act prejudicial to his dignity. The party were coming from Massi-Kessi.

It is an old custom of the Portuguese grandees travelling in Africa—a custom now in existence for three hundred years—to travel in the manner above described, and a very convenient manner, I must say, it is.

The way the natives of that part of the world greet each other when they meet is somewhat singular. To shake hands, as we do, is a practice unknown to them. Their mode of greeting is more elaborate; they rub their feet against the ground, look into each other's eyes, and clap their hands.

On our present road we passed many a deserted ox-waggon, the animals that had brought them there having been stung to death by the destructive tsetse-fly. We now journeyed through country more open than that we had passed through the day before, and we were indeed glad to quit the dense bamboo-bushes where we had to endure such depressing heat. There is really no pleasure in travelling when the road leads the traveller through a bamboo-forest; one is there not only exposed to various dangers, but all the scenery around him is shut from his view; all that he is able to see through the reeds is a little of the blue sky.

We next stopped at the side of a clear stream, and within ten minutes after our arrival there the three of us were in the water, but for fear of crocodiles we did not venture to swim. After the bath we had our breakfast, and in the afternoon we resumed the journey. After travelling some distance I missed my overcoat. I had been in the habit of keeping it in front of me on my horse, but I had once got down on the way to drink water at a streamlet, and I believe it was there that I left the overcoat behind. I was sorry to lose it, but did not think it worth the trouble returning for it; and if I *had* gone back for it, I doubt whether I should have found it.

It was half-past five when we reached Chimoyo, another Kafir station, of which a Kafir of the same name was captain. We had travelled twenty miles during the day, and we were now at the close of the ninth day since our landing at Beira.

The distance between Beira and Chimoyo is at least 190 miles.

CHAPTER X.

Bartering with Kafirs—Our followers begin to feel fatigued—I stick to my portmanteau in spite of Mr. Rhodes's generous offers—Major Johnson is charged by a wild ox—How a Kafir smokes—A lovely halting-spot.

CHIMOYO, like Mandigo, offered us everything eatable he had, and soon a throng of Kafirs, men, women and children, stood around us with various kinds of vegetables and fruits. They placed everything down, and then, as if at a given signal, they all clapped their hands. The men stood in front, the women and children behind. What struck us as curious about the females—children as well as adults—was the fact that most of them wore on the nose and lips a sort of silver plate fixed on those features like earrings. It seemed to me that those whose faces were thus ornamented (?) belonged to the upper class. But why the women and damsels were so afraid of us I could not understand. They appeared glad to see us, and they looked at us with the greatest inquisitiveness, but whenever we looked at them they sheltered behind the men, and as soon as anyone of us happened to walk round the latter they (the women) became seized with fright and ran to their huts as hard as they could. It was always best to pretend not to notice them. The men, however, showed no signs of fear, and were at any time most willing to fetch us wood and water if only we gave them the remains of our meals.

As amongst the Inhambane Kafirs, so amongst these, strong, fine-built men were to be seen—men large in limb, healthy, and created, as it were, for no other purpose than to serve as outdoor labourers.

Our Inhambane boys now began to complain of their legs becoming stiff as a result of all the walking. One after another gave up. Pikenin was already as stiff as a sore-footed goat, and Matokwa as lame as a duck. Tonie and William, however, were all right still; but no wonder, for they had the advantage over the Kafirs of wearing boots, and they had a horse between them which they rode in turn.

We left Chimoyo the following morning at half-past six, and had in our service, including the natives we had hired there, no less than twenty-five Kafirs. We made them all carry something, their burdens ranging in weight from thirty-five to forty-five pounds. My portmanteau, however, weighed over fifty pounds, but it was a good strong Kafir whose task it was to carry it. I pitied him though, and I was afraid the load would exhaust his strength, but not a word of complaint did he utter.

Since the day we had left our first cart behind, Mr. Rhodes had repeatedly urged me to cast away my portmanteau with all its contents, for, he said, at Salisbury he had a large case full of clothing of which he would let me have as much as I should care to take; but I would, of course, not listen to such advice. The cart-cushions I had used as pillows every night were gone, my overcoat had disappeared, and I was not going to lose anything more if I could help it. Besides, I had many articles in my portmanteau that were too valuable to cast away. And what a laughing-stock would I have made of myself if I were seen in Mr. Rhodes's clothes—trousers about eight inches too long for me and jackets with sleeves out of which my hands would not have had a peep! Then, too, we had received a telegram at Port Elizabeth to the effect that two of the waggons we had sent to Salisbury had capsized on the way, that a quantity of the goods was destroyed, and that one of our horses had gone astray. Well, for all I knew, Mr. Rhodes's case with clothing might have been amongst the things damaged.

I promised my Kafir that if he carried my portmanteau safely to Umtali I would give him two pretty kerchiefs. This seemed to make his burden lighter. With the exception of two, all our Kafirs were hired up to Umtali.

About two hours from Chimoyo we caught sight of a large animal, but we could not tell what it was. Riding closer up to it, we found it to be a wild ox. It was very probably one of the oxen lost there a month before. We resolved to shoot it, for we had not a particle of meat left amongst our provisions. For several days we had not been able to shoot any game, it being next to impossible to hit a wild animal in that region of woods. Traces of game were to be seen everywhere, but the game themselves kept aloof. Now and then we spied an animal, but, just as the gun was being levelled at it, away it went! And to

A NOVEL MODE OF SMOKING.

pursue the animal would have been the act of a madman. But to return to the ox. Major Johnson chased it, and, as he came within a short distance of it, it suddenly turned round and charged him; but our gallant friend, an excellent shot, was not the man to take to flight, and before the infuriated animal could touch him the Major had sent two bullets through its body—one through its shoulder and one through its head. The ox fell and died. Quickly the Kafirs were on the spot and the large animal was skinned and cut to pieces. Every Kafir had to carry a part of the meat; not even the stomach or the legs were left behind. At a streamlet bordered with the prettiest greenery we stopped and breakfasted, the fresh beef tasting very well.

By the side of the stream grew a species of tree from the bark of which our Kafirs twisted strong rope; they used it for binding together their packages.

It was amusing to watch the Kafirs smoke their pipes. The long shank is placed under the loose soil, and only the two ends of the pipe appear above the surface. The smoker kneels down, bends his head to the pipe's mouth, and in this awkward posture he gives one long draw after another, each puff being followed by a cough. Five or six smoke successively out of one pipe, and it is not tobacco they smoke, but *dagga*.

We did not stop long at the brook. Leaving it, we passed a Kafir kraal, the inhabitants of which stared at us with their mouths open. It was the first time in their lives that they had seen horses, and it was something most wonderful for them to see us sit on the backs of such animals. Nine big grey Kafir dogs thought it their duty to pursue us, but we soon got rid of them; a couple of gun-shots gave them such a fright that they quickly turned back with drooping heads and with their long tails swinging between their legs.

At five o'clock we arrived at another lovely river, and there we decided to spend the night. The water was beautifully clear; round about it there was good pasture for our horses, and in every respect the place was a very convenient one to stop at. The bath we took in the cold water was something glorious after the hot day we had had. We sat under a waterfall and let the sparkling water, running over moss-covered rocks, fall upon us. Was it not delicious! We could have sat there for hours. The spot itself was a beautiful one, one of the loveliest, in fact, that I have ever seen. Indeed, one who has not seen it for himself can hardly form an idea of its grandeur. On the one side we were faced by a stair of mossy rocks with glittering water rippling between and over them, and on the other there was the calm transparent stream with its verdant margins spotted with lovely flowers. Nature here showed itself to us in its full sublimity, and seldom has my admiration for her been excited to such a pitch. We pitched our tent, and, as we were wont to do every evening (except, of course, when prevented), we sat down together, enjoyed a smoke, and engaged in a long, jolly chat. As a rule, we took all precaution within our means to render our little camp as safe as possible against lions, but as we now had twenty-five Kafirs with us, and as some of them were well acquainted with the country as well as with the nature of the animals dwelling therein, we felt

A LOVELY COUNTRY.

pretty secure without fortifying the camp. We had become used to the growling of the king of beasts, and the last few nights his noise had grown less and less. But to the horrid yelping of the hyænas there still seemed to be no end. A hungry hyæna near a camp is an abominable nuisance; its almost incessant and most monotonous howling greatly disturbs one's rest. How different are the sounds heard at the break of morning, when the birds of the woods sweetly welcome the new day!

Before sunrise on Wednesday, the 7th of October, we left "Crystal River" (a name *we* gave it), and from thence our road took us through a lovely tract of country—down one hill and up another, all covered with pretty verdure. The grass was often taller, far taller, than our horses.

At a small stream we allowed our animals a little rest, and from there our course wended up the side of the Moosikani River. We halted on the way, took a bath in the river, and had our breakfast on its bank. About a mile from where we stopped we noticed a mealie garden, at the farther end of which stood a hut built on poles. We asked the Chimoyo Kafirs the reason why the hut was built so high, and they told us that, as the mealies began to ripen, the apes and baboons round about stole the fruit if nobody protected it; the hut was elevated not only to enable the occupier to cast his eye at one and the same time over his whole garden, but to enable him to shout with a loud open voice over the whole plantation in order to frighten these rascally animals. It often happened, our informants told us, that lions, on hearing the shouting, made for the place whence the noise came, and that, when this was the case, the inmates of the hut on poles were as safe as ever. But a lion would often lie under such a hut till late the following morning, and it had happened more than once that Kafirs, unaware of the presence of the animal, on descending the poles in the dark to go and drive the thieves out of their gardens, were caught and devoured.

Next to the stream at which we halted stood a tree on the bark of which the following was inscribed, "*Mosika River, River Pioneer Bridge, 8 Aug.* 1891," signed "*B. B.*" Though I could not make much sense out of this, it was plain that the man who wrote it was one of the party who, about three months before, while on their way to Beira with a number of ox-waggons, lost all their oxen—and consequently their waggons—before they had come within two hundred miles of their destination. Not less than twelve abandoned waggons with all their belongings did we pass on the road.

CHAPTER XI.

An historical show—The scene of a battle—Massi-Kessi—On the track of the ancient gold-seekers—We plan to sleep outside the tent, but are discovered by our Premier—Some thrilling lion stories.

AT half-past five we left the river and passed a shop belonging to the Mozambique Company. This shop had, during the petty war a few months before between the Pioneers of the Chartered Company and the Portuguese, fallen into the hands of the former, who supplied themselves with the provisions in it. The Mozambique Company thereupon demanded £100,000 from the Chartered Company as compensation for damages done to the shop, which of course they did not get. In my estimation, the entire building with all its stock was not worth 100,000 half-pennies.

At noon we arrived at Massi-Kessi, a Portuguese station over which Captain Trada has recently been appointed Governor. We unsaddled our horses at a shop belonging to a Portuguese Jew, who asked us whether he should prepare us a dinner.

"Yes," was our answer.

In the mean time he fetched us a demijohn filled with delicious Portuguese wine, and set it down before us—a temptation to which we gracefully yielded!

All kinds of provisions were obtainable here, so we provided ourselves and our horses with all that was necessary. Straight over against the shop lay the ground where the engagement took place on the 10th of May last between forty-eight of the Chartered Company Pioneers and four hundred and eighty soldiers fighting on the Portuguese side (eighty of whom were Portuguese, the rest natives), and ended in the latter taking to flight, leaving twenty of their number dead on the field. I was shown the exact positions the respective armies had occupied during the encounter; they were such as offered the Portuguese a decided advantage. Taking this fact into consideration, it is a disgrace to the Portuguese to have been defeated by such a handful of men. The above account was given me by Mr. Lorenso, a Portuguese gentleman who lives at Massi-Kessi, and who himself had been an eye-witness of the fight. He assured us that he had never before felt so ashamed of his fellow-countrymen as that afternoon when he saw the four hundred and eighty suffer defeat. It was then that the Kafir abandoned his hut, the shop-keeper his shop, the soldier his fort; it was then that the Pioneers made for the shop and took as booty as much of its store as they needed—whence the extraordinary claim sent in by the Mozambique Company. Hayman[*] was the Commander of the Pioneers, and Calas Xavier of the Portuguese. It may be mentioned that Victor Morier,[†] son of Sir Robert Morier, British Ambassador at St.

---

[*] Now Chief Magistrate at Buluwayo.—*Trans.*

[†] He died on the ship *Tartar*, on his way to the Cape in May, 1892.—*Trans.*

Petersburg, fought in the Pioneer regiment, and conducted himself gallantly.

I asked Mr. Lorenso what caused the Portuguese to retreat so soon.

"Well," said he, "the Kafirs always seem to be seized with fright when the shooting commences, and that makes them take to their heels."

"Why, then," I asked, "do you employ them to fight for you?"

"Oh," he answered, "just to have a number of fighting men together. And, you see, just as fast as the Kafirs can flee when we lose, they can pursue when we win."

Massi-Kessi has been in the hands of the Portuguese for the last three hundred years, but one can hardly believe it when one sees the place. Though limestone and other building material are to be found there in abundance, the dwellings of the Portuguese are no better than those of the natives; they are all huts built of straw; and though the soil there is of the very best for agriculture, very little of it is under cultivation. But the natural beauty of the place arrested our admiration. Massi-Kessi lies between two high hills, midway between which run two fine rivers. Bananas grow there to perfection; they are larger and have a better flavour than the best grown in Natal.

The time cannot be far distant when Massi-Kessi will be a large flourishing town. It is only waiting for the railway. It is a curious fact that where the train brings the white man, fevers rapidly disappear. This has been proved to be the case in certain parts of Spain, in Italy (especially between Rome and Naples), and in Australia; it has also been manifested at Kimberley, Johannesburg, Pretoria, Barberton and Zoutpansberg.

At half-past three we bade Massi-Kessi farewell, and our road now took us through a tract of country where denudation had strikingly been at work. In the valleys one could see that the ground had everywhere been carried away to the extent of from two to three feet in depth, and at a distance one could see hundreds of elevations, the accumulations of the washed-away soil, now covered with luxuriant grass. But stranger even than that it was to notice that all the black turf in the valleys on this side of the Umtali Mountains had been removed, a proof that in centuries past thousands of men had been washing there for alluvial gold.

At sundown we found ourselves at the foot of the Umtali Range, and there we stopped for the night. Having completed a distance of between twenty and twenty-five miles during the day, we felt very tired.

As I mentioned before, every night Mr. Rhodes, Major Johnson and I took our repose under a small oval-shaped tent. Our tent was our best friend. One of the first things we did at every place at which we halted was to pitch the tent. We never felt perfectly at ease during the nights, for when there were no wild animals disturbing us there was always a fear of those fever-producing fogs that so often arise from the damp ground. We sorely missed the three cart cushions we had cast away on our abandoning the second cart; they had served Major Johnson and myself as a mattress. Since the day we had to part with them we substituted a large woollen blanket in their stead, but the latter did not serve its purpose nearly so well as did the fine, thick cushions. We spread the blanket on the ground, placed a pillow underneath our heads, and covered ourselves with karosses. One of our tasks every evening was to level the area our tent was to encompass. Sometimes this was not necessary, but we usually preferred putting up the tent upon a spot we ourselves had cleared and levelled, because upon the grass, smooth and level though it was, it was impossible to sleep with comfort—at least, so we fancied —for the tick (a sort of ground-louse) abounded there. The Premier, of course, could enjoy a good bed, for he slept on his stretcher. Major Johnson and I, however, were not half so well provided; we had to be satisfied with sleeping on the hard ground. But we were now becoming tired of it, our bodies could stand it no longer, and we decided this night at the foot of the Umtali to sleep on the grass outside the tent. We knew the Premier would dislike our doing so, so we told him nothing about it. He was having a rest on his stretcher when the Major and I stood outside the tent planning how and where to sleep. Ticks or no ticks, fog or no fog, we were determined to have a soft bed. We had a lot of grass cut and we spread a quantity on each side of the tent. Having eaten our evening meal, we quietly betook ourselves to our green beds. It did not, however, take the Premier long to catch us there.

"What does this all mean?" he asked with surprise.

"Nothing," we answered; "but that we wish to sleep here. It is more than our bodies can endure to lie upon the hard ground."

"But what about the ticks?"

"Ticks be blowed! Tonie, William, and the Kafirs sleep upon the grass every night, and they complain less about those insects than we do, despite the precautions we take."

"Well, but why could you not bring the grass inside the tent?"

"Because," we answered, "we knew you would not like it."

"Oh, no," answered Mr. Rhodes, "I have not the least objection. Bring in the grass!"

Accordingly we had the grass carried into the tent and had our soft bed nicely made up. Soon the roaring of the lions became terrible; it was a repetition of what we had at Muda River. But we had such a large number of Kafirs with us—and they were all on the watch—that we did not feel very uneasy. We had a good night. I slept till five o'clock, when Mr. Rhodes awoke me. No ticks had disturbed us, and, thank Providence, we never slept so badly again as we had the few nights before.

In the country through which we were now passing we observed numerous spots where alluvial gold had been dug for by the ancients. All along the sides of the rivers there were patches where the ground had been hollowed out and brought to the rivers to be washed.

We were now near to the spot where Mr. Theal had so horribly met his death a month before. He had come from Umtali to trade in the districts round about. As night set in, he lay down with a Kafir attendant on each side of him, naturally thinking that in case a lion should tackle them during the night he would be the safest of the three. It was a quiet night, and no lions were to be heard, except a few a long distance off. The Kafirs slept soundly till the morning broke, when they awoke and missed their master, not having the slightest idea as to what had become of him. Later in the morning they met some fellow-Kafirs, *en route* to Massi-Kessi, who told them the shocking tale that they had passed on their way the head and feet of a white man. The horror-stricken Kafirs went to see, and they found and recognised the head of their master, Mr. Theal! Immediately they sped to Massi-Kessi and reported the terrible news to the authorities there, who at once despatched some officials to the place where the remains of the man were reported to be lying, and they found the Kafirs' story only too true. The unfortunate trader had been devoured by a lion. The footprints of the animal were traced from the spot at which the head was found up to where the cart was standing. The two Kafirs asserted they had heard nothing during the night. Very likely the head of the unfortunate man was bitten off and his body carried away before he could utter a sound.

Incidents of this kind are not at all of rare occurrence in that part of the world. Lieutenant Stanley, one of the Chartered Company's Pioneers, who joined our party in the afternoon, having been sent to us by Dr. Jameson to show us the way across the Umtali Mountains, told us that the Christmas-night before last he also slept in the neighbourhood of where we were now travelling, and also had with him two Kafir attendants. Towards midnight he was suddenly

aroused by a shriek. He grasped his gun and sprang to his feet, but too late. The lion had already disappeared with one of the Kafirs, and all that he could hear was the dismal cries of the lion's victim growing fainter and fainter as the animal receded. The other Kafir, who was now with the Lieutenant, affirmed every word his master told us.

But the most remarkable and interesting of adventures with lions is the following. Some three months ago Mr. Selous—I do not recollect whether he was alone—on his way from Umliwan to Umtali had to spend a night in the wilds not far from where the tragedies above related occurred. Having chopped some poles and branches, he constructed a little hut for himself, interlacing the boughs with grass and saplings, and leaving a few openings on each side of the structure through which to fire in the case of need. Early in the evening he heard some lions growl in the vicinity, but later all was quiet again. Mr. Selous had with him as weapons a rifle, a hatchet, and a long knife. The gun he placed near to his head, within convenient reach. He was aware that he was now in a veritable nest of lions, so to call it, and that was why he took so much precaution for his security. He fell into a slight slumber, but was soon awakened by the noise of some animal in the bushes near by. Retaining his presence of mind, he sat as still as a mouse, and soon he could faintly discern in the dark through one of his little hut windows the form of some big creature. Slowly he stretched his hand to his gun and drew it nearer; then, levelling it noiselessly to the black

object, he pulled the trigger, and the animal—an enormous lion—after a few terrific grunts, lay a carcass. Again he loaded his rifle, and again he quietly sat down. Sleep he could not and dared not, for when he fired the shot he heard some more lions near. As it happened, only a few minutes passed when a second lion made its appearance. Gently again Mr. Selous took up his gun and, to the best of his judgment in the dark, pointed it at the burglar's head. The second shot was fired, and the second lion, after a few loud moans and gasps, breathed its last. "Two lions dead! Now I may rest!" thought the adventurer, but five minutes had not elapsed when there was a third marauder, the boldest of the three. Sitting breathlessly still, Mr. Selous would not fire until he could see the animal's head. Meanwhile, however, the lion had torn some boughs from the hut, and soon its inmate, calm even in this critical situation, felt the animal sniffing at his feet. Gently Mr. Selous drew his feet in, fired the third shot that night, and mortally wounded the third lion. Now at last the man was left in peace. At early dawn he rose, crept out of his fortification, and found not far from it two full-grown lions cold and stiff. The third, if I remember rightly, was found some time afterwards at the side of a little stream. I may mention that the above tale, incredible as it may appear, has been told me as perfectly true, and that it has been confirmed by several, some of whom had themselves seen the dead lions.

CHAPTER XII.

We cross the Umtali Mountains—A good night's rest—Our Kafir boys leave us, but Pikenin and Matokwa choose to stick by their present masters—An accident to Pikenin—I am thrown into a pool—Our boys frighten the Kafir women—A Kafir burial-place.

At twenty-three minutes past five the following morning we started on our journey over the Umtali Mountains, the boundary between Mozambique and Mashonaland—between the land of the Portuguese and that of the Chartered Company. We crossed the Samba River, on the banks of which the banana grew luxuriantly, and rode down one steep mountain, then another, then along the Umtali River, which here flows through a pretty valley, and finally (at halfpast eight) we arrived at the Umtali camp, a distance of about seventeen miles from Massi-Kessi.

Here we met Mr. Heany, Dr. Jameson, and some other well-known gentlemen. It was to us a moment of rejoicing when we entered the Umtali camp. There we had huts to which to retire, and the food and drink we received were of the very best. What a difference to what we had the night before! We could now enjoy a good bed; no lion's roar or hyæna's yelping

disturbed us; no rain need we fear and guard ourselves against, and no reason had we to doubt our horses' safety.

Umtali is 252 miles distant from Beira.

Manika, the district we were now in, is a magnificent tract of country. Already some 300 white men are earning their living there. The day after our arrival we visited several of the gold-reefs in the district, and also the area marked out for the new township.

We intended to depart from Umtali towards evening, and, therefore, early in the afternoon we called our Kafir boys together and asked them whether they wished to remain at Umtali and work for Mr. Heany, who was most willing to take them into his employ and would pay and feed them well; whether they preferred returning to Inhambane; or whether they would like to accompany us farther. They went aside, discussed the question amongst themselves, and at three o'clock they told us their resolution. All of them, except two, had decided to remain at Umtali for the present and return to their homes later on. Pikenin and Matokwa were the dissentients—they chose to go with us to Capetown. We paid all the Kafirs what was due to them. To the boy that had so gallantly carried my portmanteau I gave three kerchiefs, a string of beads and a pocket-knife, and he almost jumped out of his skin, so pleased was he with those handsome presents!—presents that altogether did not cost me three shillings.

The waggon and cart that had been waiting for us at Umtali were now got ready. The waggon had harness

enough for eight horses, and the cart for four. We left it entirely in the hands of our driver and reinholder to select the horses and mules that were to draw the vehicles. Tonie, William, Matokwa and Pikenin were left in charge of the ponies.

As I mentioned above, Manika, as far as we saw it, is a lovely country; its landscape views—hills, valleys and waters—are very pretty, and, as far as its mineral wealth is concerned, the fact that 1950 claims have already been registered there speaks for itself. In my judgment the place is very rich in gold.

We left Umtali at five o'clock on Saturday, 10th October. The waggon led the way; it was one of the spring waggons with which we had travelled to Tuli on our last trip, and which had been sent on from there to Dr. Jameson at Salisbury.

Our course being downhill now, our animals could trot away at a good speed. We noticed that our grooms were rather tipsy, and we were afraid that, if we left them at their posts, ere night our cart would be overturned. We therefore halted for a few minutes, Major Johnson went over to the waggon and took its management upon himself, whilst I replaced the driver of the cart. After promising the Major to wait for him at Eight Mile Spruit, I drove in advance of the waggon. Handling the reins very cautiously, I steered clear of all the trees bordering the narrow road, successfully passed the several spruits that crossed our way, and reached the Eight Mile safely. My cart had long been outspanned when the Major arrived with the waggon. The bush of one of the fore-wheels of the waggon had been so ground by friction that it had

gone loose and dropped out—hence the delay. Fortunately we met a few Boers at the Spruit who ably assisted us in the repair of the waggon.

The following morning my boy Pikenin was not lively enough according to Mr. Rhodes's fancy when the latter ordered him to bring together the horses and mules. Angry at this imaginary laziness of the boy, the Premier gave him a few slaps, and the boy, somewhat confused, ran amongst the horses, one of which violently kicked him in the stomach. He fell unconscious to the ground, and when we picked him up he looked as if he would not recover. After a while, however, he returned to his senses, but his condition was still by no means such as to allow him to resume work. We lifted him upon the waggon and applied every remedy, for we were still afraid that his injury might prove fatal. It grieved me much to see him suffer, and I had anything but a kind feeling towards the Premier, who had been the cause of the accident, and who had no business whatever to interfere with the inspanning.

After travelling another fifteen miles we arrived at another spruit, which we named "Sunday Spruit," as it was on a Sunday that we came there. The veld round about was of a good character.

On our way to Sunday Spruit we had to drive through a drift, the sides of which were very steep and contained several dangerous holes. Our rein-holder, through careless driving, ran one of the cart-wheels over one of those holes, with the result that I was jerked out of the cart like a stone into a deep pool. I escaped unhurt, but I must say I felt rather small

when I stood up, half confused and as wet as a fish, and was received with a roar of laughter.

At the close of the day we stopped at the Umsapi River, and there we passed the night. Though we were now at another haunt of wild animals, we were not much disturbed by lions during the night. A fortnight previously a traveller who had outspanned not far from here walked a small distance from his ox-cart at evening, when suddenly the Kafirs he had left at the cart heard a sort of smothered cry and then all was quiet again. Never again did those Kafirs behold their master. Where he had trodden last the fresh footprints of a lion were to be seen.

It was at that same place that the members of the Cape Commission to Mashonaland, Messrs. Eksteen, de Waal and Vosloo, had a month previous to our arrival there shot a lion. These gentlemen, whilst hunting, came upon the animal, and Mr. de Waal and Mr. Vosloo fired at it almost simultaneously, and wounded it mortally. Whether it was the bullet from Mr. de Waal's gun or that from Mr. Vosloo's that struck the animal, remains unsettled; each claims that it was his. Anyhow, the wounded lion disappeared among the tall reeds, and the hunters forbore pursuing, knowing that wild animals are at their fiercest when injured. Three days afterwards, however, a transport-rider stopped there, and his nose coming in contact with a not very fragrant smell, he searched for the object whence the odour came, and found the decaying lion with a bullet through its back.

We left Umsapi River at six o'clock and next outspanned near to a kopje (*lit.* " little head "), on which

was built a Kafir-kraal. At the foot of this kopje there was a stone wall, built for the purpose of fortifying the kraal. Shortly after our arrival we began bartering with the natives of the kraal near by; we exchanged limbo and salt for such food-stuffs as mealies, Kafir-corn, Mozambique and other beans, Kafir-beer, meal, eggs, fowls, etc. The mealies, beans, rice and Kafir-corn were fetched from earthen vats erected upon the highest rocks on the little hill. We drove a profitable business, for we had brought plenty of limbo and salt with us. If anything struck us about the personal appearance of the Kafirs here, it was their extreme ugliness.

Leaving our cart and waggon where we had outspanned, we walked towards the kopje, and at the foot of it seated ourselves under a large wild fig-tree. There we ate and drank, and had a nap, whilst Daniel and James, two boys whom Dr. Jameson had brought with him, and whom we had made our drivers, climbed up the rocky kopje to go to the kraal. Suddenly we heard loud screaming. We looked up and saw some Kafir women standing on the edges of some precipitous rocky ridges about 150 feet high ready to jump down. Dr. Jameson at once saw what the matter was; the ignorant Kafir women were fleeing before our boys, who, they fancied, purposed to take them captive. With all the force our throats could produce we shouted to the boys to turn back immediately. They heard us and obeyed. Had the women leaped down those krantzes, they could not but have broken their limbs and been killed.

The fig-tree under which we sat was laden with fruit

"But what about the ticks?"

"Ticks be blowed! Tonie, William, and the Kafirs sleep upon the grass every night, and they complain less about those insects than we do, despite the precautions we take."

"Well, but why could you not bring the grass inside the tent?"

"Because," we answered, "we knew you would not like it."

"Oh, no," answered Mr. Rhodes, "I have not the least objection. Bring in the grass!"

Accordingly we had the grass carried into the tent and had our soft bed nicely made up. Soon the roaring of the lions became terrible; it was a repetition of what we had at Muda River. But we had such a large number of Kafirs with us—and they were all on the watch—that we did not feel very uneasy. We had a good night. I slept till five o'clock, when Mr. Rhodes awoke me. No ticks had disturbed us, and, thank Providence, we never slept so badly again as we had the few nights before.

In the country through which we were now passing we observed numerous spots where alluvial gold had been dug for by the ancients. All along the sides of the rivers there were patches where the ground had been hollowed out and brought to the rivers to be washed.

We were now near to the spot where Mr. Theal had so horribly met his death a month before. He had come from Umtali to trade in the districts round about. As night set in, he lay down with a Kafir attendant on each side of him, naturally thinking that in case a lion should tackle them during the night he would be the safest of the three. It was a quiet night, and no lions were to be heard, except a few a long distance off. The Kafirs slept soundly till the morning broke, when they awoke and missed their master, not having the slightest idea as to what had become of him. Later in the morning they met some fellow-Kafirs, *en route* to Massi-Kessi, who told them the shocking tale that they had passed on their way the head and feet of a white man. The horror-stricken Kafirs went to see, and they found and recognised the head of their master, Mr. Theal! Immediately they sped to Massi-Kessi and reported the terrible news to the authorities there, who at once despatched some officials to the place where the remains of the man were reported to be lying, and they found the Kafirs' story only too true. The unfortunate trader had been devoured by a lion. The footprints of the animal were traced from the spot at which the head was found up to where the cart was standing. The two Kafirs asserted they had heard nothing during the night. Very likely the head of the unfortunate man was bitten off and his body carried away before he could utter a sound.

Incidents of this kind are not at all of rare occurrence in that part of the world. Lieutenant Stanley, one of the Chartered Company's Pioneers, who joined our party in the afternoon, having been sent to us by Dr. Jameson to show us the way across the Umtali Mountains, told us that the Christmas-night before last he also slept in the neighbourhood of where we were now travelling, and also had with him two Kafir attendants. Towards midnight he was suddenly

aroused by a shriek. He grasped his gun and sprang to his feet, but too late. The lion had already disappeared with one of the Kafirs, and all that he could hear was the dismal cries of the lion's victim growing fainter and fainter as the animal receded. The other Kafir, who was now with the Lieutenant, affirmed every word his master told us.

But the most remarkable and interesting of adventures with lions is the following. Some three months ago Mr. Selous—I do not recollect whether he was alone—on his way from Umliwan to Umtali had to spend a night in the wilds not far from where the tragedies above related occurred. Having chopped some poles and branches, he constructed a little hut for himself, interlacing the boughs with grass and saplings, and leaving a few openings on each side of the structure through which to fire in the case of need. Early in the evening he heard some lions growl in the vicinity, but later all was quiet again. Mr. Selous had with him as weapons a rifle, a hatchet, and a long knife. The gun he placed near to his head, within convenient reach. He was aware that he was now in a veritable nest of lions, so to call it, and that was why he took so much precaution for his security. He fell into a slight slumber, but was soon awakened by the noise of some animal in the bushes near by. Retaining his presence of mind, he sat as still as a mouse, and soon he could faintly discern in the dark through one of his little hut windows the form of some big creature. Slowly he stretched his hand to his gun and drew it nearer; then, levelling it noiselessly to the black

object, he pulled the trigger, and the animal—an enormous lion—after a few terrific grunts, lay a carcass. Again he loaded his rifle, and again he quietly sat down. Sleep he could not and dared not, for when he fired the shot he heard some more lions near. As it happened, only a few minutes passed when a second lion made its appearance. Gently again Mr. Selous took up his gun and, to the best of his judgment in the dark, pointed it at the burglar's head. The second shot was fired, and the second lion, after a few loud moans and gasps, breathed its last. "Two lions dead! Now I may rest!" thought the adventurer, but five minutes had not elapsed when there was a third marauder, the boldest of the three. Sitting breathlessly still, Mr. Selous would not fire until he could see the animal's head. Meanwhile, however, the lion had torn some boughs from the hut, and soon its inmate, calm even in this critical situation, felt the animal sniffing at his feet. Gently Mr. Selous drew his feet in, fired the third shot that night, and mortally wounded the third lion. Now at last the man was left in peace. At early dawn he rose, crept out of his fortification, and found not far from it two full-grown lions cold and stiff. The third, if I remember rightly, was found some time afterwards at the side of a little stream. I may mention that the above tale, incredible as it may appear, has been told me as perfectly true, and that it has been confirmed by several, some of whom had themselves seen the dead lions.

CHAPTER XII.

We cross the Umtali Mountains—A good night's rest—Our Kafir boys leave us, but Pikenin and Matokwa choose to stick by their present masters—An accident to Pikenin—I am thrown into a pool—Our boys frighten the Kafir women—A Kafir burial-place.

At twenty-three minutes past five the following morning we started on our journey over the Umtali Mountains, the boundary between Mozambique and Mashonaland—between the land of the Portuguese and that of the Chartered Company. We crossed the Samba River, on the banks of which the banana grew luxuriantly, and rode down one steep mountain, then another, then along the Umtali River, which here flows through a pretty valley, and finally (at half-past eight) we arrived at the Umtali camp, a distance of about seventeen miles from Massi-Kessi.

Here we met Mr. Heany, Dr. Jameson, and some other well-known gentlemen. It was to us a moment of rejoicing when we entered the Umtali camp. There we had huts to which to retire, and the food and drink we received were of the very best. What a difference to what we had the night before! We could now enjoy a good bed; no lion's roar or hyæna's yelping

disturbed us; no rain need we fear and guard ourselves against, and no reason had we to doubt our horses' safety.

Umtali is 252 miles distant from Beira.

Manika, the district we were now in, is a magnificent tract of country. Already some 300 white men are earning their living there. The day after our arrival we visited several of the gold-reefs in the district, and also the area marked out for the new township.

We intended to depart from Umtali towards evening, and, therefore, early in the afternoon we called our Kafir boys together and asked them whether they wished to remain at Umtali and work for Mr. Heany, who was most willing to take them into his employ and would pay and feed them well; whether they preferred returning to Inhambane; or whether they would like to accompany us farther. They went aside, discussed the question amongst themselves, and at three o'clock they told us their resolution. All of them, except two, had decided to remain at Umtali for the present and return to their homes later on. Pikenin and Matokwa were the dissentients—they chose to go with us to Capetown. We paid all the Kafirs what was due to them. To the boy that had so gallantly carried my portmanteau I gave three kerchiefs, a string of beads and a pocket-knife, and he almost jumped out of his skin, so pleased was he with those handsome presents!—presents that altogether did not cost me three shillings.

The waggon and cart that had been waiting for us at Umtali were now got ready. The waggon had harness enough for eight horses, and the cart for four. We left it entirely in the hands of our driver and rein-holder to select the horses and mules that were to draw the vehicles. Tonie, William, Matokwa and Pikenin were left in charge of the ponies.

As I mentioned above, Manika, as far as we saw it, is a lovely country; its landscape views—hills, valleys and waters—are very pretty, and, as far as its mineral wealth is concerned, the fact that 1950 claims have already been registered there speaks for itself. In my judgment the place is very rich in gold.

We left Umtali at five o'clock on Saturday, 10th October. The waggon led the way; it was one of the spring waggons with which we had travelled to Tuli on our last trip, and which had been sent on from there to Dr. Jameson at Salisbury.

Our course being downhill now, our animals could trot away at a good speed. We noticed that our grooms were rather tipsy, and we were afraid that, if we left them at their posts, ere night our cart would be overturned. We therefore halted for a few minutes, Major Johnson went over to the waggon and took its management upon himself, whilst I replaced the driver of the cart. After promising the Major to wait for him at Eight Mile Spruit, I drove in advance of the waggon. Handling the reins very cautiously, I steered clear of all the trees bordering the narrow road, successfully passed the several spruits that crossed our way, and reached the Eight Mile safely. My cart had long been outspanned when the Major arrived with the waggon. The bush of one of the fore-wheels of the waggon had been so ground by friction that it had

was built a Kafir-kraal. At the foot of this kopje there was a stone wall, built for the purpose of fortifying the kraal. Shortly after our arrival we began bartering with the natives of the kraal near by; we exchanged limbo and salt for such food-stuffs as mealies, Kafircorn, Mozambique and other beans, Kafir-beer, meal, eggs, fowls, etc. The mealies, beans, rice and Kafircorn were fetched from earthen vats erected upon the highest rocks on the little hill. We drove a profitable business, for we had brought plenty of limbo and salt with us. If anything struck us about the personal appearance of the Kafirs here, it was their extreme ugliness.

Leaving our cart and waggon where we had outspanned, we walked towards the kopje, and at the foot of it seated ourselves under a large wild fig-tree. There we ate and drank, and had a nap, whilst Daniel and James, two boys whom Dr. Jameson had brought with him, and whom we had made our drivers, climbed up the rocky kopje to go to the kraal. Suddenly we heard loud screaming. We looked up and saw some Kafir women standing on the edges of some precipitous rocky ridges about 150 feet high ready to jump down. Dr. Jameson at once saw what the matter was; the ignorant Kafir women were fleeing before our boys, who, they fancied, purposed to take them captive. With all the force our throats could produce we shouted to the boys to turn back immediately. They heard us and obeyed. Had the women leaped down those krantzes, they could not but have broken their limbs and been killed.

The fig-tree under which we sat was laden with fruit

when I stood up, half confused and as wet as a fish, and was received with a roar of laughter.

At the close of the day we stopped at the Umsapi River, and there we passed the night. Though we were now at another haunt of wild animals, we were not much disturbed by lions during the night. A fortnight previously a traveller who had outspanned not far from here walked a small distance from his ox-cart at evening, when suddenly the Kafirs he had left at the cart heard a sort of smothered cry and then all was quiet again. Never again did those Kafirs behold their master. Where he had trodden last the fresh footprints of a lion were to be seen.

It was at that same place that the members of the Cape Commission to Mashonaland, Messrs. Eksteen, de Waal and Vosloo, had a month previous to our arrival there shot a lion. These gentlemen, whilst hunting, came upon the animal, and Mr. de Waal and Mr. Vosloo fired at it almost simultaneously, and wounded it mortally. Whether it was the bullet from Mr. de Waal's gun or that from Mr. Vosloo's that struck the animal, remains unsettled; each claims that it was his. Anyhow, the wounded lion disappeared among the tall reeds, and the hunters forbore pursuing, knowing that wild animals are at their fiercest when injured. Three days afterwards, however, a transport-rider stopped there, and his nose coming in contact with a not very fragrant smell, he searched for the object whence the odour came, and found the decaying lion with a bullet through its back.

We left Umsapi River at six o'clock and next outspanned near to a kopje (*lit.* "little head"), on which

was built a Kafir-kraal. At the foot of this kopje there was a stone wall, built for the purpose of fortifying the kraal. Shortly after our arrival we began bartering with the natives of the kraal near by; we exchanged limbo and salt for such food-stuffs as mealies, Kafir-corn, Mozambique and other beans, Kafir-beer, meal, eggs, fowls, etc. The mealies, beans, rice and Kafir-corn were fetched from earthen vats erected upon the highest rocks on the little hill. We drove a profitable business, for we had brought plenty of limbo and salt with us. If anything struck us about the personal appearance of the Kafirs here, it was their extreme ugliness.

Leaving our cart and waggon where we had outspanned, we walked towards the kopje, and at the foot of it seated ourselves under a large wild fig-tree. There we ate and drank, and had a nap, whilst Daniel and James, two boys whom Dr. Jameson had brought with him, and whom we had made our drivers, climbed up the rocky kopje to go to the kraal. Suddenly we heard loud screaming. We looked up and saw some Kafir women standing on the edges of some precipitous rocky ridges about 150 feet high ready to jump down. Dr. Jameson at once saw what the matter was; the ignorant Kafir women were fleeing before our boys, who, they fancied, purposed to take them captive. With all the force our throats could produce we shouted to the boys to turn back immediately. They heard us and obeyed. Had the women leaped down those krantzes, they could not but have broken their limbs and been killed.

The fig-tree under which we sat was laden with fruit

both green and ripe, but it was largely in the possession of small black ants. Under the tree there lay a large square rock smooth on the top, and immediately around it were piled up heaps of stones. What these signified none of us could tell; but later on some Kafir boys from the kraal came to eat figs there, and they cleared the mystery from our mind. It was their custom, they told us, to bury their dead underneath rocks and to cover the place over with stones to prevent the corpses from being devoured by hyænas.

It can be no light work for the Kafir women to carry water in calabash-shells up to that kraal, an ascent of about 200 feet; and most of them have babes to carry with them—these they tie on their backs. The calabashes or, less commonly, earthen pitchers in which they carry the water are never borne otherwise than on their heads. To us, who had nothing to carry but our own weights, it was pretty tough work to climb up there; how those poor creatures manage to clamber up the steep hill with those burdens surpasses my comprehension. But what else are the poor souls to do? They have to secure themselves as far as they possibly can against the raiding Matabele, and so have to choose as residences the spots most difficult to reach.

CHAPTER XIII.

Beautiful farm sites—Eccentricities of Kafir hair-dressing—We take shelter from the storm—Left without food—Major Johnson loses his bet.

WE inspanned at four o'clock, and rode on till we came to a fine, clear stream, on one side of which we halted and passed the night. We had only completed fourteen miles that day, and this slow-coach travelling put me in a bad humour.

Early the next morning we left the river and journeyed through a region the scenery of which was exceedingly pretty—more picturesque I have hardly ever seen. Hills and valleys, spruits and rivers, grass and trees—all combined to present a most charming variety of landscape views.

Major Johnson and I were driving in the cart some distance ahead of the waggon, and, when we arrived at the summit of a small hill, we stopped and waited for Mr. Rhodes and Dr. Jameson. I was so struck with the beauty of the country there that I decided to choose the site of the farms, which Mr. Venter and myself were to have in Mashonaland, at the foot of that hill. Mr. Rhodes soon guessed my thoughts, for when he came up to our cart he said to me, before I had spoken a word,—

aroused by a shriek. He grasped his gun and sprang to his feet, but too late. The lion had already disappeared with one of the Kafirs, and all that he could hear was the dismal cries of the lion's victim growing fainter and fainter as the animal receded. The other Kafir, who was now with the Lieutenant, affirmed every word his master told us.

But the most remarkable and interesting of adventures with lions is the following. Some three months ago Mr. Selous—I do not recollect whether he was alone—on his way from Umliwan to Umtali had to spend a night in the wilds not far from where the tragedies above related occurred. Having chopped some poles and branches, he constructed a little hut for himself, interlacing the boughs with grass and saplings, and leaving a few openings on each side of the structure through which to fire in the case of need. Early in the evening he heard some lions growl in the vicinity, but later all was quiet again. Mr. Selous had with him as weapons a rifle, a hatchet, and a long knife. The gun he placed near to his head, within convenient reach. He was aware that he was now in a veritable nest of lions, so to call it, and that was why he took so much precaution for his security. He fell into a slight slumber, but was soon awakened by the noise of some animal in the bushes near by. Retaining his presence of mind, he sat as still as a mouse, and soon he could faintly discern in the dark through one of his little hut windows the form of some big creature. Slowly he stretched his hand to his gun and drew it nearer; then, levelling it noiselessly to the black

object, he pulled the trigger, and the animal—an enormous lion—after a few terrific grunts, lay a carcass. Again he loaded his rifle, and again he quietly sat down. Sleep he could not and dared not, for when he fired the shot he heard some more lions near. As it happened, only a few minutes passed when a second lion made its appearance. Gently again Mr. Selous took up his gun and, to the best of his judgment in the dark, pointed it at the burglar's head. The second shot was fired, and the second lion, after a few loud moans and gasps, breathed its last. "Two lions dead! Now I may rest!" thought the adventurer, but five minutes had not elapsed when there was a third marauder, the boldest of the three. Sitting breathlessly still, Mr. Selous would not fire until he could see the animal's head. Meanwhile, however, the lion had torn some boughs from the hut, and soon its inmate, calm even in this critical situation, felt the animal sniffing at his feet. Gently Mr. Selous drew his feet in, fired the third shot that night, and mortally wounded the third lion. Now at last the man was left in peace. At early dawn he rose, crept out of his fortification, and found not far from it two full-grown lions cold and stiff. The third, if I remember rightly, was found some time afterwards at the side of a little stream. I may mention that the above tale, incredible as it may appear, has been told me as perfectly true, and that it has been confirmed by several, some of whom had themselves seen the dead lions.

CHAPTER XII.

We cross the Umtali Mountains—A good night's rest—Our Kafir boys leave us, but Pikenin and Matokwa choose to stick by their present masters—An accident to Pikenin—I am thrown into a pool—Our boys frighten the Kafir women—A Kafir burial-place.

At twenty-three minutes past five the following morning we started on our journey over the Umtali Mountains, the boundary between Mozambique and Mashonaland—between the land of the Portuguese and that of the Chartered Company. We crossed the Samba River, on the banks of which the banana grew luxuriantly, and rode down one steep mountain, then another, then along the Umtali River, which here flows through a pretty valley, and finally (at half-past eight) we arrived at the Umtali camp, a distance of about seventeen miles from Massi-Kessi.

Here we met Mr. Heany, Dr. Jameson, and some other well-known gentlemen. It was to us a moment of rejoicing when we entered the Umtali camp. There we had huts to which to retire, and the food and drink we received were of the very best. What a difference to what we had the night before! We could now enjoy a good bed; no lion's roar or hyæna's yelping

disturbed us; no rain need we fear and guard ourselves against, and no reason had we to doubt our horses' safety.

Umtali is 252 miles distant from Beira.

Manika, the district we were now in, is a magnificent tract of country. Already some 300 white men are earning their living there. The day after our arrival we visited several of the gold-reefs in the district, and also the area marked out for the new township.

We intended to depart from Umtali towards evening, and, therefore, early in the afternoon we called our Kafir boys together and asked them whether they wished to remain at Umtali and work for Mr. Heany, who was most willing to take them into his employ and would pay and feed them well; whether they preferred returning to Inhambane; or whether they would like to accompany us farther. They went aside, discussed the question amongst themselves, and at three o'clock they told us their resolution. All of them, except two, had decided to remain at Umtali for the present and return to their homes later on. Pikenin and Matokwa were the dissentients—they chose to go with us to Capetown. We paid all the Kafirs what was due to them. To the boy that had so gallantly carried my portmanteau I gave three kerchiefs, a string of beads and a pocket-knife, and he almost jumped out of his skin, so pleased was he with those handsome presents!—presents that altogether did not cost me three shillings.

The waggon and cart that had been waiting for us at Umtali were now got ready. The waggon had harness

P

enough for eight horses, and the cart for four. We left it entirely in the hands of our driver and reinholder to select the horses and mules that were to draw the vehicles. Tonie, William, Matokwa and Pikenin were left in charge of the ponies.

As I mentioned above, Manika, as far as we saw it, is a lovely country; its landscape views—hills, valleys and waters—are very pretty, and, as far as its mineral wealth is concerned, the fact that 1950 claims have already been registered there speaks for itself. In my judgment the place is very rich in gold.

We left Umtali at five o'clock on Saturday, 10th October. The waggon led the way; it was one of the spring waggons with which we had travelled to Tuli on our last trip, and which had been sent on from there to Dr. Jameson at Salisbury.

Our course being downhill now, our animals could trot away at a good speed. We noticed that our grooms were rather tipsy, and we were afraid that, if we left them at their posts, ere night our cart would be overturned. We therefore halted for a few minutes, Major Johnson went over to the waggon and took its management upon himself, whilst I replaced the driver of the cart. After promising the Major to wait for him at Eight Mile Spruit, I drove in advance of the waggon. Handling the reins very cautiously, I steered clear of all the trees bordering the narrow road, successfully passed the several spruits that crossed our way, and reached the Eight Mile safely. My cart had long been outspanned when the Major arrived with the waggon. The bush of one of the fore-wheels of the waggon had been so ground by friction that it had

gone loose and dropped out—hence the delay. Fortunately we met a few Boers at the Spruit who ably assisted us in the repair of the waggon.

The following morning my boy Pikenin was not lively enough according to Mr. Rhodes's fancy when the latter ordered him to bring together the horses and mules. Angry at this imaginary laziness of the boy, the Premier gave him a few slaps, and the boy, somewhat confused, ran amongst the horses, one of which violently kicked him in the stomach. He fell unconscious to the ground, and when we picked him up he looked as if he would not recover. After a while, however, he returned to his senses, but his condition was still by no means such as to allow him to resume work. We lifted him upon the waggon and applied every remedy, for we were still afraid that his injury might prove fatal. It grieved me much to see him suffer, and I had anything but a kind feeling towards the Premier, who had been the cause of the accident, and who had no business whatever to interfere with the inspanning.

After travelling another fifteen miles we arrived at another spruit, which we named "Sunday Spruit," as it was on a Sunday that we came there. The veld round about was of a good character.

On our way to Sunday Spruit we had to drive through a drift, the sides of which were very steep and contained several dangerous holes. Our rein-holder, through careless driving, ran one of the cart-wheels over one of those holes, with the result that I was jerked out of the cart like a stone into a deep pool. I escaped unhurt, but I must say I felt rather small

when I stood up, half confused and as wet as a fish, and was received with a roar of laughter.

At the close of the day we stopped at the Umsapi River, and there we passed the night. Though we were now at another haunt of wild animals, we were not much disturbed by lions during the night. A fortnight previously a traveller who had outspanned not far from here walked a small distance from his ox-cart at evening, when suddenly the Kafirs he had left at the cart heard a sort of smothered cry and then all was quiet again. Never again did those Kafirs behold their master. Where he had trodden last the fresh footprints of a lion were to be seen.

It was at that same place that the members of the Cape Commission to Mashonaland, Messrs. Eksteen, de Waal and Vosloo, had a month previous to our arrival there shot a lion. These gentlemen, whilst hunting, came upon the animal, and Mr. de Waal and Mr. Vosloo fired at it almost simultaneously, and wounded it mortally. Whether it was the bullet from Mr. de Waal's gun or that from Mr. Vosloo's that struck the animal, remains unsettled; each claims that it was his. Anyhow, the wounded lion disappeared among the tall reeds, and the hunters forbore pursuing, knowing that wild animals are at their fiercest when injured. Three days afterwards, however, a transport-rider stopped there, and his nose coming in contact with a not very fragrant smell, he searched for the object whence the odour came, and found the decaying lion with a bullet through its back.

We left Umsapi River at six o'clock and next outspanned near to a kopje (*lit.* "little head"), on which

was built a Kafir-kraal. At the foot of this kopje there was a stone wall, built for the purpose of fortifying the kraal. Shortly after our arrival we began bartering with the natives of the kraal near by; we exchanged limbo and salt for such food-stuffs as mealies, Kafir-corn, Mozambique and other beans, Kafir-beer, meal, eggs, fowls, etc. The mealies, beans, rice and Kafir-corn were fetched from earthen vats erected upon the highest rocks on the little hill. We drove a profitable business, for we had brought plenty of limbo and salt with us. If anything struck us about the personal appearance of the Kafirs here, it was their extreme ugliness.

Leaving our cart and waggon where we had outspanned, we walked towards the kopje, and at the foot of it seated ourselves under a large wild fig-tree. There we ate and drank, and had a nap, whilst Daniel and James, two boys whom Dr. Jameson had brought with him, and whom we had made our drivers, climbed up the rocky kopje to go to the kraal. Suddenly we heard loud screaming. We looked up and saw some Kafir women standing on the edges of some precipitous rocky ridges about 150 feet high ready to jump down. Dr. Jameson at once saw what the matter was; the ignorant Kafir women were fleeing before our boys, who, they fancied, purposed to take them captive. With all the force our throats could produce we shouted to the boys to turn back immediately. They heard us and obeyed. Had the women leaped down those krantzes, they could not but have broken their limbs and been killed.

The fig-tree under which we sat was laden with fruit

enough for eight horses, and the cart for four. We left it entirely in the hands of our driver and reinholder to select the horses and mules that were to draw the vehicles. Tonie, William, Matokwa and Pikenin were left in charge of the ponies.

As I mentioned above, Manika, as far as we saw it, is a lovely country; its landscape views—hills, valleys and waters—are very pretty, and, as far as its mineral wealth is concerned, the fact that 1950 claims have already been registered there speaks for itself. In my judgment the place is very rich in gold.

We left Umtali at five o'clock on Saturday, 10th October. The waggon led the way; it was one of the spring waggons with which we had travelled to Tuli on our last trip, and which had been sent on from there to Dr. Jameson at Salisbury.

Our course being downhill now, our animals could trot away at a good speed. We noticed that our grooms were rather tipsy, and we were afraid that, if we left them at their posts, ere night our cart would be overturned. We therefore halted for a few minutes, Major Johnson went over to the waggon and took its management upon himself, whilst I replaced the driver of the cart. After promising the Major to wait for him at Eight Mile Spruit, I drove in advance of the waggon. Handling the reins very cautiously, I steered clear of all the trees bordering the narrow road, successfully passed the several spruits that crossed our way, and reached the Eight Mile safely. My cart had long been outspanned when the Major arrived with the waggon. The bush of one of the fore-wheels of the waggon had been so ground by friction that it had

that he had been going on in that way for three weeks running, for I was afraid that our provisions would run short ere we reached the end of our journey. We had still to travel some 1200 miles in a land about which we knew, as yet, exceedingly little. What also annoyed me was to see how fast the whiskey that Mr. Lange and I had bought at Capetown to serve us on our journey was being consumed.

Well, after dinner I went to bed, and I was the first of our party to do so, though the others were no less tired than myself. I was pretty sound asleep when, between eleven and twelve, Captain Tyson came into the waggon in which I was lying, and I awoke. The Captain undressed himself, lit his pipe, took a book in his hand, and began to read in bed. Well, I had not the slightest objection to his sleeping next to me, for there was plenty of room for two, but what I was opposed to was the burning of a candle by my side and the smoking. Being as yet very little acquainted with the gentleman, I did not wish to disturb him, much less quarrel with him, so I adopted another plan; I quietly stood up, put on my boots, and stepped out of the waggon.

"Where are you going?" asked Captain Tyson.

"Oh, it's all right!" was all I answered.

I called Tonie and asked him where my rug and pillows were.

"What do you want to do with them?" exclaimed the Captain out of the waggon; "I can let you have half-a-dozen."

"Well, thanks!" I replied, "let me have them, then."

when I stood up, half confused and as wet as a fish, and was received with a roar of laughter.

At the close of the day we stopped at the Umsapi River, and there we passed the night. Though we were now at another haunt of wild animals, we were not much disturbed by lions during the night. A fortnight previously a traveller who had outspanned not far from here walked a small distance from his ox-cart at evening, when suddenly the Kafirs he had left at the cart heard a sort of smothered cry and then all was quiet again. Never again did those Kafirs behold their master. Where he had trodden last the fresh footprints of a lion were to be seen.

It was at that same place that the members of the Cape Commission to Mashonaland, Messrs. Eksteen, de Waal and Vosloo, had a month previous to our arrival there shot a lion. These gentlemen, whilst hunting, came upon the animal, and Mr. de Waal and Mr. Vosloo fired at it almost simultaneously, and wounded it mortally. Whether it was the bullet from Mr. de Waal's gun or that from Mr. Vosloo's that struck the animal, remains unsettled; each claims that it was his. Anyhow, the wounded lion disappeared among the tall reeds, and the hunters forbore pursuing, knowing that wild animals are at their fiercest when injured. Three days afterwards, however, a transport-rider stopped there, and his nose coming in contact with a not very fragrant smell, he searched for the object whence the odour came, and found the decaying lion with a bullet through its back.

We left Umsapi River at six o'clock and next outspanned near to a kopje (*lit.* " little head "), on which was built a Kafir-kraal. At the foot of this kopje there was a stone wall, built for the purpose of fortifying the kraal. Shortly after our arrival we began bartering with the natives of the kraal near by; we exchanged limbo and salt for such food-stuffs as mealies, Kafircorn, Mozambique and other beans, Kafir-beer, meal, eggs, fowls, etc. The mealies, beans, rice and Kafircorn were fetched from earthen vats erected upon the highest rocks on the little hill. We drove a profitable business, for we had brought plenty of limbo and salt with us. If anything struck us about the personal appearance of the Kafirs here, it was their extreme ugliness.

Leaving our cart and waggon where we had outspanned, we walked towards the kopje, and at the foot of it seated ourselves under a large wild fig-tree. There we ate and drank, and had a nap, whilst Daniel and James, two boys whom Dr. Jameson had brought with him, and whom we had made our drivers, climbed up the rocky kopje to go to the kraal. Suddenly we heard loud screaming. We looked up and saw some Kafir women standing on the edges of some precipitous rocky ridges about 150 feet high ready to jump down. Dr. Jameson at once saw what the matter was; the ignorant Kafir women were fleeing before our boys, who, they fancied, purposed to take them captive. With all the force our throats could produce we shouted to the boys to turn back immediately. They heard us and obeyed. Had the women leaped down those krantzes, they could not but have broken their limbs and been killed.

The fig-tree under which we sat was laden with fruit

speaking, a very large one. I could hardly believe my eyes when I saw the immense store of groceries it contained, and not less surprised was I to behold the stock of ploughs, picks, spades, shovels, galvanised iron, and other such articles. There were also stored thousands of bags of flour and mealies, and as many cases of biscuit, sardines, pickles, potted meat, and what not.

As I cast my eye over the town, I could not help marvelling at the sight. "Is this the place," I thought to myself, "which Major Johnson and his Pioneers came to only twelve months ago and found an abode of the lion and the hyæna?" Wonderful! A year before the place was a lonely wilderness; now it was a busy town, and on its way to become an extensive city.

The great majority of the inhabitants of Salisbury are speculators and tradesmen. The actual digger is not to be seen in the town; he is to be met with at various places in the country outside.

Before we came to Salisbury we had been told by some that great dissatisfaction prevailed in the town owing to a general scarcity of food, and that an insurrection had broken out amongst its citizens against the Company, but this report we found to be incorrect. Not of food, but of drink there was a want. It is true, however, that there were some discontented spirits at Salisbury, and these now came to the Managing Director of the Chartered Company and tried to make him believe that they were very nearly starved, not having been able for a long time to obtain anything but mealie porridge.

"Well," Mr. Rhodes answered them, "I know that when the rivers were full the waggons could not cross, but I could not help that. You certainly cannot expect to be already provided with roads, telegraphs, bridges, post-carts, etc., all within the short space of twelve months. You have any amount of linen goods, beads, and such-like articles, have you not?"

"Yes," was the reply; "but we can't eat them."

"Well," the representative of the Chartered Company rejoined, "if you were really hard up for food, why did you not take them to the Kafir kraals in the neighbourhood and exchange them for eatables, as *we* did on our way?"

They felt rather in a corner, and had hardly anything to say.

"Every kraal," continued the Premier, "is stocked with mealies, meal, rice, pumpkins, beans and eggs. What more do you want? No," he concluded, "your agitation has not arisen from want of food, but from something else: it is want of *liquor* that displeases you!"

Soon all the grumbling was at an end and all seemed satisfied. What greatly went against their arguments was the fact that the town had a sufficient supply of groceries just then to last the population a very long time, and that a large quantity of liquor had just arrived. If they did not have enough before, they had more than enough now. However, to do them justice, I must admit it is very hard for one who has been used to enjoy a drink at his meals to go without it, especially in a country like Mashonaland. I know this by experience; whiskey and water, wine, brandy, or beer, never were more welcome to me than in that country.

As on the night before, so again, a large party was invited to take dinner with us. The recollection of my son's death, just twelve months before, made me feel low-spirited that evening, so I withdrew myself early from the gay company and betook myself to my waggon. I had no desire to spend my time with the Salisbury commanders, colonels, captains, lieutenants, sergeants and other office-bearers; besides, I cared but little to see how our food and drink were being consumed by strangers. I was more than once greatly annoyed at Salisbury, not only at the way our provisions were being wasted, but at having to spend my time with a lot of men I had never seen before and knew nothing about. Every Johnny to whom I was introduced was a major, a commander, a captain, a colonel, a lieutenant or a sergeant, but common soldiers I saw none. Those titled gentlemen earn large salaries—for what I cannot tell.

A couple of days previous to our coming to Salisbury a waggon arrived there with some cases of champagne. The liquor was immediately removed to a certain bar-room, and a certain gentleman pretty well known at Salisbury, hearing of it, went to that bar-room, stopped in it all day, and emptied no less than seven bottles, for each of which he had to pay the modest sum of five pounds; his stomach thus received £35 worth of liquor in one day. Similar excessive drinking I myself witnessed on the road between the Orange River and Kimberley when the railway line was being laid there.

Mr. Lange and I left at five o'clock on Sunday evening for the Mazoe Gold Fields with one of our waggons drawn by a team of spirited oxen. Jacky was the leader and Fortuin the driver.

When it began to grow dark we stopped, unteamed the oxen and tied them to the yoke. We were now near to a river, the banks of which were adorned with most beautiful flowers. Soon a fire was kindled and a meal prepared, which my friend and I, free—thank goodness!—from the Salisbury military society, very much enjoyed.

We had our rifles with us, and being aware that we were again in a lion neighbourhood, we warned our boys to be on the alert and to wake us if at any time during the night the oxen showed any signs of fright. However, we passed the night more pleasantly than we had expected. Up to two o'clock in the morning we enjoyed sound rest, but at that hour Fortuin awoke us and told us that the oxen were very restless. We immediately got up and, standing on the fore-part of the waggon, we noticed the animals fidgeting, but could neither hear nor see anything unusual. However, we fired a few shots in the dark, to frighten off any wild animals, if such there were; and all was quiet. The oxen seemed glad at our having made our appearance, and one by one they laid themselves down again. We sat upon a box on the waggon for a little, then returned to our bed and slept unmolested till late in the morning. We had heard no lions during the night except a few very far off, and, though the hyænas around us created as much noise as ever, we did not bother ourselves much about them,

When we got up next morning the first thing we did was to go and see whether there were any fresh traces of lions near the waggon. We found none. The only new foot-prints to be seen were those of hyænas—that dreadful nuisance of the night.

After partaking of coffee, we left at six for the Mazoe Valley, a beautiful and most fruitful bit of country. Arrived there, we outspanned. On both sides of the extensive valley high hills rise, and a number of Mashona kraals is to be seen on them. The inhabitants have fine gardens laid out in the vales below, where Kafir-corn, mealies, pumpkins, beans and other vegetables thrive to perfection. A lovely stream runs through the valley, and on both sides of it the soil is as fit for agriculture, in my judgment, as in any other part of the world. The plough may be put into the soil at almost any part of the valley and drawn along in a straight line for miles without being lifted. Millions of bags of mealies, grain, beans, peas, potatoes, sweet-potatoes, etc., could be produced there yearly.

Having allowed our oxen to eat as much as their stomachs could carry, at noon we put them in harness again and drove on until we came to the tent of the Commissioner of the Mazoe Gold Fields, where we stopped and outspanned.

Shortly afterwards some Kafirs appeared at our waggon with a few hundred of as pretty lemons as ever I had seen. We bought a hundred for a bagatelle, and learnt that they had been picked from trees not far from there. We went to see the Gold Commissioner, and he informed us that thousands of lemon-trees were growing on the banks of the Mazoe River (a tributary of the Zambezi), and he expressed it as his firm conviction that the Phœnicians of old had introduced them there; and the undisputed fact that the Mazoe Gold Fields had been worked by thousands in past ages strengthened his statement. He was certain that Mazoe was the part of Africa from which King Solomon had obtained his gold. To convince us of it, he showed us the skull of a man's head which he had dug out from some débris, and which, judging from its formation, was undoubtedly that of a white man. The Mazoe Gold Fields lie about thirty miles north of Salisbury and eighty from Tete, a little Portuguese town situated on the Zambezi.

At four o'clock we took a bath in the river, and, an hour later, we walked to the lemon-trees. They were a sight worth seeing. Countless trees, small as well as big, old as well as young, and all heavily laden with fruit, adorned the Mazoe's banks. Whether it was the Phœnicians, the Egyptians, or the Portuguese, who introduced the lemon there, I cannot tell; but if there is one thing certain about it, it is this, that it was the *white* man who had introduced it. Equally certain is it that the gold mines there had been worked in previous ages by *white* nations.

CHAPTER XVI.

Lord Randolph Churchill—An ancient gold-seeker—Political discussions—I grow warm, and give the English ex-Chancellor my views without fear or favour—The Blue Rock Reef—Dr. Jameson and I inspect an old mine—Lord Randolph prefers to prepare his own breakfast.

Towards evening Mr. Rhodes, Lord Randolph Churchill, Mr. Borrough, Dr. Jameson and Dr. Harris also arrived there. They had come with a cart drawn by four horses. The two doctors were shown the skull, of which I have made mention, and both of them, after carefully examining it, declared it to be that of a European or Asiatic—certainly not of an African negro. It had been found in the Rothschild Mine, at a depth of 35 feet. It was in that same mine that, shortly after the discovery of the skull, a human skeleton was found, which Mr. Bent minutely examined, and pronounced to be that of a European. Some ancient instruments were also found there.

As evening set in we drew the waggon and the cart close together, and spread the sheet of canvas we had brought with us over the two vehicles. We were thus protected from dew, and were comfortably housed.

After supper Lord Randolph began to express his

views on certain South African political points, and during the course of his remarks he railed against the Boers for being such a lazy people! Though I was already disgusted with the man, owing to the letters he had written to the *Daily Graphic*, I quietly and attentively sat listening to all he said. The more he spoke the more he exposed his ignorance on the subject he was trying to handle, and it appeared only too plain by his utterances that he cherished bitter animosity towards the Boers. Having listened to all his absurd talk, I begged him to tell me what were the actual reasons for his aversion to the Boers.

"They are lazy, dirty, and barbarous," was the cutting reply.

"How do you know that? Have you been to their farms?"

"Yes," he replied, "at a couple of them."

"But surely you cannot judge the whole country by a couple of farms in it!"

"Well," said he, "I have seen and heard enough of them."

"No," I told him frankly; "you fancy that because you have seen a few farms—the worst in the country, for all I know—you have gathered sufficient knowledge to write a lengthy article in one of the leading London newspapers about the Transvaal and its inhabitants. I would draw a black stroke through every line of that article, and don't be angry with me if I declare its contents for the greater part to be untrue and slanderous. To judge from that letter, I must say, you have as little knowledge of the Transvaal as a sucking-baby has."

A hot discourse now ensued. My opponent defended himself as best he could, but his statements met with the approbation of none present. When I told him a few facts about the Cape Colonial farmers, he said,—

"It was not the *Colonial* farmers I criticised."

"But," I asked, "did you not distinctly say in that letter of yours '*the South African farmer*'? and is not the Cape Colony in South Africa?"

"Yes," he replied; "but it was the farmer of the Transvaal I meant."

"Well, do you mean to say that the farmer of the Transvaal does not come up to the farmer of Ireland, England, or Scotland?"

"Well," said he, "I described what I had seen."

"If you did," I retorted, "you would not have had much to describe. I know a gentleman who in 1882 gave a description of Holland. He crossed over from England to Holland, sailed up the Maas, landed at Rotterdam, and there got into an express train bound for Berlin. He travelled with it to Utrecht, thence to Arnheim, and, before he had spent more than three or four hours in the Netherlands, he found himself in Germany. He then travelled to some other countries on the Continent, never again saw Holland, except on the map, perhaps, and a couple of months later he arrived at Capetown, where he declared he had seen every country in Europe and had found none in such a bad state as Holland; all that had struck his notice there was mud and water; the ground was untilled, and the grass only served to keep the crows alive in winter! Well, *you* remind me of that gentleman. You seem to know nothing of South Africa; you are entirely ignorant as to what South African farmers are, and it appears that, though you have passed over a portion of their country, it has never been your object to come in contact with the people."

No sooner had I done speaking when our good Premier took the word, and, gently though forcibly, tackled the noble Lord, bringing to his notice how much evil he had wrought through the articles he had written, and how he was busy stirring up hatred between the rival races in South Africa, and adding that the ex-Chancellor of the Exchequer of England was the last man from whom he had expected that.

The stubborn man, however, would not give in, though not a single listener agreed with anything he said. He was beaten out of the field altogether. I hope the lessons he received will do him good.

It was late when we went to bed. Twice in the night our horses were frightened by hyænas.

Having taken our coffee the following morning— Randy having drunk the coffee he himself had prepared—Mr. Rhodes, Lord Randolph and Dr. Harris, in company with the Gold Commissioner, went to the Blue Rock Reef; and they were surprised on arriving there, to find the reef "pitched out," *i.e.*, run to its end. Mr. Perkins, the gold expert, (who had come along with Lord Randolph,) and the English nobleman, both of whom seemed greatly interested in the reef, were quite upset at the discovery, so much so that neither of them took any interest in anything else for the rest of the day.

Whilst they were looking at the Blue Rock Reef, Dr. Jameson and I went with a few Kafirs to a mine about half an hour's walk from our waggon. Arrived there, the doctor was the first to descend it. He stepped into a bucket and was lowered into the mine by means of a rope and pulley to a depth of one hundred and nine feet. I, meanwhile, stood waiting for him outside. He was soon out again, and expressed much pleasure at what he had seen. I then got into the bucket. The poles to which the pulley was attached bent a little as I went down, but I reached the bottom safely. To my surprise, I observed down in the mine, at a depth of more than a hundred feet, an old, worn cavity in the ground, the remnant of an ancient tunnel; and I found that the diggers had sunk a shaft from the top of this old piece of tunnel and had struck the previously-worked gold reef, a reef about four feet broad. I was greatly interested in it, and my thoughts were far away as I looked around me and remembered that I was standing in a mine which so many thousands of years ago had been worked by the people of the great King Solomon —at least, so think the best authorities.

We returned to our camp, and next drove to Rothschild's Gold Mine, of which Mr. Bell was the manager. We stopped within a small distance of the mine and took breakfast. At a quarter past eleven, Mr. Rhodes, Lord Randolph and the Gold Commissioner also arrived there, but Dr. Harris was not with them. He had lost his way. We knew that Lord Randolph would be hungry, so we had a good meal ready for him; it was warm and well prepared.

"What have you got there?" he asked.

"A fine breakfast!" answered Mr. Lange. "We

have splendid ham and eggs, cold meat, coffee, milk, etc."

Lord Randolph looked at the food we had been kind enough to keep for him, shook his head and said,—

"None for me, thank you!"

"What's the matter with it?" I asked.

"Badly prepared," was the surly reply. "Give me some eggs and ham, and I shall make my own breakfast."

We complied with his wish. He placed six eggs in the pan, added some fat pieces of ham to them, and sat at the fire acting his own cook. When the eggs were fried, he put his own coffee into the kettle, cooked it himself, and then began enjoying the fruits of his toil. I could not help casting a look upon his plate, for I was inquisitive to know what difference there was between the meal *we* had offered him and the one he himself had prepared. The only difference I could see was, that he had used much more fat for the eggs than we; his lordship was apparently exceedingly fond of fat, for it was astonishing to see how eagerly he ate the rich bacon.

When he had finished his breakfast I asked him whether he had seen Rothschild's Mine.

"Oh, yes, " replied he, "and I have bought half a share in it for £2000."

I congratulated him upon his purchase, and expressed my conviction that he would make a profit out of it.

CHAPTER XVII.

The Rothschild Mines—Output of gold—How Lobengula treated his advisers—Traces of the Phœnicians—Lemon-trees—Crossing the Hunjani River—Hunting the Setsiebies bucks—I prefer to shoot nothing to being shot—We have to return empty-handed.

NEXT we visited the Rothschild Mines lying at the foot of a hill, and surrounded by dense mimosa trees. There were three distinct reefs, and each was supplied with its own shaft. The shafts were from thirty-five to sixty feet deep. One of the mines particularly arrested our interest. It had been discovered by Mr. Bell; he had noticed a little opening in the ground there, and at once surmised that there was an old mine underneath. His conjecture proved correct. Sinking a shaft he struck upon a rich little reef nine inches thick at a depth of twenty-five feet. He followed it, and, ten feet deeper, found its thickness increased to two and a half feet. In this mine also were to be seen old tunnels and other excavations made by the miners of days long past—in all probability by the Phœnicians. These people had evidently considered it waste of time and trouble expending labour on a vein only nine inches broad, not knowing that if they followed it a little farther they would find it grown to thrice that width. I can attest to the richness of this mine, for I myself brought a piece of its quartz to Capetown and had it examined by Government analysts, who declared it to contain no less than 17 ozs. of gold to the ton.

The other reefs, too, were broad and rich. Dr. Jameson and I visited all the mines, and we had every reason to be pleased with what we saw. The Premier, also, was highly satisfied. Lord Randolph uttered not a word; he was afraid, I dare say, to expose himself, for there was already on its way to England a letter of his to the *Daily Graphic*, wherein he condemned Mashonaland as far as its auriferous character was concerned. If his chosen, confidential friend, Perkins, had now been with him he would have had some one to whom to confide his feelings; but as that gentleman was not there, his lordship was wise enough to remain quiet.

We had the horses saddled and the vehicles inspanned. Dr. Jameson and myself drove ahead in the cart; Mr. Rhodes, Lord Randolph and Mr. Heany following on horseback, whilst Mr. Lange came on behind with the waggon.

Dr. Jameson told me that Lobengula, the notorious Matabele king, had the year before put his chief induna (adviser) to death, because it was by the latter's advice that the monarch signed the Concession to the Chartered Company. The unfortunate counsellor was slain like a dog, his wife and children maltreated, his grain forfeited to the despot, and his cattle—seven thousand head—added to the king's stock. It took several days to bring the grain over from Luchi's kraal (the kraal at which the induna was slain) to Buluwayo.

We were back at Salisbury a little before night. On our way thither we descried a small camp in the distance, and learnt that the Count de la Panouse was having his temporary residence there. He was prospecting the land. The Count visited us at Salisbury the same evening. He told us that the Mazoe River flowed close by his camp, and that he was every night being molested by lions, some of which had already carried off three oxen of his, two goats, five dogs, four fowls, and a few lambs. Only the night before there had been a lion at his camp. The animal at first made for a hut in which an aged Kafir was sleeping, put its nose through the shutter of the little window and struggled to get in. The poor old chap inside did not know what to do; helpless he stood there and in the greatest anxiety. The lion, failing to force an entrance, withdrew for a while, and the Kafir seized the opportunity to cross over to another hut of his. There he discovered that the only pet he had possessed, a faithful little dog, had been devoured by the dreaded burglar. The lion returned to the hut, but, finding its attempts to enter it unsuccessful, uttered some loud growls and retired.

The Count also told us that hundreds of lemon-trees were growing on the river sides near to his temporary dwelling, that he at present had five bags of lemons in his house, and that his wife was making lemon-juice from them. He, also, felt certain that the first lemon-trees on the Mazoe had been planted by men from the northern hemisphere; so, too, were the orange-trees which he had seen growing in luxuriance on the shores of the Odzi. We spent an exceedingly pleasant evening with this gentleman.

We left Salisbury the next morning, October the 20th, with three waggons (each drawn by a team of twelve oxen), and five saddle-horses. Sergeant James, the same gentleman who had conducted us some distance on our journey the previous year, was again our guide. Tonie was our cook, and he was assisted by Matokwa and Pikenin, the two Inhambane Kafirs. Bandmaster was the waiter at our table. Mr. Eduard Lange had the control of the waggons, and Captain Tyson was charged with the duty of looking after the victuals. Our five horses were left in charge of Roeping, a fine young Basuto-Kafir. Dr. Jameson, Mr. Duncan (the Surveyor-General), and Mr. van der Bijl accompanied us with a cart drawn by six strong mules. I cannot say I felt sorry when we left Salisbury.

We journeyed on until we came to a native village, where we outspanned and passed the night.

At four the next morning we started again. As we were crossing the Hunjani River the waggon in which I was sitting drove against a rock in the stream and stuck; it took a long time to get it loose again. Mr. Rhodes, Dr. Jameson and Mr. van der Bijl, who had remained behind with the cart, caught us up at nine o'clock. We had then already outspanned and were busy preparing coffee.

We went to bathe, and, as we were both hungry and tired—for we had been up since four and it was now eleven—the bath was followed by a big and substantial breakfast.

Having spread the canvas over the waggons, which were standing in the cool shade of some large trees, we all lay down under it for a nap, after which we had coffee.

At four o'clock Mr. Rhodes, Dr. Jameson, Sergeant James and I had our horses saddled, and we went out hunting. We came across three wild pigs, and some red-bucks and riet-bucks, but we would not shoot at them, for we were desirous rather to aim at some setsiebies-bucks, deer as large as donkeys, which we knew were to be found there, and which we did not wish to frighten. Just as we were crossing an elevation, we caught sight of some fifty of these bucks grazing a little distance in front of us. On seeing us they made off bewildered, scattering into a number of little groups, but they ran so clumsily that they seemed to have difficulty in getting along. However, they gave such long strides that, contrary to appearance, they moved along very swiftly. We pursued them, and bom! bom! the shots came from all sides, but all in vain. With a steady gallop, though with no apparent hurry, the animals gradually gained distance. Some bullets from the guns of my companions flew past my head. "Heavens!" I thought with alarm, "this won't do!" I held in my horse and allowed the excited hunters to pass me by. "Rather shoot nothing," I thought, "than be shot!" At last the excitement was over and the bucks had fled. All the sportsmen assembled again and each had something exciting to tell, but none could say, "I shot one of them." I also had something to tell—not that I very nearly *shot* a buck, but that I was very nearly shot *like* a buck. Really, more than one bullet whistled past my ear, and I still shudder to think of it.

The sun set and we were still far from our waggons. No time was to be lost. It was a pity that we had not sighted the game earlier than we did. With a feeling of shame at not having overpowered a single buck, we returned to our camp, and it was pretty dark when we reached it. Mr. van der Bijl and Mr. Lange had a hearty laugh at us for returning with an empty bag. Captain Tyson, however—though he also smiled—I noticed, was disappointed at our ill-luck, for he remembered how I had foretold at Salisbury that he would regret, ere we reached the end of our journey, his lavish hospitality at that place.

CHAPTER XVIII.

Hunting again—The Premier Nimrod this time—I shoot a crocodile—Mr. Scott's narrative—Our oxen missing, and we are all out of humour—A tropical storm.

EARLY the following morning we—the same party as the day before—went out for another hunt. We passed some quaggas, wild dogs, wild pigs, red-bucks and riet-bucks, but left them all in peace. Ultimately we caught sight of a group of setsiebies bucks. Immediately on seeing us they took to flight. Resolved, however, not to return to our waggons before we had at least felled one of their number, we chased the animals for a distance of five or six miles, when the River Hunjani, a tributary of the Zambezi, prevented them from fleeing any farther. No alternative was left them but to force their way back if possible, and this was the course they adopted. But just as they were turning the Premier and Dr. Jameson fired at them, the former succeeding in shooting one through the shoulder. When I saw the bucks turn back I sprang from my horse and awaited them, and I had not waited long when five passed me at a distance of about fifteen yards. I pulled the trigger, but, to my disappointment and annoyance, the shot failed to go off. It was a double-barrelled gun I had, but only one barrel was designed for a bullet. By the time I had loaded it with another cartridge the bucks were as far from me as when the chase was begun.

Two young Kafirs, who had also been hunting, met us in the field. We immediately employed them to skin and cut up the buck the Premier had shot. With wonderful skill and in very little time the animal was flayed and sliced. We took as much of the meat on our horses as could conveniently be carried, and made the Kafirs bring the rest.

All, except myself, returned straightway to the waggons. I preferred to take the longer course along the river. Lose my way I knew I hardly could, because our camp stood on one of the sides of the river, and I wanted to kill a crocodile. I had spied more than one during the day basking in the warm rays of the sun. I had not ridden long when I arrived at a small spruit of the river, and there I noticed a large black creature quickly move through the tall grass in the direction of the water. I dismounted, and, on approaching the animal, I saw that it was a monstrous crocodile. I fired, but—fortune that day seemed to be against me—I missed it (I think), and the ugly reptile disappeared into the water. It was at least ten feet in length.

Riding on, I noticed on a small island in the river a little crocodile basking in the sun. I rode nearer to it, dismounted again, took accurate aim, and sent a bullet through its head. There it lay kicking. Close though I was to it, I would not venture to fetch it, for in that part of the world it is risking one's life to swim across even the narrowest rivulets.

At four o'clock our vehicles were inspanned again, and after journeying four and a half hours we met Mr. Kirton with his waggons, one of which was under the control of Mr. John Scott. These gentlemen had just unteamed their oxen. We outspanned close to them.

Mr. Scott related to us a little of his interesting African experiences. In company with two other gentlemen he set out from Salisbury, on the 11th of January last, for Tete, a small Portuguese town on the Zambesi, in order to procure provisions for the Pioneers of the Chartered Company. One of his companions (Smith) contracted fever on the way, and died. All Mr. Scott's attendants (natives) then deserted him, but he was fortunate enough to procure the services of a strong-built, handsome young Kafir six feet tall. By this boy he was led through grass ten feet high and always damp at the stalks, since, owing to its height and density of growth, the sun had very little power to evaporate the moisture there deposited. By this means he caught fever on the Lucia River, a two-days' journey from Tete, to which place he had to be carried back. There he was carefully attended to, and soon afterwards he was as well as ever. Shortly after his illness he purchased for the Chartered Company, from an Indian merchant, sufficient goods for two hundred men to carry, and from this trader he learnt, to his surprise, that the Kafir that had so nobly attended him (Scott) when he became ill had sold to him (the trader) seventy-seven ounces of alluvial gold which he had brought with him from Mashonaland. The Indian had a large supply of ivory, ostrich feathers, hides, nuts, gold, and a variety of other articles, which he was then about to send to the mouth of the Zambezi by a small vessel.

After some delay Mr. Scott returned to Mashonaland, successfully accomplishing his errand, though not without having undergone a very trying journey.

Tete, Mr. Scott told us, had between forty and fifty white inhabitants, and was provided with seven or eight stores. The Governor of the place, an enterprising man, had turned it into an attractive spot. Tete lies about 250 miles from Salisbury and 260 from the mouth of the Zambezi. A swift boat, the *Turn Wheeler*, runs at frequent intervals between Tete and the coast, touching at stations on the banks of the river, where rapid progress is being made in sugar plantations. Mealies, pumpkins, potatoes, rice, etc., also thrive there.

We continued the journey the following morning to Klip River and in the clear water we had a refreshing bath. After the bath we had our breakfast, and after breakfast we went for a hunt. Meeting, however, with no large game, we soon again returned to our waggons.

The district in which we were now travelling has lately been the scene of many a tragedy; several human beings and a comparatively large number of oxen and mules have there been torn to pieces by lions. Strange to say, however, we neither saw nor heard a single animal of that description.

We had intended to resume the journey at half-past three; but neither ox nor mule was to be seen when we wanted to inspan. Mr. van der Bijl saddled his horse, Mr. James his, and I mine, and we set out in different directions in search of the strayed animals. We also sent our Kafirs on the same errand. After a long and tedious search, we one by one gave it up as useless and returned to the waggons, where we found to our joy that the animals had already been discovered by the Kafirs. Fully an hour and a half did we waste in this quest.

At half-past five we were able to move on again; but the party was altogether out of humour. Roeping and Jas, the former rather unjustly, each received a thrashing for not having kept better watch over the animals.

We had hardly been on our way half an hour, when there was every indication in the sky of an approaching storm, and soon the lightning flashed on every side. Every minute the weather grew worse, and the oxen became so seized with fright that it was with the greatest difficulty that we compelled them to proceed. Still the storm increased in violence. Peal after peal of thunder shook the sky above us, and every moment we expected the lightning to strike our animals, if not ourselves. To add to our misfortunes, rain now came down in torrents, and much thwarted our progress. At seven o'clock it was so dark that we could hardly see our hands before our eyes. Of course, we halted then.

CHAPTER XIX.

The Umfuli River—Ant-heaps a thousand years old—The climate of Mashonaland—The Makalaka Kafirs—A meeting in the wilds with friends—Young colonists—Captain Tyson's stores are replenished—We receive a visit from Mr. Selous and travel on the road he constructed—More lion stories.

At half-past two the following morning—the heavens being then again at rest—we set forward again, and at five we crossed the Umfuli River, another tributary of the Zambezi. At six we stopped and drank coffee, and at seven we again set forth, our road taking us over a pretty, open field. We passed some fine old tree-plantations, the indications of some of the spots where the ancient Phœnicians built their huts and pitched their tents. Now and then, also, a green picturesque valley appeared in view and added to the variety of scenery. But what struck us more than anything else was the immense size of the ant-heaps. It is difficult for one who has not seen them to realize their magnitude; and when one bears in mind that they have been raised solely by the tiny ant, one cannot but be struck with wonder when he sees them. Judging by their enormous size, every ant-heap there—ant-mountain, I might say—is more than a thousand years old. Around each of them the common Cape sweet quick-grass grows in abundance, a grass which horse, ox, ass, goat, and sheep all deem a luxury, and is most nourishing.

The climate in that part of the country is all that can be desired. Though the place is called by some a lion's nest, not a single lion disturbed us during all the time we spent there. Heavy and destructive winds are unknown, and so are snow, sleet and frost. Now and then a heavy rain would fall—accompanied by thunder and lightning perhaps—that was all. Taken all round, the climate is excellent. Drought is unknown in that region. Should the grass upon the hills become dry, the valleys may be resorted to; these never fail. With many a veteran hunter, who had had much experience in Mashonaland, did I converse, and everyone assured me that oxen in that land would grow beautifully fat; and, I may add, that I did not meet a single team of oxen in Mashonaland but what was in excellent condition. Transport-oxen often enter that country thin and ugly, but they are always fat and pretty when they leave it.

No doubt many of my readers will think that I am speaking too highly in praise of the country; but what I have stated above is the perfect truth, and my fellow-travellers will bear me out; so also will Mr. Ferreira of Uitenhage, Mr. Herman Morkel of Somerset West, Mr. Kirton of Marico, Mr. Botha of Heidelberg, and many others—men who have themselves seen the land.

Not far from where we were now travelling live a Kafir tribe (the Makalaka), who eat the largest and filthiest hair-worms they can catch from the tops of trees. They make a sort of pap—*pudding* they would prefer me to call it—of them, and treat it as a dainty.

At half-past five we arrived at Fort Charter, a small fort built on a high elevation. Lieutenant Cordington was the commander here. Five waggons were standing outspanned near to the fort; they belonged to Mr. Lourens van der Bijl, who, immediately when he noticed our waggons, came to meet us. He invited us to his waggons, and the invitation was of course accepted. Arrived at his camp, we were heartily cheered by Mr. van der Bijl's young companions. The boys seemed all in the best of spirits. We spent two pleasant hours in the tent of the much-esteemed trekker, who entertained us with an interesting account of his experiences on his journey to Mashonaland. He had been on the road now for five months and had not yet reached his destination. Just a week previously, he was grieved to tell us, he had to bury one of the youthful twenty-five Colonials that he had brought with him; but, despite the numerous misfortunes the young immigrants had had to contend with, we found them joyful and in high spirits. Not a word of complaint did we hear from their lips; with everything they were satisfied. Meat or no meat, it was all the same to them: so long as they could get their mealie porridge, they were quite content. It was a great pleasure to me to meet them. We advised Mr. van der Bijl not to settle until he had come to Marandella's district, a magnificent piece of country between Salisbury and Umtali—the district in which I had the farms measured out for Mr. Venter and myself. Mr. van der Bijl took our advice. His settlement to-day bears the name of Lourensdale.

We left Fort Charter at two o'clock the following morning, and halted in a small valley where there was fine grazing for our draught animals. Shortly after breakfast we were met by a gang of Kafir women and children, who were eager to barter with us. They had with them—besides a large quantity of vegetables—beer, fowls and eggs. It was a pleasant hour for Captain Tyson. The poultry and eggs he was particularly happy to obtain, for he was aware that our provisions were rapidly growing less, and he had already seriously been troubling his mind about it, the more so since we had so frequently cautioned him to be less extravagant. Well, he now did lively business with the natives, and the latter were as happy to get our salt and limbo as we were to relieve them of their produce.

At four o'clock, just as we were ready to advance again, Mr. Selous, the famous huntsman, who had already spent nine years in the interior of South Africa, and whom we had ardently been longing to meet, made his appearance. He had come from Victoria, and had brought with him our newspapers and letters addressed to that place.

Allowing our waggons to proceed, we decided to stop behind for a while with our cart and riding-horses in order to have a long interview with the great Mashonaland pioneer. We offered him some refreshments, and, seating ourselves by his side, we listened with the keenest interest to all he had to tell, and we were so absorbed in the vivid account he gave of his experiences in Mashonaland that we would not allow him to leave us. He was the very man we had been most eager to meet, and he had arrived at a very opportune time.

We left Fort Charter at one o'clock in the morning, and our road—one that Mr. Selous himself had devised and ordered to be constructed—took us on a long range of upland. By means of that road all the spruits, which are to be found on both sides of the hill, have been avoided. The elevation serves as a watershed to two large rivers: the waters on the one side of it flow eastward into the Sabi, and those on the other westward into the Zambezi. The veld, which had been burnt a month before, was as green and pretty as might be seen anywhere. Mr. Selous assured us that, long as he was acquainted with Mashonaland, he had never seen an ox there die of hunger, thirst, or disease, nor had he *heard* of a single such case, but he recollected deaths by accidents. Speaking of the dangers of the country, he told us that lions in some parts of Mashonaland seemed to have made it a special object of theirs to prey upon human beings, for they had already devoured hundreds of Kafirs, especially women and children. The people of Chilimanzi and Indarman, for instance, had very materially been reduced in number within recent years by such lions. In fact, these cannibals had become so dangerous that Kafirs were compelled to desert their kraals and build new ones in other districts. According to Mr. Selous, a lion that has once caught and eaten a human being would go far out of his way to get hold of another—and what trouble would it have to catch an old Kafir woman? The adventure Mr. Selous had at the foot of the Umtali Mountains I have already recounted; but he had several other interesting lion stories to tell us. On one occasion—it was last June—a white man, whilst on his way to Salisbury with three donkeys, was approached within a short distance of that township by four lions. The terrified traveller had just sufficient time to climb into the nearest tree, and whilst he was sitting in it he saw how one of his donkeys was being caught and devoured by the lions. Nothing of the poor animal being left, the lions left the place and he the tree. He arrived safely at Salisbury, but he never again saw anything of any of his donkeys.

At the close of the day we arrived at Incasithe, which lies 5000 feet above the sea-level. We had travelled thirty miles that day. This was rather too much of a good thing, for it told considerably upon the animals.

CHAPTER XX.

Remarks on Mashonaland—The natives' fear of the Matabele—A profitable exchange—The houses of the Mashonas—Their fondness for rats as food, and surprise that we do not share it—How the climate compares with other parts of South Africa.

WE continued our journey on the plateau we had entered upon at our start the previous morning, but the road was now sandy and heavy.

The high, and consequently healthy, veld of Mashonaland covers an area of about 150 by 400 miles, and, roughly speaking, it could be divided into 10,000 farms, each containing 2000 morgen, *i.e.* nearly 4000 acres.

I cannot speak of Selous's road but in the highest praise. The course its designer has given it cannot be improved upon even by the most skilful of engineers. The views from that road over the hills, plains, valleys and rivers are truly grand. Now and then we spied some game, but none near. Game, as a rule, keep far from the high road.

We generally rode on horseback during our journey except during the earliest part of the day, when we still lay warm beneath our blankets in our waggons, but even at that inconvenient time we had often to mount our horses, as, for instance, when the waggons came to a spruit; we preferred to miss a little sleep, and take the trouble of riding on horseback through the drift, rather than to remain in the waggon and stand the chance of being knocked about in it or flung out altogether. Since the day on which Mr. Lange upset two of our waggons at the Nionetse, when on the road to Salisbury, he was very cautious—and he had made us no less so—when coming to a spruit. As a rule the air was pleasantly cool at night. In fact, on the whole, we had no reason to complain of the weather.

A few generations back Mashonaland was in the possession exclusively of the Mashonas. Between the years 1810 and 1812 a large band of Zulus left their native land and migrated as a conquering people to this country, where they were known as the Mongoni. Later on Gungunhana, with his large train of followers, also left Zululand and settled in a part of the same region, his subjects being termed the Abagaza. As might have been expected, the two warlike tribes soon began to quarrel, and a long, fierce war was the result. The Mongoni ultimately had the worst of it, and were driven across the Zambezi, where they settled on the plateau-land on the west of Lake Nyassa. The Abagaza were then acknowledged by all native tribes as the master of the beautiful territory along the Sabi River, and Gungunhana* is still their paramount chief, his land being called Gazaland. In 1820 the Matabele also migrated out of Zululand and settled in

* After a short war recently with the Portuguese he was taken captive by them, and it is reported that he will be conveyed to Lisbon.—*Trans.*

the Marico district, whence they were driven by the Boers in 1837 across the Limpopo. The Matabele then steadily trekked further and further northward, and repeatedly raided upon the Mashonas, butchering thousands of the men and carrying off their wives and children as slaves.

Judging from the foundations of huts that the Mashonas of previous generations had inhabited and which are still to be seen, the Mashonas of former times were certainly more respectable as a nation than those of to-day. The former used to live in fine, spacious, comfortable straw-built houses; the latter dwell in narrow little huts, and these are only to be met with on the kopjes and upon the highest krantzes. But even there the unhappy beings are far from safe; they are still frequently being attacked and plundered by the dreaded Matabele under Lobengula. No wonder they look upon Mr. Rhodes as their deliverer! But what can the latter as yet do? As matters stand at present, I fear the Matabele are too strong for the Chartered Company's force. The whites in Mashonaland have often to witness their Mashona servants slain in front of them by the heartless Matabele. Only a short time ago an aged Kafir captain who refused to pay taxes to Lobengula was murdered, his cattle and grain carried away, his wives and children made slaves, and his sons-in-law put to death.

We stopped at a small Kafir kraal, and exchanged some limbo and a number of empty cartridges and some beads—all of which were only a few shillings in value—for eighteen young fowls and a lot of eggs. Captain Tyson's countenance was again "all smiles."

We set out again at half-past two the next morning, leaving Roeping behind with a horse to bring on the four oxen which were too tired to be inspanned. At ten o'clock he arrived at our waggons without any of the oxen, saying he could not find them. Mr. Rhodes immediately sent him back, along with Mr. James, to go in search of the animals. They returned by the road for a distance of twelve miles, and at four o'clock they arrived at the waggons with the oxen. It was clear that Roeping had been afraid to be alone in the dark, and had followed the waggons without troubling himself about the animals.

We outspanned upon an elevation between two kraals built on rocks, and we had not been there long when we were again encircled by a crowd of Kafirs (men, women and children), who wished to sell us their products—meal, beans, peas, mealies, rice, pumpkins, wild oranges, figs, loquats, mapels, maconas, honey, eggs and fowls.

Sibaberossa was the captain of these kraals, and he in turn was a subject of the chief, Zimuto. Mr. Selous told me that in certain parts of Mashonaland hundreds of huts were to be found, which were built so high on rocks that their inhabitants could not reach them except by means of long ladders. These ladders they drew up every night and let down every morning. This was of course done through fear of the Matabele. There was a time when thousands of cattle and sheep were to be met with in the country, but Lobengula's men had carried away almost all of them. The cattle and sheep of the Mashonas are small in size, but they look very well. The same may be said of Mashona fowls.

An enormous fig-tree, patronised chiefly by the bee and the starling, stood close to where we had outspanned. I shot some of the birds, not for sport, but to eat. Of smaller birds than the starling, as, for instance, the sparrow, the finch, the robin or the red-beak, I saw none, except the little blue parrot. The previous year, however, on our way to Tuli, we saw hundreds of these birds. I cannot understand how it is that they do not inhabit the part of the country we were now travelling through. The hawk is very common here, and probably that accounts for the absence of the smaller birds: the hawk very probably does with the weaker bird what the Matabele does with the Mashona.

As far as rats are concerned, Mashonaland cannot complain of having too few. These little mischievous animals exist there in thousands. The natives, however, are fond of them; they catch them and eat them. It happens now and then that a Kafir would smilingly appear at a camp with a number of rats tied to a stick, and offer them for sale; and he is greatly surprised at the taste and the manners of the white man when the latter shudders at the sight and tells him immediately to be off with rats and all!

The climate of Mashonaland is fairly mild. In summer the highest degree of temperature would be 87 in the shade, and in winter 41 in the sun. At Kimberley we meet with far greater extremes; there the thermometer sometimes reads 100 degrees in summer in the shade, and I know it to have descended to 25 degrees in winter. From these facts we see that, as far as temperature goes, the climate of Mashonaland is precisely the same as that of the south-western corner of the Cape Colony, viz., between Capetown and the Paarl. The above information I received from Mr. Selous, who himself made the observations with sound apparatus which he had brought with him from Europe.

CHAPTER XXI.

Formation of rocks at Fort Victoria—Lord Randolph Churchill's opinion of the Mashonaland Gold Mines—Will not accompany us to the ruins of Simbabe—I cannot understand such conduct in a news correspondent—He invites the Premier and myself to be his travelling companions, but we decline.

AT nine o'clock in the morning of the 13th October we reached Fort Victoria, and outspanned about half a mile from it. The fort is situated on an elevation, at the back of which rise some high hills. It gets its water supply from some fine clear streams running near by, which empty themselves into one or two green-skirted spruits a little further off.

Shortly after our animals had been unteamed we rode to the telegraph office, which had only been opened the day before, and was three miles from Victoria. The office was a waggon. Mr. Rhodes was the recipient of three telegrams—one from Mr. Merriman, one from Mr. James Sivewright, and one from Mr. Currey. The Premier and I next sent away some: it was then twelve o'clock. I was very anxious to have some tidings from home, for I knew absolutely nothing of what had happened there within the previous six weeks. At half-past two we received long answers to our telegrams, and at three we returned to the waggons.

The formation of the rocks near Fort Victoria struck my attention. They all appeared more or less gold-bearing.

Lord Randolph's camp stood a little distance from our own. His lordship came over to us towards evening, Mr. Perkins, his friend, again accompanying him. We invited him to join our company the following day to visit the Simbabe ruins, but Lord Randolph stoutly declined to do so, saying that he had seen enough of old débris-heaps in his day and had no desire to see more.

"But," he added, "if you can take me to a reef bearing two ounces of gold to the ton, I will go and see it."

"Well," answered Dr. Jameson, "then we shall take you to-morrow to Dickens' Reef and to Long's Reef, both of which yield from six to nine ounces to the ton."

"What's the use!" retorted the nobleman. "Follow them a little deeper and they stop."

"I do not understand you," interrupted the Premier. "Because you have seen *one* reef pitched out you denounce all others!"

"I take Perkins' word," was Lord Randolph's abrupt reply.

Mr. Perkins, on being asked what his opinion was of Long's Reef, said that it was twelve feet broad and looked very pretty, but that its proprietors were afraid to open it any farther because they knew it would soon run to its end.

"Do you hear that?" asked Lord Randolph with a triumphant smile.

It was no use arguing with them.

"You must be either prejudiced against Mashonaland," I said to Perkins, "or you have some private reason for denouncing it."

Lord Randolph then compared the gold fields of Mashonaland with those of the Transvaal, and showed the contrast between the outputs of the respective places.

"But are you aware, Lord Randolph," I said to him, "that Witwatersrand is six years old, whereas this place is barely a year? I should like to meet you five years hence and then hear what you and your Mr. Perkins, with all his ability as a gold expert, will have to say."

Here the argument on the gold fields dropped.

Again our distinguished visitor was requested to accompany us to the Simbabe ruins, which lay about twenty-five miles by cart, and only half that distance on horseback, from Victoria. But the stubborn gentleman was not to be moved, much less would he visit the gold reefs. His friend Perkins hardly spoke a word, and when he did he spoke in such a low voice that I could not help contracting a feeling of distrust towards the man.

It was to me something really strange that a man like Lord Randolph Churchill, who was receiving £200 for each letter he inserted in the *Daily Graphic*, should not think it worth his while going to see the rich newly-discovered reefs, nor even the intensely interesting Simbabe ruins, which, to other travellers — I don't include fortune-seekers—was the chief attraction in the country. Possibly the explanation of his conduct lay in the fact that he had already sent to England public letters in which he had expressed the opinion that Mashonaland was worth next to nothing as far as its gold-producing character was concerned.

The following morning Lord Randolph asked Mr. Rhodes to travel with him to Capetown: he had a spider drawn by twelve mules and was travelling at a much faster rate than we with the oxen.

"Well," answered the Cape Premier, "I must hear what my fellow-traveller says. I should not like to part with him."

"Oh, no," was the reply; "I mean that he should also come with us; there is ample room for the three of us in the spider."

Mr. Rhodes, I dare say, knew well that I would not exchange the company of my friend Lange, and of the genial Captain Tyson, for that of so sour a man as Lord Randolph Churchill, a man who had written in bitter malignity against my fellow Africanders, and who was now accompanied by a little conceited doctor and by Perkins. Besides, I know that he had not intended to include me when he invited Mr. Rhodes; it was only the clever dodge of the Premier—the observation that he would not like to leave his friend behind—that made the nobleman extend his invitation.

Mr. Rhodes now formally, in the presence of the English ex-Chancellor, communicated to me the latter's desire. I felt very surprised, for although I had been sure that Lord Randolph would ask the Premier to travel with him I had never expected him to invite me, seeing that he and I disagreed on nine points out of every ten and that there was very little sympathy between us.

"Oh, no, Lord Randolph," I courteously answered, "I should not like to leave my waggon until I come to Tuli, and it may be that I shall go with it to Kimberley. However, I am much obliged to you for your kind offer. I intend to stop at least two days at the Boobi River to hunt large game there; but," I added, addressing Mr. Rhodes, "*you* may journey with Lord Randolph; I shall not in the least take it amiss of you."

"Well," replied Mr. Rhodes to the nobleman, "then I am sorry to say I shall not be able to go with you."

"I am also very sorry indeed," responded Lord Randolph, who seemed very disappointed.

At two o'clock in the afternoon he left with his spider drawn by four horses and four mules, with a coach drawn by twelve mules, and with a waggon drawn by sixteen oxen.

I dare say the noble correspondent of the *Daily Graphic* burnt with anger and disgust when he had to drive away without the Premier, seeing that he had waited for us at Fort Victoria fully six days. He had left Salisbury two days before we did, and he had travelled with horses and mules while we had to get along with oxen.

Lord Randolph's drivers and "reinholders" had a thousand complaints to make against their master. According to them the nobleman must possess a very bad temper, and through it the poor draught animals had often to suffer a great deal.

CHAPTER XXII.

We start for Simbabe—A perilous ford—The great Simbabe temple—We find our arrival is expected, and don't altogether like our reception at first—Explanations make everything clear—We climb the walls—An early cup of coffee.

THE following morning Captain Tyson was to leave by cart with the provisions, the karosses, etc., for Simbabe, and Mr. Rhodes, Mr. Selous, Dr. Jameson, Mr. Brabant and myself were to follow later in the day. It was a beautiful morning. While Captain Tyson was preparing to proceed to the ruins I took a walk up the hills on the other side of Victoria, and from there I had a magnificent view over the hills, valleys, and woods around. Some beautiful large flowers were to be seen on some of the krantzes. I picked a few, and with my stick dug out the bulbs of two.

I was back at the camp at twenty minutes past eight. Captain Tyson was then on the point of starting for Simbabe. There was a seat vacant in the cart and the Captain pressed me to take it. In a moment I was ready, and at half-past eight we left with our cart drawn by six choice mules. The driver and reinholder sat in front, Captain Tyson and I at the back. We drove across a field and were guided, not by a road, but by some wheel-tracks. We passed over hills, through kloofs, and across spruits, the scenery being sublime on every side. At length we approached a deep river, with banks steep and dangerous, but we did not notice it until we were within a short distance of it. We were going down hill at a rapid speed, with animals not strong enough to stop the heavy cart in time; and the prospect of man, mule and cart being thrown into the river stared us in the face. Captain Tyson knew not what to do; but in an instant I formed a plan. I jumped down, seized from the mules every leather strap that they could spare, and with the assistance of my companion I quickly tied the straps to the sides of the cart and by their means we pulled with all our might in the direction opposite to that in which the cart was going, whilst the boys in the cart did their utmost to hold the mules in, and in this way the speed of the vehicle was slackened and we got it safely—though barely so, and not without the expenditure of much exertion—through the river.

At eleven o'clock we arrived and stopped at a river, on the banks of which many an old heap of soil pointed out the spots where the ancients had been washing gold-quartz. We cooked coffee and roasted a piece of meat—our midday meal—and a very nice meal it was.

At one o'clock we proceeded again, our course winding through some narrow passages between green hills. Soon Simbabe Hill came in sight, and after passing some gardens belonging to natives we arrived at our destination and outspanned. We were now confronted by the massive ruins of the great Simbabe temple, and the historical hill that rises close to it. A strange feeling ran through me as I stood there and cast my eyes upon the ruins; it was the same sensation I felt when I beheld the remains of ancient Rome, and, at a later date, those of Pompeii and Herculaneum.

Shortly after we had unteamed the mules we found ourselves encircled by a wide ring of some two or three hundred Kafirs, old as well as young. I at first took no particular notice of them, much less did my companion, but when I observed that their number was gradually increasing, that all of them were armed—some with bows and arrows, some with axes and a segais, some with knob-kieries and others with guns —and that every eye was fixed on us with unusual gravity, my suspicions were aroused, and I said to Captain Tyson—

"I wonder what this means. Everyone is armed; and look at that old man with the tiger-skin as shield, with his plumed hat and his weapons of war!"

"Do you not see," replied my friend, "that they have just returned from a hunt?"

"Don't you believe that!" I rejoined; "this is not the way that Kafirs dress when they go out hunting; besides, they would not go out in so large a body."

I then told the driver, who could speak Kafir, to tell the Kafirs to fetch some mealies and corn for our horses and we would give them pretty things in return. He did so, but not the slightest heed was given to his request. This was the strangest of all.

"What may this mean?" said my companion as he earnestly looked at me.

"Man," I said, "I do not understand it. Something must be wrong. Keep your eye upon our guns."

"Ask them," I bade the driver, "why they have armed themselves? whether they have returned from a hunt?"

"Yes," replied one of the number, "we have been hunting."

"Ask them why, if they do not wish to barter with us, they don't return to their kraals?"

To this question the old armed warrior answered—

"We have come to see the 'great master.' Is he one of you gentlemen?"

"No," replied the boy, "but he is on his way to this place on horseback."

"With how many men," inquired the old man eagerly.

"With three."

"With no more?"

"No."

"Then the whole party consists of you four and three more?"

"Of those few only," replied the boy.

"What are the 'great master' and his people coming to do here?" was the next question.

"They are coming to see the ancient temple which once upon a time belonged to white men."

Feeling quite at ease now the old man began to speak freely. To the question why he and his men were in arms, he replied that he had received a message a week previously that he must be on his guard, because the "great master" of the land had arrived, and he purposed killing all the male Kafirs and taking their wives and children into captivity. They had been expecting him many days.

"Tell the captain," we ordered the boy, "that if he fears that we have come to put him to death he can take our guns and keep them till we leave this place. We have only come to see the temple that former white men had built and occupied. And tell him that the 'great master' will, if possible, protect every Mashona and will never carry away a single woman or child."

This announcement was received with great joy. The Kafirs clapped their hands and bowed down to us, and the plumed captain then withdrew with his large retinue. The few that remained behind we asked to fetch us wood and water. Within an hour afterwards a gang of natives of both sexes appeared at our cart with mealies, rice, corn, eggs, etc., and four fowls were sent us as a token of goodwill from the Kafir captain. Captain Tyson again made a profitable exchange.

At four o'clock the Premier arrived with Mr. Selous, Dr. Jameson and Mr. Brabant. After taking coffee we went in one company to see the remains of old Simbabe. We did not at first sight think the ruins nearly so gigantic as on viewing them more closely we found them. Dr. Jameson and I climbed up the massive but elegantly-built walls, which at some parts are between twenty-five and thirty feet high, and we walked on them almost right round the ruins. We were much interested in the Phallus or Phalli, the Phoenician god, the top part of which had fallen in. Inside the temple there grew a large wild tree, the branches of which bowed about thirty feet over the walls.

At sundown we returned to our cart.

The country round about the ruins exhibits most picturesque scenery. Look where you will, all is green and beautiful.

There being no waggon in which we could sleep we spread our beds on the ground and, though numbers of hideous centipedes were creeping there, and though our beds were almost as hard as stone, we tried to sleep. Mr. Rhodes lay in the cart. It was a quiet, cool night; nothing but the night-bird broke its silence. As I lay there with everything appearing so gloomy and solemn around me, it was strange to me to think that the place, which was now as desolate and quiet as a churchyard, was once the abode of thousands of white men, and a place at which, in all probability, great festivities had frequently taken place in honour of the Phallus. At last I slumbered, but I had hardly been asleep two hours when the smell of smoke awaked me, and I was startled to find a fire kindled next to me and Captain Tyson busy gathering wood.

"My dear man," I said, "are you possessed by the devil, or is the spirit of Simbabe haunting you? It is not two o'clock yet and you are making a fire! How can I sleep like this?"

"My good friend," he replied, "I want to let you enjoy a delicious cup of coffee early this morning."

"Very kind of you," I answered, "but we don't want it in the *night*. Leave your fire and come to bed. At four o'clock I'll wake you."

But my words were waste of breath. Nothing remained for me but to take up my karosses and spread my bed upon another spot farther from the fire. However, my rest was entirely broken, and it was in vain that I tried to sleep again. At five we were all up, and then we drank the coffee that Captain Tyson had prepared for us three hours before.

(275)

CHAPTER XXIII.

Inspecting Simbabe—Mr. and Mrs. Bent's discoveries—Early history of the temple—Supposed to be built by Solomon—The connection of the Moors with Mashonaland—Early gold fields—Simbabe Hill—The ancient prosperity of the place to be surpassed in the future.

This done, we went to inspect the remains of the old Simbabe temple. Entering its sacred grounds we proceeded through a wide dilapidated porch, on some stones of which certain words were to be seen engraved, but the lapse of ages had obliterated them almost entirely. To the back part of the temple there led three narrow passages, and at their entrance were to be seen some fallen cross-walls, overgrown with shrubs, and a few heavy trees almost sixty feet high. We also went through the aisles leading to the Phallus, the idol, and we could see that that part of the religious house had been divided into a number of distinct sections—probably one was for the priests, another for the aristocrats, and another for the common people. In the middle of the temple there was a large hall, which had evidently been used for dancing festivities in honour of the idol. How many thousands of people the temple was able to contain is difficult to say, but the number certainly must have been enormous, the dome bearing some resemblance to the Colosseum at Rome. From the discoveries that Mr. and Mrs. Bent had made in that temple there can be left no doubt that the building had been erected by a white nation. Mr. Bent dug out of the ruins fine porcelain, bronze chains and rings, bronze parrots, peculiar old coins, broken pots, vases, beads, knives, axes, assegais, slabs of marble, pieces of cement and bronze phalluses. I saw the spots at which " the white man and the white woman " had been digging. A lot of old pieces of wood—remains, I presume, of the roof of the temple—were to be seen lying there. I once more climbed up the big wall and from its top had another view of the temple. It was strange for me to imagine that what was now the home of the lizard and the weasel was once the place of glory of Phœnicians. On the right of us stood Simbabe Hill, which rose about 500 feet above the level of the neighbouring land, and was enclosed by a heavy stone wall. It was inhabited by the Kafirs with whom we had the memorable meeting the day before.

In the fifteenth and sixteenth centuries Simbabe was frequently visited by Portuguese, who, it is stated, carried away many valuable articles from the temple, but the people were afterwards driven from there by Kafir tribes. Since that time nothing was heard of Simbabe until in 1871 Manch, the famous traveller, discovered it anew. The story goes that Simbabe was the capital of Manikaland, the country lying between Umtali and the present Fort Victoria, and measuring about 400 miles long and 160 broad. Judging by the old diggings, almost all that country must once upon a time have been gold-producing, and if the land was rich in gold in former ages—as history says it was—it must be rich in gold still, though the veins of gold may no longer be met with *on*, or even *near*, the surface. But there are gold experts who say with Lord Randolph Churchill (though on grounds no longer tenable) that all the gold the land had contained had been carried away by the ancient miners, and that this accounts for the reason why Simbabe, once a town of thousands of inhabitants, had been abandoned.

Simbabe was called "Simboae" in earlier days, and it is known by some to-day as "Simbambye." It is the opinion of Manch that Sofala Bay was the landing-place of the people who in olden days dug for gold in the neighbourhood of Simbabe, and that the magnificent temple, judging from the style in which it had been built and the way in which the town had been laid out, had been erected either by the order of King Solomon, or of the Queen of Sheba, or else by the Persians; and he does not think it at all impossible that the Ophir, of which we read in the Bible, is Simbabe. This was the opinion also of the Portuguese of the sixteenth century. History tells us that 600 years before the birth of Christ a Phœnician fleet, equipped by Necho in the Red Sea, sailed round the coast of South Africa, and it also informs us that the Arabians in the fourteenth century largely traded with the natives of Sofala, exchanging Asiatic products for Manikaland gold.

The Moors, too, who dwelt upon Quilloa, an island in their occupation close to Sofala, at one time extensively bartered with the Sofala inhabitants. In the fifteenth century the Portuguese defeated the Moors, took Quilloa in possession, and opened trade with the Sofalans, which consisted chiefly in the exchange of European articles for gold and ivory. Both the Arabians and the Moors used to have important commercial towns on the East Coast. We read that the Moors on a very large scale traded with Monomotapa, the great and wealthy negro king of the land of gold; that the King of the Moors paid Monomotapa more than one visit, and that Monomotapa had a magnificent Court, at which sixty princes received their education in lordly style. We read also of the fine stables that that monarch had for his own use; of his high officials, men imported from Arabia and India; of his beautiful grain fields; of his sugar plantations; of his fields of rice and cotton; of his large flocks of sheep, goats and pigs; and of the multitude of slaves, both male and female, in his service. In those days copper was considered by the Sofalans as a more valuable metal than gold, being much scarcer.

In 1569 Francisco Barreto was appointed by the Portuguese the Captain-General and Governor of the East Coast of Africa, with the additional title of "Governor of the Gold Mines of Monomotapa." We read how this Francisco Barreto was sent from Lisbon with a force of 1000 men, all well equipped, to conquer Monomotapa, "the King of the Gold and Silver Mines," and how a body of Moors from Algiers, provided with horses, mules and camels, followed to assist him. Barreto defeated the great negro monarch, not, however, before he (Barreto) had suffered several reverses. All his horses were killed by the tsetse-fly, and he himself died soon afterwards, probably of fever and over-exertion. Vasco Homen succeeded him to the command the following year, and he brought with him to Sofala Bay, from Lisbon, 1500 fighting men. By stratagem Homen fell upon the King of Quiteve unexpectedly, and subsequently attacked Monomotapa (who was then still in possession of the mines), but did not much further reduce the latter's power. By clever tactics he afterwards succeeded in seizing the gold mines, and he endeavoured also to get the silver mines into his possession. When the news of this reached the ears of Monomotapa, the latter immediately and secretly marched his men to the gold mines, suddenly fell upon the Portuguese and Moors and slew them almost to a man. The handful that escaped fled towards the East Coast, and after encountering many hardships on the way, reached Mozambique. Monomotapa followed this onslaught by attacking the 200 Portuguese stationed at Fort Chicona. With 400 natives he laid siege to the fort. The Portuguese held out until all their provisions became exhausted and then made a desperate attack on the besiegers, from whose swords, however, not a single Portuguese or Moor escaped. At a later date the Portuguese again captured the gold mines, but the silver mines they never could discover.

Now, knowing for a fact that the Phœnicians, the Persians, the Moors, the Portuguese, and the natives of whom Monomotapa was king, obtained gold from Mashonaland, a man who has travelled in that country and sat on the walls of the Simbabe temple cannot fail to be convinced that the Mashonaland gold mines are the same from which King Solomon got his gold (through the Phœnicians), and he is strengthened in this conviction when he has seen the very places at which the smelting had taken place.

Since, then, the gold fields have been a source of wealth to so many nations—first, as far as we can trace history, to the Phœnicians, then to the Persians, then to the Moors, then to the people of Monomotapa, then to the Portuguese, and then, to some extent, to the Mashonas—we cannot but expect that they will also fill the coffers of the Chartered Company, and we heartily hope they will, because the prosperity of Mashonaland means to a great extent the prosperity of the Cape Colony, not only because it is the coming market for our wines and other produce, but because there is every prospect of its soon becoming amalgamated with, if not annexed to, the Cape Colony. We trust that the fate of Vasco Vernandes and of Homen is not also awaiting Rhodes and Jameson, and that Mashonaland will ere long have its fame of old restored.

We left the temple and visited the other ruins, but they were so covered with shrubs and a sort of wild vine that we could hardly see anything of them. Next we decided to ascend Simbabe Hill. Passing the old walls surrounding the hill —which were about six feet wide—and slowly ascending the hill, we came to the remains of several ancient villas surrounded by high walls. To each of these villas there was a wide porch with pillars on both sides. These pillars were constructed of long granite blocks, and they stood as firm as if they had only recently been put up. All over the hill the remains of terraces were to be seen, which, I have very little doubt, were the residences of the aristocracy.

Some walls I found to be thirteen feet wide and built of small smooth granite stones of the size of bricks. No doubt those enormous walls about Simbabe —there are hundreds of them—are the works of slaves. Many an ancient fort is still to be seen there, and there are several ruins which appear to be remains of temples and palaces. I climbed up a large rock, and from there I had a splendid view of all the ruins on the mountain-side. All was solemnly still around me, the only noise that I could hear—and that was very faint—being the dismal music coming from some peculiar Kafir instruments at the foot of the hill, and I cannot express the strange feeling with which I was seized as I sat on that rock and gazed on the sight in front of me.

It is not improbable that Simbabe Hill had once been worshipped, and that hymns of praise had there been sung to the sun, moon and stars, as was common in the days of the Galicians, the Phœnicians, the Assyrians and other nations. It is, however, not my intention to enter into the history of these peoples and detail their connection with Simbabe, nor to show how Manch, the well-known natural philosopher, who made the ruins a special study, agrees with Barras, with the Portuguese of the sixteenth century, and with others, that the ruins are the remains of large buildings raised by white men, and *not* by natives; nor to recount how Marco Polo, the Venetian traveller, in 1292 met a "brown nation" on Africa's east coast, "having swords and lances and shields, and riding camels and elephants"; nor to relate how, 600 years B.C., a Phœnician fleet, fitted out by Necho, doubled "the most southern point of Africa"; nor to tell what influence the Saracens exercised on the East Coast after the time of Christ. Suffice it for me to say that I am thoroughly convinced that the ruins in and round about Simbabe are a proof to demonstration of the existence in earlier days of thousands, yea tens of thousands, of white men there. This was also the opinion of Livingstone. I say again it is my sincere wish—and I am sure that my fellow-colonists are sharing the wish with me—that Mr. Rhodes—who is now reopening those rich mines of Mashonaland, and by whose means the white man (amongst others the Boer, the best of pioneers) is fast coming into possession of the country—may meet with all success and prosperity. Our Premier may be sure of gaining the hearty support of the vast majority of the farmers in the Cape Colony, the Free State, the Transvaal and Natal in his undertakings in Mashonaland. I trust that the little mistrust and jealousy that some still cherish towards him will soon die away, for discord and strife amongst the white population in a country like ours can only tend to injure all parties. Let us remember that we have not only to take account of foreign countries, but we have to keep a watchful eye on the internal interests of our own land; we live in a land in which there are millions of natives, a fact that gives rise to an obviously serious question. If, therefore, the white races in the different parts of South Africa do not live in harmony with each other the future is certain to yield us bitter fruits.

The discoveries of minerals that are daily being made in Mashonaland are already to a great extent attracting the attention of the world, and I am fully persuaded that the day will soon come when we shall see large cities round about Simbabe, and when the produce of that country will surpass that of any other country in Africa. Just as once the eye of Europe was turned to America, and a great migration thither followed, so it shall fall on Africa—and with the same result. I fear that the time will come when thousands of the sons of our soil will regret that they had not moved to Mashonaland. *Now* is the time to trek! Mashonaland is still open to all, and I would be glad to see the descendants of the daring South African voortrekkers occupy that fine, healthy, fertile land. Indeed, to my fancy, they are the very people who would best get on there. Let not our people hesitate whether they should proceed thither or not, but let them set out at once to inhabit a region than which there are few, if any, more beautiful on the globe.

CHAPTER XXIV.

We return to our travels—The thriving condition of the Simbabe Kafirs—Their pretty children—The little ones suspicious of the meat-tins—One of our animals taken ill—A visit to Dickens' Gold Reef—Stamping the quartz—Dr. Jameson displays his horsemanship and comes a cropper.

LET me, however, return to our travel. As we slowly descended the mountain we passed several huts built among the ruins, and if there was anything that struck us about their inhabitants it was their physical condition. The little boys and girls we saw there were as fat as human beings could be. How the young women looked I have not seen enough of them to tell. We now and then noticed an inquisitive damsel peeping out of the hut door, but as soon as we approached the hut she disappeared, and, awe-stricken, she would so bolt the door from inside that not a mouse could pass through it. The poor creatures were filled with fear and suspicion—and what wonder! Past experiences at the hands of the Matabele have taught them the wisdom of exercising extreme precaution.

The little children of the Simbabe Kafirs are really pretty. I felt inclined to catch a couple, take them to Capetown, and bring them up. Now and then, to show his good-will, a Kafir would come to us with a few eggs and make us a present of them. The Mashona cows that we passed on the hill-side took after their masters as far as their condition was concerned—fine, strong and fat every one of them looked.

Having spent two hours and a half upon the hill we returned to our camp, where Captain Tyson had meanwhile prepared us a splendid dinner. I now forgave the philanthropic Captain the sin he had committed during the night in depriving me of my rest, and we heartily drank each other's health.

The remains of our dinner we gave to the little Kafir children who had been flocking around us, but it was strange to see how cautious they were with regard to what they ate, being afraid, I suppose, there might be poison in the food. The lemonade and the meat-tins they would at first not touch at all, for these really looked too suspicious. I took a spoonful out of a tin and ate it in their presence to show them that it was free from anything malignant. One or two of the bolder youngsters then grabbed a tin each, and soon all were greedily eating and drinking everything that they could get.

At half-past one Captain Tyson and I left Simbabe with the cart. The rest of the party having their horses with them could cross to Victoria by a short cut, and so they decided to leave Simbabe at a later hour.

When we had gone about three miles from Simbabe one of our fore-mules began to cough, and trot badly, but we did not trouble ourselves much about it. The farther we drove, however, the more the poor creature coughed and the weaker it seemed to become, till at last foam began to run from its nose. Our Zulu rein-holder then assured us that the animal had the "horse sickness," and he advised us to have the mule immediately removed. We stopped the cart and unharnessed the animal, which Mr. Brabant, who came on horseback behind us, kindly drove on, choosing the shorter road to Victoria. Our cart was now being drawn by only four mules. The odd one, the one that had been harnessed to the invalid, we tied to the mules at the back.

We stopped at the same river at which we had outspanned the day before, took a refreshing bath in it and then prepared coffee, which, though we had to take it without sugar—and the Africander is very fond of sugar—tasted as Scotch whisky would to a thirsty Scotchman.

We soon set off again, and towards evening we arrived at the camp. Mr. Brabant shortly afterwards turned up with the diseased animal, but the valuable creature died within an hour after its arrival.

The next morning at a quarter to six Mr. Rhodes, Dr. Jameson, Mr. Selous, Mr. Lange and I left on horseback for Dickens' Gold Reef, nine miles from Fort Victoria. We rode through pretty veld, passed some beautiful running streams, and at a quarter to eight we arrived at the reef. The reef was only eighteen inches wide when first struck; now, however, at a depth of thirty feet its width was four feet. Mr. Runsman, the overseer there, asked us to take some pieces of the quartz and he would stamp and wash them for us at the nearest spruit. We each then took some quartz from different parts of the reef and, provided with pestle, mortar and basins, we went to the stream. There the quartz was stamped and washed, and everyone of us was surprised at its richness.

At ten o'clock we again saddled our horses, and after riding a few miles we came to a little river. There we dismounted, tied our horses to some trees, had a swim and took breakfast. Riding on from there, Dr. Jameson was cock of the walk. Sitting upon a fine horse he took delight in showily riding ahead of us; but we had not gone very far when, as the doctor put his spirited steed into a gallop, the animal stumbled and went head over heels with its rider. We were alarmed and thought that our friend had been seriously injured, but when we came up to him he quietly rose to his feet as if nothing at all had happened, though the colour of his face showed that he had been greatly shaken, and though his hand was bruised. This attitude of the Administrator was manly, of course, but it permitted us to indulge in the laugh which the ludicrous picture he and his horse had presented during the fall deserved. It was indeed too comical to see him roll like a pumpkin whilst his horse flew over him. The incident created much amusement all the way, especially since we had so often warned the doctor not to ride so fiercely. In hunting, too, he was wildness personified, never seeming to care a straw what became of him.

We were back at the fort at noon, and to our sorrow we learnt that another of our comparatively few mules had died.

We now began to prepare for our departure, for we

intended to leave the next morning as early as possible. During our stay at Victoria the keen eye of our Premier had observed much. He ordered that barns should without delay be erected there to store the mealies, corn and flour, and that they should be covered over with grass in order that the damp might be kept out.

At Victoria, as at Salisbury, we met none but commanders, captains, corporals, sergeants, etc. Those gentlemen bear so many titles to their names that it is no wonder they forgot to bring the mealies under roof.

CHAPTER XXV.

A new team—Mr. Lange, Captain Tyson and I are teamsters—A mad rush down hill—A bathe in the Crocodiles' pool—Providential Pass, in the haunts of the gold-seekers—Long's Reef—Mr. Long can give reasons for his actions—Lord Randolph much in error.

A LARGE number of oxen was brought together, and from it January, Fortuin and Bosbok had each to choose his team of twelve. Of course the very best were selected.

Leaving Mr. Rhodes, Mr. Selous, Dr. Jameson and Mr. Barrow to follow us on horseback later in the day, and substituting Bosbok, a good Kafir, for that curious Hottentot, Petrus, as driver, Mr. Lange, Captain Tyson and I set out with the waggons at half-past seven in the morning (November 3rd). Mr. Lange sat on the front waggon, Captain Tyson on the second, and I on the third. We had taken these respective places in order to watch how the new oxen pulled, and to lend a helping hand to the drivers if anything should go wrong. At the outset all fared well; our road was uphill and all the oxen worked steadily. Those at the rear pulled a little harder than those in front, but that did not matter—*all* pulled, and with that we were satisfied. But, gracious me, what a

U

spectacle there was when we had reached the top of the hill and had to go down the other side! Some of the hind oxen furiously ran between those in front as though determined to take the lead. Mr. Lange had to do his utmost to keep ahead in order to prevent the waggon behind from colliding with his. Captain Tyson's task was harder still. On the one hand he had to try to keep his waggon from running into Mr. Lange's, and, on the other, he needed to drive as hard as he could to keep his waggon clear of mine. This was too hot for him; seized with fright, he jumped down from his waggon and ran as hard as he could to that of Mr. Lange, where he thought he was more secure. On my waggon no whip was needed, but "ho! ho! ho!" we had to shout until our throats were as dry as corks. Of stopping or arranging the oxen in proper order we could, of course, not think. Madly they rushed down the hill, causing the waggons to run now on two wheels, now on four, whilst our poor bodies were being shaken about most mercilessly; and yet, strange to say, we reached the end of the slope without the slightest accident having happened. Thank Providence, we could breathe again! We stopped the waggons, got down, and congratulated each other on our safety. Captain Tyson, who was still trembling with excitement, now gave us a very humorous exposition of what he thought and felt and did during the mad descent, and he openly confessed that he had been seized with fear when his oxen could not be controlled, and that he had therefore thought it best to desert his waggon.

We changed the oxen, putting several that had

drawn in front to the rear, and *vice versâ*, and bringing some over from one team to another, until we had them all more or less in correct order. It was fortunate that Mr. Rhodes was not with us when we came down the hill; if he were, I wonder what orders he would have given!

At half-past eleven we arrived at Fern Spruit, and, thinking it a very suitable spot to halt at, we outspanned. Mr. Lange, Captain Tyson and I decided to take a bath in the little river that ran close by. A part of the stream was fenced in, but that did not matter; we crept through the wire, walked a little distance along the spruit, and came to a fine, deep pool. The Captain and I took our bath there, Mr. Lange walking farther on. It struck us as rather strange that all the large pools alongside the river were enclosed with wire, but we did not bother our heads much about it.

When we had taken our bath and returned to the waggons, the other gentlemen turned up. The Premier found fault with the outspan-place, and he was dissatisfied also at our having covered so big a distance during the morning. However, soon again all were in good humour.

"Have you bathed?" asked Dr. Jameson.

"Yes," said we.

"Where?"

"In that fine pool!" I answered, pointing to it.

"What!" he exclaimed with surprise—"In that pool there enclosed with wire?"

"Yes—why, what's the matter with it? As to the wire, we don't know why it's there."

"And you became aware of nothing?"

"Of nothing unusual," we replied.

"My dear friends," said he, "must I tell you why that pool is fenced in? It is to prevent cattle from drinking water there and being caught by crocodiles. In fact, this is one of the most dangerous crocodile-places in all Mashonaland."

Others told us the same afterwards. Well, I am glad we had not been warned *before* we went into the water, because, "where ignorance is bliss, 'tis folly to be wise."

We were now at the entrance to Providential Pass, a narrow way leading through some mountains. It is the pass through which the Pioneers were led by Mr. Selous into Mashonaland. It was believed at one time that that was the only way from the south by which a waggon could get into Mashonaland, and that it was by the guidance of Providence that the passage had been discovered—hence the name.

The range of hills on the right of us was the Injaguzwe. All about this place diggers were busily engaged in opening reefs, and their waggons and tents gave the place a lively appearance. Mr. Rhodes, Mr. Selous, Dr. Jameson, Mr. Barrow and I had our horses saddled and we rode to Long's Reef. Past kopjes, over hills, and through streams we rode, and within an hour and a half we reached our destination. We dismounted, tied our horses to trees, and went to inspect the reef of which we had heard so much. And we were not disappointed at what we saw. The reef projected between six and eight feet above the surface of the ground and was about twelve feet wide, showing visible gold on every side. Upon the top of one of the rocks not far from there twelve round holes were to be seen, which no doubt had been made by natives, who stamped and ground the quartz. Indeed all the hill seemed to be auriferous. We took some pieces of the quartz and stamped and washed them at a stream close by, and it was really wonderful to see how much gold they contained. The reef had been opened only three feet! This arrested the attention of the Premier.

"Why do you not sink your shaft deeper, say thirty or forty feet?" he inquired of Mr. Long, purposely in our presence, for, as the reader will remember, Mr. Perkins, the gold expert, had declared that Mr. Long was afraid to sink his shaft deeper because he (Mr. Long) knew that he would find the reef at its end.

"Well, Mr. Rhodes," answered Mr. Long, "you ask me the same question Mr. Perkins asked me, and I can only give you the same answer I gave him. How can you expect me to continue shaft-sinking and so allow the rain to wet everything, and leave water standing where we are working, which would certainly produce fever amongst us? No, sir; the gold-bearing quartz is here, and even though this reef should run out at a depth of *five* feet, I can make my fortune out of it. However, when I have finished the dwelling-house, which, as you see, I am now building, and have erected some barns, I shall go on sinking the shaft."

"Bravo! Mr. Long," I exclaimed; "you have answered well!"

"What do you think," asked Mr. Rhodes, "will be the depth of this reef?"

"Judging by what the top of it was," replied Mr. Long, "and by what I find it at this depth, I would say it runs very deep."

"That is also as it appears to me, Mr. Long," rejoined the Managing Director of the Chartered Company, who seemed very pleased both with the reef and Mr. Long. "My good man," he continued, "when your dwelling-house and your barns are ready, do not delay sinking the shaft as deep as you can, and, if this reef does not run out, Mashonaland is made! For a richer reef than this I have neither seen nor heard of."

While we were speaking to Mr. Long some other miners came to us and invited us to come and see the reefs that they were working. They brought some quartz with them, which also appeared very rich. We had before been told of their reefs, but had no time now to visit them. I put a few pieces of quartz in my saddle-bag to give one or two of them to Mr. Lange in fulfilment of my promise to him, and to take the rest to Capetown for analysis.

Towards evening we set out to our camp, and rode at a very hard pace, in order to avail ourselves, for the direction of our course, as much as possible of the daylight still left us. However, it was pitch dark when, at eight o'clock, we reached our waggons.

When I think that Lord Randolph Churchill passed within three miles of Long's gold mine—apparently the richest mine hitherto discovered in Mashonaland—and would not so much as go and look at it, I cannot help shaking my head in surprise.

Why Perkins dissuaded him from going, and said that Mr. Long was afraid to follow the reef deeper, is another puzzle, for Mr. Long had told him precisely the same as he had told us; besides, he was not so stupid as not to know that Mr. Long would erect no dwelling-house and other permanent buildings if he (Mr. Long) did not feel sure of having struck a mine which would take him long to exhaust. I suppose Lord Randolph knew that he would get his money for each letter he inserted in the *Daily Graphic* whether he went to see the most important sights in Mashonaland or not, so he did not think it necessary to ride twelve miles out of his way to see the interesting ruins of Simbabe, nor worth his while to visit Dickens' Reef, near Victoria, or Long's Reef, near Providential Pass.

Ah! Johannesburg, you are for the present the centre of attraction of the gold-loving world, but what will you be in comparison with Mashonaland when its hidden treasures are brought to light!

CHAPTER XXVI.

Again on the march—An accident to my portmanteau—I am sad in consequence—A hard alternative before Roeping and January—Off to Chibe to learn the truth about the Adendorff concession—An uphill climb—Chibe does not confirm the concession—We learn more details about Lobengula—My new boy.

At two o'clock the following morning we again advanced with the waggons. I sat upon the waggon that January drove. Our road was not a very pleasant one, being overgrown in several parts by obstructing shrubs, and dangerously bordered by large trees. I had my portmanteau tied to one of the sides of the waggon, and there, I thought, it would be perfectly safe. About an hour after our start, as I was lying half-asleep in the waggon, I heard something tear, but, thinking that it was the waggon-canvas, and forgetting altogether about my portmanteau, I was not much concerned about it. At half-past five we arrived at the Tukwi River, and outspanned on the other side of it. On going to see where the canvas had got torn, I found, to my sorrow, that not the canvas but my portmanteau was the thing rent. It had been torn by a tree almost right in two, and many of the articles I had stowed in it were missing, amongst them the palm-nut that I would not have sold for ten pounds, and some pipes, beads, and jerseys. I felt vexed with January, but more so with Roeping, for he had been following the waggons, and should have seen and picked up the lost articles. I felt so sad and out of humour about it that I abandoned my intention of going with the rest of the party to Chibe's kraal, and resolved to set out instead in search of my palm-nut. But the rest of the party would not hear of my turning back and not accompanying them. So it was at last decided that Roeping and January should return on the waggons' track and find the missing things, failing to do which we promised to give them each twenty-four lashes; we had to add this threat or else be pretty sure that those sly fellows would go halfway and then turn back to tell us—as Roeping did the day he had to seek the oxen—" We cannot find them."

At seven o'clock we had our horses saddled, and Mr. Rhodes, Dr. Jameson, Mr. Selous, Mr. Brabant and I rode to Chibe's town to hear from the mouth of the chief himself how much of what had been told us about him was true. He was the Chief with whom the Adendorff concession was said to have been drawn up, and who was represented by the Adendorff-Vorster clique as the true owner of Mashonaland—at least, of a part of it. Mr. Adendorff, it will be remembered, received the support of a considerable number of irresponsible Transvaal burghers, among them the Malans, one of whom, I may mention, was the son-in-law of General Joubert. Several citizens of the Orange Free State and Cape Colony favoured the movement. Three parties were despatched to the Free

State, there to promote the cause of Mr. Adendorff by pleading the rights which had been obtained from the great paramount chief, Chibe! Circulars were spread in the Transvaal urging the burghers to resist Rhodes taking possession of Banyailand. This led to commissions being despatched from the Cape to the Transvaal, to negotiate with the misinformed—the *misled*, I should say—parties; and proclamations were issued in the Cape Colony, as well as in the Transvaal, that none should take part in the hostile trek-movement. This naturally set some newspapers in agitation and led to numerous meetings being held to discuss the question. When any one of any public significance in the republics expressed his decision in favour of Mr. Rhodes, he was stigmatised as bribed by the latter. Well, we were now on our way to Chibe, the man who was said to have granted Messrs. Adendorff and Vorster their "Banyailand Concession."

It was a beautiful morning. On our left chains of hills were facing us, and on our right the pretty Tukwi flowed. The country there is rich in woods and abounds in all kinds of wild fruits, amongst which are the medlar, the fig, the loquat, the date, the "German polony," the orange and the nacuna. We also passed several kraals and grain-fields.

At ten o'clock we reached the foot of the mountain upon which the town of Chibe stands. There we stopped and took rest under three large wild fig-trees, then in full foliage, allowing our horses to graze in the meantime. After breakfast, Mr. Rhodes asked Mr. Brabant to go and inquire from Chibe whether we could meet him, and, if so, when. Mr. Brabant, who could speak Kafir fluently and was personally acquainted with Chibe, being Secretary for Native Affairs in Mashonaland, then walked up the mountain to do his errand. Meanwhile hundreds of Kafirs, men, women and children, came to have a look at us, all as naked as Father Adam except the women, who wore a slight covering, not more, however, than a scarf of ordinary size could serve to clothe. They stood at a distance from us, staring at us as if we were beings of a supernatural world. Many of them had calabashes or pitchers upon their heads wherein to fetch water; but, in order to reach the stream, they would have to pass us by, and this they were afraid to do. When, however, they were at last convinced that we intended them no harm, they went on with their work.

The sheep, goats and cows we saw there looked remarkably well.

I counted around us eighty-two children between eight and fifteen years of age; seventy-two men, who sat there with not a square inch of clothing on their bodies; and sixty women, mostly young, who scanned us as though we were sitting in a glass case for exhibition. The longer they watched us the less they seemed to fear us, and the nearer they came.

Whilst still waiting for the return of Mr. Brabant, Chibe kindly sent us a large calabash filled with Kafir-beer; it was very welcome, for the day was warm, and we were thirsty. After staying away for more than two hours, Mr. Brabant returned with a message from the chief that he would be glad to see us. At two o'clock the five of us ascended the mountain. The road was very steep. How the Kafir women could walk it up and down every day with babes tied on their backs, and heavy calabashes filled with water on their heads, I could not understand. But what else are the poor creatures to do? They are compelled to dwell on the highest ridges of the mountains in order to be as secure as possible against the enemy. Indeed, it was no pleasant task we had: not only was the road steep, but it was slippery, and therefore dangerous—if one slipped and fell, the chances were that he would also roll some distance down the slope. Mr. Brabant, who acted as our guide, led us past several krantzes and huts, whilst we were being treated with instrumental Kafir music from the little mountain-tops. Having completed all the turnings leading up to the Kafir town, we reached our destination—Chibe's residence. We found the chief sitting on a small chair in front of his hut, with about eight aged indunas around him. Mr. Brabant was to be our interpreter, though Mr. Selous could also speak Kafir. As we approached the hut, the chief and the counsellors courteously bowed to us, and we returned the salutation. We could at once recognise which one was the chief. Mr. Brabant opened the conversation.

"What is your name?" he asked the Banyai ruler.

"Chibe is my name," was the reply.

"Are you the only captain in this country known by the name of Chibe?"

"Yes," the chief answered, "but my eldest brother also used to be called Chibe." [This elder brother was the predecessor of the present ruler.]

Upon the request of Mr. Rhodes, Mr. Brabant asked

Chibe how he happened to be placed at the head of his race.

"Thirteen years ago," he replied, "my brother was taken prisoner by Lobengula, carried to Lobengula's town, and flayed alive. Since that time I have ruled over this tribe."

"If your eldest brother's name was Chibe, how is it that you have the same name?"

"Chibe is not a man's name," was the response; "both of us had other names—Chibe means headman or chief—Chibe is only a title."

Mr. Brabant then asked the chief whether he knew anyone with the name of Shebassa. This question was put because Mr. Adendorff, when he began to waver as to Chibe, asserted that he had received his concession from Shebassa, a greater man even than Chibe!

"Yes," answered the chief, "I know Shebassa well; he is a grandson of mine and a petty chief, but he is also one of my subjects."

"And has Shebassa the right to make a concession of land to anybody without your permission?"

"No, certainly not!" was the answer. "He has no right to give away the smallest bit of ground without my consent."

"But has not Shebassa perhaps made a concession to somebody without your knowing of it?"

"No, I do not think so, because he knows that he is not allowed to do it, and that he would lose his life if he did. But even if he *should* have made such a concession it would have no value, for it is in my land that he lives, and he has no right to dispose of my property."

"But did you not grant a concession to white people to seek for gold in your land?"

"No, to none! My land is hardly large enough for myself and my people; why should I be so foolish as to allow white men to occupy it?"

"But you have signed a document—and your counsellors have signed it as witnesses—conceding your land to Mr. Adendorff?"

"No! no!" answered Chibe excitedly; "who told you that?"

"Mr. Adendorff says so," answered our interpreter, "and he has such a document in his pocket."

"That is a lie!" replied the chief with emphasis. "I have given no concession of land to anybody."

"Well, Mr. Adendorff has a document which he pretends to have received from you, and in which it is written that you have granted him a right over your entire land."

"How could I make such a concession?" rejoined the chief. "I am a ruler over a part of this land, but *all* the land does not belong to me. Here are many chiefs—some greater than myself—and what right have I to give away of their land? You have been deceived, that is all."

Mr. Selous then came forward and addressed the counsellors—

"Perhaps your captain has forgotten—but do you not recollect anything about such a concession?"

"No, nothing," was the unanimous reply; "such a concession must be false."

"What are the boundaries of your land?" asked Mr. Selous.

"The Lundi river on the west, the Indymas land on the north, the Simuto and Chellemanzi on the east, and the Mapan Zula on the south," answered the chief.

"Is all your land of the same character as this part?"

"Yes, all the same."

"Have you no open veld such as the wildebeest inhabits?"

"No," he replied; "the open veld upon which the wildebeest is to be found belongs to the chiefs of the Lundi near Matabeleland, and of Chellemanzi's land on the other side of the Indymas."

"How far," asked Mr. Selous, "does your country extend toward the highland?"

Chibe rose from his chair, and, accompanied by a few of his veteran indunas, walked a little way with us to a spot where we could have a good bird's-eye view of his land, and from there he pointed with his finger beyond the Inyaguzwe, that is, ten miles on this side of Fort Victoria.

"Do you acknowledge anyone as overmaster in all these lands?" we asked.

"Yes," answered the aged chief, "we acknowledge the great rogue as the mighty chief to whom we have to pay taxes every year."

"And who is this 'great rogue'?" asked Mr. Selous.

"The son of Umziligazi—Lobengula," responded Chibe.

"Are there also other *mambos* (chiefs) who pay taxes to the son of Umziligazi?"

"Oh, yes," was the answer, "there are many."

"Tell us to whom the regions belong over which the following chiefs rule: Chellemanzi, Guto, Umtigeni, Matebi, Sitoutsi, Simuto, Indina, Berrezema, Lomogendi, Kwetella, etc."

"All these," answered Chibe, "belong to King Lobengula, and all those chiefs must pay an annual tax to him."

I asked one of the indunas to show me from where we were standing, if he could, in which directions and how far the land of Chibe stretched. This he gladly did.

"In what time of the year," I asked him, "have you to pay your tribute to Lobengula?"

"*Now*," replied the induna, and, pointing with his finger to a Kafir camp at the foot of the mountain, he said, "Do you see that? Well, they are tax-gatherers from Lobengula. They are Matabele men, and they have come to get cattle and grain from us."

"How much must you give?" I inquired.

"As much as they demand and can carry away. There is no fixed tariff. Sometimes they are satisfied with a little, but at other times they want a large quantity of everything."

"How many of them are there in that camp?"

"About sixty."

"And since when have they been here?"

"Since noon yesterday."

Mr. Selous then resumed questioning Chibe.

"Why," he asked, "do the Matabele tax-gatherers all enter the land at one and the same time?"

"Ah, that they do in order that, if any dispute arise on the amount of contribution demanded, or if any chief offer resistance, all the tax-gatherers that have been sent to the various chiefs may be able quickly to assemble in order to attack and slay the rebel, and to take away by force as many of the women, children, cattle, sheep, and as much of the grain, as they are able to convey to the king."

"Then you mean to say that if you refuse to comply with the demands of those sixty, all the men who have been sent out to the various chiefs to exact taxes will, immediately on receiving word of the matter, gather together, and with their combined force attack you?"

"Yes, exactly so,—every party of tax-collectors have their messengers, who in time of danger run as swiftly as they can from the kraal of one chief to that of another, to summon the men together, and in this way, within the space of a few days an army of some hundreds is raised, by which the rebellious chief is attacked and plundered and butchered."

"Thus," remarked Mr. Selous, "you must have as much respect for the sixty as for the six hundred!"

Chibe nodded. "And though," said he, "I should be strong enough to repulse and rout the six hundred, I would be very stupid if I did it, because Lobengula would then lead two thousand or three thousand men against me and would put me to death. Such has happened before to other chiefs."

"But if one of the chiefs who is subject to Lobengula has a fall-out with the tax-collectors, do none of the others lend their aid?"

"No! oh, no! None dare! None would risk it. If they do, they can only expect to be put to death and to have their wives and children captured and made slaves."

We were further told that the tax-collectors were the choice soldiers of the Matabele king. It was strange that we should have come there at the very time when the Matabele were going about demanding contributions.

From one of the indunas I received as a present a walking-stick, with which I was much taken up, but which I lost soon afterwards. All the time we were engaged in the interesting interview with Chibe, Kafir women were to be seen inquisitively peeping through every hut-door near at the curious white men! I stepped towards Chibe's hut to see in how far it differed from others, but suddenly the door was slammed before my eyes by one or two females inside, and barred. Oh, these poor beings are terribly afraid of the white man! At a little distance from us some Kafir maids were playing the flute and the ramkee; the music sounded rather pretty.

We were highly satisfied with our visit. We thanked Chibe for the important information he had so kindly given us, bade him farewell, and went to saddle our horses. It was now four o'clock.

I may mention that, though Chibe * is a man of at

* A year later, *i.e.*, 1892, Chibe, foolishly relying on the expectation that Lobengula would not dare to attack him owing to the presence of so many whites in the country who were known by the natives to entertain great aversion to cruelty and oppression, refused to pay the taxes demanded by Lobengula, with the result that a Matabele force was sent against him, his town plundered, a large portion of his people massacred, and he himself captured and slain.—*Translator.*

least eighty years of age, he has still a very fair memory and considerable intelligence.

There was a pretty boy of about twelve at the kraal on whom my eye had fallen, and whom I more than once treated with coffee and pieces of biscuit, and I was soon much attracted to him. He was very obedient to me; every time I told him to run for the horses and bring them nearer to us, he gladly did so, and when at last we were ready to leave, he stood ready for departure also. I told Mr. Brabant to ask him what he intended to do.

"I want to go with that master," replied the lad as he pointed his finger to me.

"How can you do that?" said Mr. Brabant.

"I go," he replied, "with the two Kafirs who are carrying the food-baskets to the waggons, and from there I go with that master."

"But, my dear boy," I said to him, through our interpreter, "I live very, very far from here, and what will your parents say if you go with me? You cannot leave your father and mother without their consent?"

"Yes, I can," he answered; "my father and mother have many children besides me."

When I saw that he was really determined to follow us, I asked the two Kafirs who were carrying the food-baskets whether they thought the parents of the child would miss him much if he left them.

"No, sir," was the answer; "the parents will know that he has gone with you, and will not care much about it."

I then asked Mr. Rhodes what he thought of it.

"Well," he replied, "if the boy earnestly wishes to

x 2

go with you, take him! He seems a good and funny little fellow."

The boy almost leaped out of his skin from joy when we told him he could go with us.

We then bade Chibe's town "Good-bye," and, with Mr. Brabant again as leader, we once more walked down the steep, winding, slippery road. Here and there we passed a small group of Kafirs. Very slowly we descended the hill, and very cautiously, in order to escape falling. We took the shortest cuts to our waggons. The two Kafirs followed us closely, and so did my boy, who ran like a little buck over the way, and every now and then brought me some wild fruit, among them a few wild oranges, which I took with me to Capetown.

At six o'clock, we arrived at our waggons, having travelled the distance in half an hour less time than in the morning. I there immediately inquired of January and Roeping whether they had found the things that I had lost on the road. To my joy, they had, though not all—the palm-nut and some pieces of clothing were returned to me, but my pipes and some other articles the boys assured me they could not find, but I did not mind that. My portmanteau and some of the canvas the thoughtful Captain Tyson had meanwhile got repaired by a German who was living near the Tukwi River and understood work of that kind. My portmanteau was now again as strong as ever.

My little Kafir attendant seemed greatly pleased with the large company, but Mr. Selous made a bet with Mr. Rhodes that the boy would very soon run back to his kraal.

We enjoyed a fine supper, and spent our last night with Mr. Selous, Dr. Jameson and Mr. Brabant in a very pleasant way. At three the following morning we bade these gentlemen God-speed, and again took up the journey. My Kafir boy was nowhere to be seen; no doubt he had turned back with the Kafirs who had carried the baskets. Perhaps this was best, after all.

CHAPTER XXVII.

Captain Tyson's dip—How Mr. Vluggi lost his way—A grim game—A meeting with some disappointed diggers—The scene of young Hackwell's death—A foolish hunt—I shoot an alligator—Captain Tyson proposes a race—I accept the challenge, and come off victorious.

Mr. van der Bijl, son of the much-respected Lourens, now joined our party with the intention to accompany us up to Tuli, whence he would return with the waggons together with Dr. Jameson and Mr. James.

At a quarter to seven we arrived at a green spruit. Some beautiful large trees, amongst which was a huge fig-tree, stood near the stream. We had hoped to have a nice nap under them, but on our return from our bath we found the place occupied by six diggers and six donkeys. Nothing was left for us but to return to our waggons and have our nap there.

Close to where we had outspanned there was a pool into which a smooth rock projected. At the lower side of this rock Captain Tyson, who was as much afraid of crocodiles as men of old were of ghosts, stood in Adam's apparel washing himself. The soapy water naturally caused the stone to be very slippery, but the captain apparently did not think of that. Finished with washing, and having dried his body, he wanted to get to the top of the rock, there to dress; but lo! he had hardly taken his second step when his foot slipped and he tumbled head over heels into the pool, disappearing from our sight for a few seconds. When his head appeared above water again, there was such an expression of bewilderment in his eyes, such a look of terror, that, if we had known no better, we would have sworn a crocodile had got hold of him. Oh, I shall never forget those eyes! Help him we could not, and try the slippery rock again he would not venture; the only course open to him was to swim with all his might to the bank, a little distance from the rock. But misfortunes don't come singly. The side of the pool at which the poor captain climbed out was so muddy and dirty that he looked, when he again stood on shore, like a pig that had been rolling in the mire. Tears of laughter ran down the eyes of Mr. Lange, Mr. van der Bijl and myself, as we stood beholding the amusing sight. We sent a Kafir with a bucket of clean water to wash our unfortunate friend.

Mr. Vluggi, a German gentleman, here took breakfast with us. It was interesting to hear how he had once lost his way in Banyailand. Early in the morning of the 22nd of October last he sprang out of his waggon with only his pyjamas on, and went in pursuit of some guinea-fowls. The birds drew him farther and farther from the waggon, until, when he wanted to return, after having chased them two hours, he was completely nonplussed as to which direction to take. He ran now this way, now that, but only to find himself each time at a place he had never seen before. He was still in his pyjamas, and all that he had with him was a shot-gun and a game-bag. What was he to do? He now became seized with anxiety; but indefatigably he continued seeking his way. But hours and hours elapsed and he had not made any progress; he had shouted, he had fired, but all to no effect. At about six in the evening he arrived at a grassy spot near to a pool of water, and there, tired out and abandoning all expectation of finding his way ere night, he sat down in the faint hope that some Kafir might turn up and relieve him from his plight. Night approached and Vluggi still found himself alone. Fortunately he had matches in his game-bag. Before darkness set in, hundreds of animals came to drink water at the pool, and Vluggi, who noticed all this, became aware that his situation was more dangerous than he had expected. He collected some branches and grass and arranged a little shelteringplace for himself, and there he was left undisturbed till midnight, when some lions in the reeds close by began to roar. The fire he had lit he made larger, thinking by that means to keep the beasts from him; but, instead of retreating, the animals came nearer, and Vluggi was startled by two lions making their appearance. His anxiety was now raised to the highest pitch; but, retaining his presence of mind, he ran to the one side of the fire when the lions were on the other, the animals keeping at a radius of some ten yards from the fire. If they had had the sense to separate—the one to lie in wait for the man whilst the other drove him round—they would soon have had a good meal, but they were too stupid to do that. Well, as it was, the circular chase continued for a while. Mr. Vluggi had his shot-gun in his hand, but he would not shoot at the animals, for he knew he could not kill them with guinea-fowl shot, and to have injured them would only have infuriated them and have made his position worse. He decided to fire one or two shots in the open air. The lions answered the report by a few loud growls, and trotted away. The moon at last appeared above the horizon, and at four o'clock in the morning Mr. Vluggi discovered which direction he should take. Keeping in the correct course, he arrived at nine o'clock at the telegraph wire. Guided by this wire, he continued his way northwards until he came to the river on the banks of which his waggon was standing. Naturally he was then exceedingly fatigued; he fired off some shots, and his Kafirs, hearing them, ran towards the place whence the report came, and there found their master in tattered pyjamas.

"Never," said Mr. Vluggi, "shall I forget those thirty hours!"

Mr. Vluggi and a fellow-traveller of his, Mr. Forbes, went through a rather unpleasant business the day previous to our meeting them. Some Kafirs had stolen an ox from Mr. Vluggi. Discovering this, his companion and he endeavoured to find the thieves by means of tracing their footsteps, and in this they succeeded. The footprints led them to a kraal, and there they found the skin and some of the flesh of the ox. The punishment they inflicted on the guilty party was fifteen lashes with the sjambok to each

man, and a payment to be made by them of nine goats and a number of assegais. The punishment was carried out in full. The assegais we were shown. Mr. Vluggi is a gentleman well known to our Premier, as well as to Captain Tyson and Mr. Lange. He was now on his way to Mashonaland as manager there of the De Beers Syndicate.

At four in the afternoon we were ready to resume the journey. But before we set out I thought I would pay a visit to the six diggers, who were still sitting under the fig-tree with their donkeys. I asked them where they came from.

"From the so-called gold-fields," answered one.

"And where are you going?"

"To the Cape Colony," they replied.

"And why did you not stay a little longer to test your fortune?"

"Because that's all nonsense!" was the surly answer.

"Look here," I said, "do you see the sun?—well, as true as you see that sun, you will regret that you have left Mashonaland. You are treading upon gold-fields and you don't know it; fortune lies beneath your feet, and you won't have it. Mark my words, you will repent this blunder."

One of the six earnestly looked into my eyes and said, "Sir, every word you have just uttered is true. I have told my friends the same, but they won't listen to me."

"Too late, sir," replied another; "Capeward we go!"

I left them, and we departed with our waggons. Towards evening we outspanned upon an elevation, and the following morning at two we again set forth and

journeyed through a very pretty region, fertile and in every way fit for cattle and sheep. At six we stopped on the border of the Lundi, and, before we allowed our waggons to cross it, we rode through it on horseback to ascertain its depth. The Lundi is a wide, strong river, bearing some resemblance to the Tuli. It was at this river that, twelve months before, it was expected the Matabele would attack the Pioneers, under command of Major Johnson; and it was also this river in which several brave young men, during the last rainy season, lost their lives in their attempt to cross it. Near to the stream are to be seen the graves of seven men, whose names are written on a board serving as a tombstone. It was here also that the gallant young Hackwell met his death. For several successive days he had been continually passing from one bank of the river to the other, carrying provisions across to the Pioneers. Eventually he caught a cold, the cold grew into fever, and the fever resulted in his death.

The river still presents much inconvenience to passengers during the rainy season; and it is very dangerous for the traveller to linger for any length of time on its banks, inasmuch as the muddy soil renders the air very humid and, consequently, fever-producing. But what is one to do when one comes to a stream and finds it too strong to cross?

At six o'clock Mr. Rhodes, Mr. James and I went out hunting. We rode down by the river's side for some miles, and chased up guinea-fowls, pheasants, hares, etc., but they did not give us much chance of shooting at them. Next we saw, at a distance, five koodoo-cows with calves, but failed to shoot any.

man, and a payment to be made by them of nine goats and a number of assegais. The punishment was carried out in full. The assegais we were shown. Mr. Vluggi is a gentleman well known to our Premier, as well as to Captain Tyson and Mr. Lange. He was now on his way to Mashonaland as manager there of the De Beers Syndicate.

At four in the afternoon we were ready to resume the journey. But before we set out I thought I would pay a visit to the six diggers, who were still sitting under the fig-tree with their donkeys. I asked them where they came from.

"From the so-called gold-fields," answered one.

"And where are you going?"

"To the Cape Colony," they replied.

"And why did you not stay a little longer to test your fortune?"

"Because that's all nonsense!" was the surly answer.

"Look here," I said, "do you see the sun?—well, as true as you see that sun, you will regret that you have left Mashonaland. You are treading upon gold-fields and you don't know it; fortune lies beneath your feet, and you won't have it. Mark my words, you will repent this blunder."

One of the six earnestly looked into my eyes and said, "Sir, every word you have just uttered is true. I have told my friends the same, but they won't listen to me."

"Too late, sir," replied another; "Capeward we go!"

I left them, and we departed with our waggons. Towards evening we outspanned upon an elevation, and the following morning at two we again set forth and

journeyed through a very pretty region, fertile and in every way fit for cattle and sheep. At six we stopped on the border of the Lundi, and, before we allowed our waggons to cross it, we rode through it on horseback to ascertain its depth. The Lundi is a wide, strong river, bearing some resemblance to the Tuli. It was at this river that, twelve months before, it was expected the Matabele would attack the Pioneers, under command of Major Johnson; and it was also this river in which several brave young men, during the last rainy season, lost their lives in their attempt to cross it. Near to the stream are to be seen the graves of seven men, whose names are written on a board serving as a tombstone. It was here also that the gallant young Hackwell met his death. For several successive days he had been continually passing from one bank of the river to the other, carrying provisions across to the Pioneers. Eventually he caught a cold, the cold grew into fever, and the fever resulted in his death.

The river still presents much inconvenience to passengers during the rainy season; and it is very dangerous for the traveller to linger for any length of time on its banks, inasmuch as the muddy soil renders the air very humid and, consequently, fever-producing. But what is one to do when one comes to a stream and finds it too strong to cross?

At six o'clock Mr. Rhodes, Mr. James and I went out hunting. We rode down by the river's side for some miles, and chased up guinea-fowls, pheasants, hares, etc., but they did not give us much chance of shooting at them. Next we saw, at a distance, five koodoo-cows with calves, but failed to shoot any.

At last Mr. Rhodes shot a pheasant. We could see in the sand the distinct traces of hippopotami, lions, bucks and many other animals, small as well as large; but the animals themselves kept out of sight. Nothing was passed which was not admired—trees and shrubs, hills and dales, and, crowning all, the majestic river itself, which ran now wide, then narrow, now straight, then winding, now smooth, then rippling, whilst here and there a crocodile was to be noticed on a sandbank.

To have reached the place where the game was usually met with we should have continued our course for another hour; but for that we did not feel inclined. We decided to cross the Lundi, so as to return to our waggons by a different way to that by which we had come. In the middle of the stream stood a little green island. We made for it, tied our horses to each other upon it, and took a bath. I must say it was foolish of us to turn back to our waggons so soon. We should have taken breakfast and gone out for a day's hunt. If we had taken a three or four hours' ride up the river we very probably would have met the giraffes whose footprints we saw almost everywhere. But, instead, we had acted like children who knew no better. We had set out in the morning before we had breakfasted and before the horses had had anything to eat. As was to be expected, when eleven o'clock arrived our empty stomachs craved for food, as did those also of our horses. Nothing was left us but to return to our camp. Such hunting was indeed ridiculous. I am glad to say that I was not the initiator of it.

On the other side of the stream we found the trees

and shrubbery no less dense than on the banks from which we had just crossed over. Strange to say, though the fresh footprints of hippopotami, as well as those of lions, were to be observed on the ground wherever we looked, not a single hippopotamus or lion did we see. For all I know, however, we might have passed several of the latter, because on the shores of the Lundi the growth is very dense at some parts, and it is in such places that lions generally hide during day-time. At half-past eleven we were back at our waggons. The first thing we did there was, of course, to take breakfast, and an unusually large one it was.

At three in the afternoon we visited an old ruin which, to a small extent, resembled the temple at Simbabe and appeared to be the remains of a building of burnt brick.

At half-past four we left the Lundi, and next stopped at the Sugar-Loaf River, or, as the Kafirs call it, the Ingwesi. It was striking to see how much the Sugar-Loaf Hill (from which the stream gets its name) resembled a real sugar-loaf.

We left the river at two the following morning and at seven we outspanned again. After taking coffee we once more set out for a hunt. My horse was very slow and could not keep pace with those of my two companions, Mr. Rhodes and Mr. James. I therefore ceased accompanying them, and began parrot-shooting instead, but the birds were so wild that I had no chance of hitting any. However, I shot some turtle-doves. Riding up the side of the stream, I came to a beautiful bathing-place. I tied my horse to a tree and began undressing myself to take a dash in the cool, clear silly though they thought we were, took a lively interest in the race. My rival soon lost ground, and the farther we walked the greater became the distance between us. The hill, which was three hundred feet high, I climbed like a boy. I had lost much weight during my travel from Beira to Umtali, so I was able easily to stand a little exertion. Captain Tyson, on the other hand—who had been living a kingly life in a waggon during the time Mr. Rhodes, Major Johnson and I were journeying from Beira to Salisbury and had to contend with so many adversities—had considerably *gained* in weight. Well, soon he began to breathe like a whale. I rested on the summit at the telegraph-office for a few minutes, and when my friend was half way up the hill I made my way down again. He walked with a stick, I with nothing. At a quarter to two I was back at the waggons. I again rested a while and then partook of a bath along with Mr. Rhodes, Mr. Lange and Mr. van der Bijl. When we came out of the water Captain Tyson returned from his walk; he was as wet with perspiration as a man who had been playing football for the first time. I had compassion on him, for he looked sorely fatigued. His gentle, friendly glance at me deprived me of the heart to chaff him.

"Good friend," I said to him, "I have beaten you! In walking, there's no doubt, I am your master. Now, let us have a whiskey together. Your five pounds you may keep, for you have already been sufficiently punished."

We enjoyed a fine supper, and spent our last night with Mr. Selous, Dr. Jameson and Mr. Brabant in a very pleasant way. At three the following morning we bade these gentlemen God-speed, and again took up the journey. My Kafir boy was nowhere to be seen; no doubt he had turned back with the Kafirs who had carried the baskets. Perhaps this was best, after all.

at a place he had never seen before. He was still in his pyjamas, and all that he had with him was a shot-gun and a game-bag. What was he to do? He now became seized with anxiety; but indefatigably he continued seeking his way. But hours and hours elapsed and he had not made any progress; he had shouted, he had fired, but all to no effect. At about six in the evening he arrived at a grassy spot near to a pool of water, and there, tired out and abandoning all expectation of finding his way ere night, he sat down in the faint hope that some Kafir might turn up and relieve him from his plight. Night approached and Vluggi still found himself alone. Fortunately he had matches in his game-bag. Before darkness set in, hundreds of animals came to drink water at the pool, and Vluggi, who noticed all this, became aware that his situation was more dangerous than he had expected. He collected some branches and grass and arranged a little shelteringplace for himself, and there he was left undisturbed till midnight, when some lions in the reeds close by began to roar. The fire he had lit he made larger, thinking by that means to keep the beasts from him; but, instead of retreating, the animals came nearer, and Vluggi was startled by two lions making their appearance. His anxiety was now raised to the highest pitch; but, retaining his presence of mind, he ran to the one side of the fire when the lions were on the other, the animals keeping at a radius of some ten yards from the fire. If they had had the sense to separate—the one to lie in wait for the man whilst the other drove him round—they would soon have

We enjoyed a fine supper, and spent our last night with Mr. Selous, Dr. Jameson and Mr. Brabant in a very pleasant way. At three the following morning we bade these gentlemen God-speed, and again took up the journey. My Kafir boy was nowhere to be seen; no doubt he had turned back with the Kafirs who had carried the baskets. Perhaps this was best, after all.

man, and a payment to be made by them of nine goats and a number of assegais. The punishment was carried out in full. The assegais we were shown. Mr. Vluggi is a gentleman well known to our Premier, as well as to Captain Tyson and Mr. Lange. He was now on his way to Mashonaland as manager there of the De Beers Syndicate.

At four in the afternoon we were ready to resume the journey. But before we set out I thought I would pay a visit to the six diggers, who were still sitting under the fig-tree with their donkeys. I asked them where they came from.

"From the so-called gold-fields," answered one.

"And where are you going?"

"To the Cape Colony," they replied.

"And why did you not stay a little longer to test your fortune?"

"Because that's all nonsense!" was the surly answer.

"Look here," I said, "do you see the sun?—well, as true as you see that sun, you will regret that you have left Mashonaland. You are treading upon gold-fields and you don't know it; fortune lies beneath your feet, and you won't have it. Mark my words, you will repent this blunder."

One of the six earnestly looked into my eyes and said, "Sir, every word you have just uttered is true. I have told my friends the same, but they won't listen to me."

"Too late, sir," replied another; "Capeward we go!"

I left them, and we departed with our waggons. Towards evening we outspanned upon an elevation, and the following morning at two we again set forth and

journeyed through a very pretty region, fertile and in every way fit for cattle and sheep. At six we stopped on the border of the Lundi, and, before we allowed our waggons to cross it, we rode through it on horseback to ascertain its depth. The Lundi is a wide, strong river, bearing some resemblance to the Tuli. It was at this river that, twelve months before, it was expected the Matabele would attack the Pioneers, under command of Major Johnson; and it was also this river in which several brave young men, during the last rainy season, lost their lives in their attempt to cross it. Near to the stream are to be seen the graves of seven men, whose names are written on a board serving as a tombstone. It was here also that the gallant young Hackwell met his death. For several successive days he had been continually passing from one bank of the river to the other, carrying provisions across to the Pioneers. Eventually he caught a cold, the cold grew into fever, and the fever resulted in his death.

The river still presents much inconvenience to passengers during the rainy season; and it is very dangerous for the traveller to linger for any length of time on its banks, inasmuch as the muddy soil renders the air very humid and, consequently, fever-producing. But what is one to do when one comes to a stream and finds it too strong to cross?

At six o'clock Mr. Rhodes, Mr. James and I went out hunting. We rode down by the river's side for some miles, and chased up guinea-fowls, pheasants, hares, etc., but they did not give us much chance of shooting at them. Next we saw, at a distance, five koodoo-cows with calves, but failed to shoot any.

At last Mr. Rhodes shot a pheasant. We could see in the sand the distinct traces of hippopotami, lions, bucks and many other animals, small as well as large; but the animals themselves kept out of sight. Nothing was passed which was not admired—trees and shrubs, hills and dales, and, crowning all, the majestic river itself, which ran now wide, then narrow, now straight, then winding, now smooth, then rippling, whilst here and there a crocodile was to be noticed on a sandbank.

To have reached the place where the game was usually met with we should have continued our course for another hour; but for that we did not feel inclined. We decided to cross the Lundi, so as to return to our waggons by a different way to that by which we had come. In the middle of the stream stood a little green island. We made for it, tied our horses to each other upon it, and took a bath. I must say it was foolish of us to turn back to our waggons so soon. We should have taken breakfast and gone out for a day's hunt. If we had taken a three or four hours' ride up the river we very probably would have met the giraffes whose footprints we saw almost everywhere. But, instead, we had acted like children who knew no better. We had set out in the morning before we had breakfasted and before the horses had had anything to eat. As was to be expected, when eleven o'clock arrived our empty stomachs craved for food, as did those also of our horses. Nothing was left us but to return to our camp. Such hunting was indeed ridiculous. I am glad to say that I was not the initiator of it.

On the other side of the stream we found the trees

and shrubbery no less dense than on the banks from which we had just crossed over. Strange to say, though the fresh footprints of hippopotami, as well as those of lions, were to be observed on the ground wherever we looked, not a single hippopotamus or lion did we see. For all I know, however, we might have passed several of the latter, because on the shores of the Lundi the growth is very dense at some parts, and it is in such places that lions generally hide during day-time. At half-past eleven we were back at our waggons. The first thing we did there was, of course, to take breakfast, and an unusually large one it was.

At three in the afternoon we visited an old ruin which, to a small extent, resembled the temple at Simbabe and appeared to be the remains of a building of burnt brick.

At half-past four we left the Lundi, and next stopped at the Sugar-Loaf River, or, as the Kafirs call it, the Ingwesi. It was striking to see how much the Sugar-Loaf Hill (from which the stream gets its name) resembled a real sugar-loaf.

We left the river at two the following morning and at seven we outspanned again. After taking coffee we once more set out for a hunt. My horse was very slow and could not keep pace with those of my two companions, Mr. Rhodes and Mr. James. I therefore ceased accompanying them, and began parrot-shooting instead, but the birds were so wild that I had no chance of hitting any. However, I shot some turtle-doves. Riding up the side of the stream, I came to a beautiful bathing-place. I tied my horse to a tree and began undressing myself to take a dash in the cool, clear water. Looking up to a rock in front of me, I was startled to see what I took to be a large cayman. The animal, instead of fleeing out of my sight, remained sitting at perfect ease, and gazed at me contemptuously. "My friend," I thought, "this impudence I will not tolerate, and possibly you intend to make closer acquaintance with me, and — prevention is better than cure." I took up my gun and shot the animal, sending it spinning down the rock. Going to look what it was, I found it to be a young alligator. I took my bath in peace and returned to the waggons.

Shortly afterwards the other huntsmen arrived, bringing with them nothing more than a couple of turtle-doves. We left the Ingwesi, and at seven in the evening we halted at an open spot surrounded by a few trees.

We resumed the journey at half-past three the following morning, and at six we were compelled to stop again because of an accident to our waggon; it ran against a tree, the axle broke, and one of the fore-wheels fell out. This caused great disappointment, and was a source of much trouble. We could do nothing with the waggon but leave it behind, for it was now utterly useless to us. All the goods that had been packed upon it we removed to the other waggons.

The next river we came to was the Nionetse. Here we stopped and invigorated our bodies in the fresh stream. This was the place from which Captain Tyson wired us in November last that two of his waggons had capsized, and that a horse had gone astray.

The weather was exceptionally hot, the thermometer reading 100 deg. in the shade. The sky soon became overcast with clouds, and we expected a heavy storm. After we had taken our bath and had finished breakfast, Captain Tyson and I happened to get into conversation about the hill near by on which the telegraph-office was standing. The Captain declared that it was high and dangerous to climb, and he felt very indignant when I told him that I could walk up to the office and back without feeling that I had done so.

"Well," he said, "the shortest time *I* took to walk up and down the hill was two hours, and *you* won't do that!"

"Gracious me!" I thought, "what does the man take me for?"—"Well," I said to him, "let's go for a race, and I'll bet you that I'll walk the distance in less time than you will."

"Done!" he exclaimed. "How much do you bet?"

"Well, what would *you* like to bet?"

"Five pounds," he readily suggested.

"All right," I answered; "but remember that it is twelve o'clock now, and it is so warm that every crow is yawning, and we have just been having our meal."

The Captain smiled triumphantly, expecting that I was going to give in or propose a compromise; but he was mistaken—I was too proud to do that. Both of us then got ready for the race, Mr. Rhodes smilingly looking on.

"You are like two little children!" remarked the latter. "It is an act of folly to walk that height in this great heat."

But neither of us would yield to the other, and off we started. Mr. Rhodes, Mr. Lange and Mr. James, silly though they thought we were, took a lively interest in the race. My rival soon lost ground, and the farther we walked the greater became the distance between us. The hill, which was three hundred feet high, I climbed like a boy. I had lost much weight during my travel from Beira to Umtali, so I was able easily to stand a little exertion. Captain Tyson, on the other hand—who had been living a kingly life in a waggon during the time Mr. Rhodes, Major Johnson and I were journeying from Beira to Salisbury and had to contend with so many adversities—had considerably *gained* in weight. Well, soon he began to breathe like a whale. I rested on the summit at the telegraph-office for a few minutes, and when my friend was half way up the hill I made my way down again. He walked with a stick, I with nothing. At a quarter to two I was back at the waggons. I again rested a while and then partook of a bath along with Mr. Rhodes, Mr. Lange and Mr. van der Bijl. When we came out of the water Captain Tyson returned from his walk; he was as wet with perspiration as a man who had been playing football for the first time. I had compassion on him, for he looked sorely fatigued. His gentle, friendly glance at me deprived me of the heart to chaff him.

"Good friend," I said to him, "I have beaten you! In walking, there's no doubt, I am your master. Now, let us have a whiskey together. Your five pounds you may keep, for you have already been sufficiently punished."

CHAPTER XXVIII.

Secluded huts—Evidence of a struggle between animals—A view of a huge crocodile—Captain Tyson deceived—He has a nasty fall—At the Boobi River—In search of water—The snake hunts the cayman and the boys hunt the snake—Van Riet's wonderful adventure.

BETWEEN three and four there was a heavy downpour of rain, and the atmosphere in consequence became much cooler and fresher.

Early the next morning Mr. Rhodes, Mr. James and I went out hunting. We rode by the side of the river until we came to a tributary, up along which we turned. On the top of a steep kopje some distance off we discerned three Kafir huts built upon rocks. This we thought strange, because all the country round about was a lonesome wilderness in which there was no trace of human beings, and in which we did not in the least expect to find any. We made in the direction of the huts, and soon we arrived at the gardens belonging to the Kafirs on the kopje, but of the Kafirs themselves we spied none. A drizzling rain now came down, and instead of the air—which had been misty during the morning—becoming clearer in consequence, it grew darker, and so prevented us from seeing far ahead. No wonder, therefore, that we saw

Y

no game, although we were constantly coming across fresh footmarks.

We crossed a brook, and in the soft drift-sand on one side of it we could clearly see that a struggle between two large animals had taken place there a little previously. We alighted from our horses in order to examine the marks in the sand more closely, and we distinctly observed the fresh footprints of a lion and a koodoo. The only conclusion to be drawn was that a lion had there sprung upon a koodoo and dragged it away. I was then anxious to trace the lion on its "spoor," but, unfortunately, none of us had any experience in lion-hunting, and we knew it would be dangerous to attack such an animal when on its prey. It is a pity we did not have Mr. Selous with us at this juncture.

Riding farther we soon found that we had taken a wrong course. Luckily, however, the weather soon afterwards cleared up, and we again descried the three huts we had noticed on the rocky cliff, so we knew whereabout we were and which way to take. Crossing some streamlets, on the side of which there were some large pools, Mr. James and I, riding side by side, discerned on the brink of one of them a large black object. We rode a little nearer to it to find out what it was.

"Man," said my companion, "it is a monstrous crocodile."

"Well," I suggested, "let us dismount here and creep nearer before we shoot at it."

"No," said Mr. James, "let us ride a little further before we get down."

As I had expected, just as we were about to dismount the crocodile leapt into the water. It was the largest crocodile that I had ever seen.

A little before eleven we were back at our waggons, and at half-past three in the afternoon we left the Nionetse.

At seven we outspanned upon a fine sheltered spot, but we had hardly done so when the noisy hyænas again began provoking us.

"Trouble to-night again!" I heard one of our boys say.

We commanded the Kafirs to collect a large pile of wood, so that we might keep the fire lit all through the night. As we had expected, the hyæna's howling was soon followed by the lion's roaring. The latter kept a long way off, but the impudent hyænas repeatedly frightened our oxen, and would certainly have tackled them had our boys not done their best to keep them away. Only a few nights previously, near to the same place, some hyænas tore open the belly of an ox whilst it was tied to the draught-rope of the waggon of a transport-rider. The latter heard the ox pull about and bellow, so he jumped from his waggon with his gun to see what the matter was, expecting to meet a lion, but when he came to the ox he was just in time to see some half-dozen hyænas run off. He fired at them, but, as the night was very dark, his aim was bad and he missed. The following morning he was obliged to cut the throat of the poor animal.

We resumed our journey at half-past four in the morning, and at six we arrived at the Sawie River. Captain Tyson rode on horseback and kept a long distance ahead of us. He did not expect that we would outspan at the river, nor had it been our intention to do so; but when we came to it the water was so tempting that we resolved to tarry there a while. Captain Tyson, ignorant of this, steadily rode on until, twenty-five minutes afterwards, he discovered on looking round that no waggon was following. He at once turned back, and three-quarters of an hour after we had seen him last he arrived at the waggons, where he was hailed by a row of laughing faces. The good captain felt somewhat perplexed.

We went into the river. Poor Captain Tyson! He undressed himself, stepped into the water, then got upon a large smooth stone, but he had hardly done so when his foot slipped, he lost his balance, and, as he fell, bang! struck his head against another stone. As quick as thought, however, he stood upon his legs again and feigned not to have been hurt in the least. Of course we had another jolly laugh at the expense of our unlucky friend.

"My dear man," I said to him, "what is the matter with you? Why have you made it a rule to fall like that? You'll break your neck if you go on like this!"

"Well, old man," he replied, "if *you* had fallen as *I* had, you would certainly have made no joke of it!"

"But, my friend," I said, with a show of sympathy, "I *started* when I saw you fall—I started very much—but when you rose so suddenly and showed so calm, innocent a face, I could not help laughing."

Seeing that the Captain's head had really had a bad collison with the stone, I tried my utmost to be serious and show him due compassion, but, as the picture of the ludicrous mishap and the Captain's sedate attitude following it reappeared to my mind, I found it impossible to retain my serenity, and, much to the irritation of my friend, as well as to my own dissatisfaction, I could not prevent another hearty outburst.

I myself had had two falls similar to those of the Captain, though not nearly so serious.

We returned to our waggons and had our breakfast, after which we had some fun in teasing Captain Tyson about his clumsiness. The Captain, who sat near to me, then made me feel the part of his head that had struck the stone. There was a big bump. Three minutes afterwards he suddenly and unexpectedly fell forward in an unconscious state, his head dropping on my breast. Fun was now changed into seriousness. We washed his head with vinegar and resorted to every means available to get his senses restored. Soon after he recovered.

The land round about us was hilly and woody, and the veld of a good character. Polony-trees, so called from the shape of their remarkably large fruits, grew there in abundance. I picked a "polony" twenty-two inches in length, sixteen inches in circumference, and fifteen pounds in weight. It is dangerous to sit under a polony-tree when its fruits are ripe: the fall of a fruit upon one's head would stun him.

At two o'clock the following morning we inspanned, and at six we stopped at the Boobi River. Half an hour later Mr. Rhodes, Mr. James and I went out hunting. We stayed out more than two hours and came across some half-a-dozen koodoos, but it was in vain that we shot at them. At eleven o'clock we returned to our waggons to take breakfast. It was at this place, the Boobi, that Lord Randolph shot the lions, quaggas and koodoos—at least, so he *said* in his letters. It is, however, true that the shores of the Boobi has a reputation for abounding in numerous kinds of large game.

We were met by Messrs. Fry and Elliott at the river. These gentlemen complained that there were not sufficient huts and barns for the whites in the country.

At four we left the Boobi and at seven we had finished our day's journey. At two the next morning we started again, and at seven we arrived and stopped at the Umshabetsi, a tributary of the Limpopo, and a large, dry, sandy river closely resembling the Buffalo, Dwyka and Gamka in the Cape Colony—an indication that we no longer found ourselves on the plateaux of Mashonaland. We had to dig in the sand for water, and our oxen had to be sent several miles down the river to drink at some pools. The dusty road and the oppressive weather had made our bodies sorely need a bath, but there was no water near in which to take it. Captain Tyson, Mr. Lange and I decided to saddle our horses, ride down the river and take a plunge into the first pool at which we should arrive. We rode and rode—and it was not before we had ridden at least eight miles that we came to some pools. Our thirsty oxen had to walk the same distance. We told the boys who were driving the poor animals to let them graze round about the water, there being plenty of grass, that we would send them their dinner with some

A SNAKE AND A CAYMAN FIGHT.

of the other Kafirs, and that they need not return to the waggons before half-past three.

Feeling fresh again we returned to our camp. Mr. Rhodes meanwhile had his elastic bath filled with water, and so was able to enjoy a bath without going eight miles for it.

Not far from our waggons some transport-riders had outspanned. I had a short chat with them. They told me that one of their oxen had been seriously bitten by a hyæna the previous night, despite their dogs' barking.

As we were sitting in our camp we heard some exciting noise outside. On going to see what was the cause of it, we found Fortuin, January and a few others busy seeking a snake. Fortuin and January had been taking a nap under a tree when they were suddenly startled by a heavy object falling between them—it was a cayman. Hardly had they sprung to their feet when down came another creature —it was an immense snake in pursuit of the cayman. The boys then tried to kill the hideous peace-disturbers, but failed, the animals finding their way into some thorny thickets where they were lost sight of. All along the river grew prickly trees and shrubs—another proof that we were no longer on the high land.

The Umshabetsi we left at four, and from there we rode in one continuous cloud of dust till seven, when we halted on a hill, there to pass the night. As on the previous evening we were again greatly annoyed by hyænas. Lions, too, were near; but we were now upon an open place, and so we felt ourselves pretty secure; besides, it was moonlight. It was a warm night

—an exceedingly warm one—so much so, that we could hardly sleep. In the waggon the air was too close, so Mr. Lange and I spread our karosses outside on the bare ground, and lay there without any covering. The Premier's couch was of a different kind. An armchair was his bed. Throwing himself into it with his head resting over the back of it, he slept in that posture all night.

At ten minutes past two the following morning we set out again and had to put up with as much dust as we had had the day before. At sunrise we came to the Umzingwane, a broad stream with densely wooded banks.

It was between this river and our last halting-place that van Riet, a youth much liked by all who knew him, spent those memorable, miserable forty days of his life. He was on his way to Salisbury with some Sisters of Mercy, when, one day, having walked too far from his waggons, he lost his way. The Sisters on missing him naturally grew alarmed, and sent out men in search of him; but, after waiting for him for several days and discovering no trace of him, they naturally presumed that he had met his death somehow and somewhere in the wilds, and so continued their journey to Salisbury without him. To their extreme amazement and joy, however, the lad was again found and handed over to them. To relate in detail the sufferings and anxiety the young fellow had had to endure during those forty days he wandered in the wilds would require as many pages. The huntsmen who discovered him had been in search of water when they observed the boy's footprints in the sand.

Following them, they eventually arrived at the spot they sought. There the boy sat with bent back and in utter despair and misery in front of a little hole of water that he had dug with his hands. His finger-nails were worn away up to the naked flesh, having been employed for digging into the hard earth for roots and water, and his teeth were blunt and broken, owing to the hard wild dates he had been chewing. He was not far from dead when discovered, and was already semi-unconscious. In fact, he would not have lived a day longer had he not been rescued. The kind hunters did all within their power to restore his strength, and in this they happily succeeded.

CHAPTER XXIX.

A koodoo shot—Mr. Rhodes' light waggon—I over-persuade my companions, and we all start together for Bechuanaland—Pikenin leaves me—On the track of our previous journey—An invitation at Macloutsi in which I am not included.

Not far from us some waggons stood outspanned. Two of the gentlemen belonging to them—the one a Mr. Malherbe and the other a Mr. Vivier—came to us and invited us to accompany them on a giraffe-hunt. They assured us that they were experienced huntsmen and knew the country well. We accepted the invitation. The hunting-party consisted of Mr. Rhodes, Mr. Malherbe, Mr. Vivier, Mr. James, Roeping and myself, all on horseback. Having ridden a couple of hours, we came to a place where the footmarks of various large animals were to be seen, amongst them those of the giraffe. We rode on and met a group of koodoos. Becoming excited, everyone, except myself, dashed in mad pursuit after the animals, each choosing a different course, with the result that within a few minutes I could not see a man, not even Roeping. Bang! bang! bang! I heard on every side, but my fellow-travellers were soon such a distance from me that not the firing even could I hear. I rode on, but, coming across neither man nor koodoo, I decided to ride back along the river; but I had hardly started doing so when Mr. Malherbe appeared—he was chasing a koodoo he had wounded. As he passed me, he pointed to the sand to drops of blood of the injured animal. Shortly afterwards Mr. Rhodes, Mr. James and Roeping also turned up. We followed Mr. Malherbe, and soon heard him call, "Here he is!" The poor koodoo could not proceed one step farther. The hind part of the animal rested on the ground, whilst its fore-legs supported its front, the bullet having passed through the poor creature's spine. It was a beautiful full-grown bull with fine horns. We killed it, skinned it, cut it in pieces, and took with us as much of the meat as we could carry. Mr. Malherbe took the skin and the horns with him.

We were now undecided as to what to do, to continue the hunt or return to our camp. If we went farther we would in all probability come across giraffes, whose fresh footprints we observed in abundance, but the weather was so warm and depressing that we felt more inclined to cool ourselves in our camp than pursue game. We returned, leaving Mr. Vivier behind. On our way back we rode through a spruit of the Umzingwane, where we noticed a young crocodile leaping into a small pool. We tried to get the animal out of the water by means of sticks, but in vain.

We reached our waggons a little before noon. Mr. Vivier arrived at one. He had found the giraffes, he said, and had pursued them some distance, but, on becoming aware that none of us were following him, gave up the chase as not worth the trouble, for he knew that, supposing he shot a giraffe, without assistance he could do nothing with it. He was displeased that we had left him so soon, but we cared but little for that.

We left the Umzingwane at four in the afternoon, journeyed right on for five hours, and outspanned upon an open plain. Night set in and, with it, the vexatious yelping of the hyænas. Nothing would have pleased me more that night than to see every hyæna in the land a carcass. Mr. Rhodes again slept in his armchair.

At two the next morning we set off again, and at three we passed the River Spagi, on one of the borders of which there stood a small straw-built hotel—an ordinary hut. At six we came to a spruit within five miles of Fort Tuli. After stopping there three hours we again advanced, and at half-past ten—Saturday, November the 14th—we reached Fort Tuli. On our previous trip to the North we arrived at the fort on the 1st of November; it was now, therefore, a little more than a year since we had last visited it. The previous year on my arrival there I felt as though I had reached the northern end of Africa—so far the place seemed to be from Capetown; now, however, I felt as though I stood on the border of the Cape Colony. It being a hot day, the Tuli River was a boon to us; if it had not been there, I do not know how we would have borne the excessive heat. In the afternoon it began to rain, and the air became cooler in consequence.

The light waggon for which Mr. Rhodes had wired to Palapye had arrived at Tuli. Mr. Lange and I went to examine it. To my judgment, the vehicle, though very light, was pretty strong. Not so, however, did it appear to the eye of my friend; in no way did it suit his taste, and he denounced it as being too frail to carry the combined weight of Mr. Rhodes, Captain Tyson, himself and me. He therefore proposed that we should leave it and ride instead in the coach of Mr. Zeederberg, and he succeeded in getting the Premier to agree with him. To Captain Tyson it was immaterial what we did. I, however, pleaded for the little waggon, and I ordered a blacksmith to tightly tie some leather straps around its springs so as to strengthen them.

The following day the weather was just as oppressive as, if not worse than, it had been the day before. In the morning we rode on horseback to the river, once more to take delight in the sweet, clear water. On our return, the fore-feet of my horse sank into the clayey sand of the river, with the result that I slid over its head into the water, which was four feet deep. Of course my clothes became soaking wet, but I did not mind it—in fact, I rather liked it—for the rays of the sun were scorchingly hot. My horse easily got up again.

In the afternoon Mr. Zeederberg arrived at Tuli with his coach drawn by eight dapple-grey horses, which looked very attractive. Mr. Zeederberg urged the Premier to get into the coach and travel with him to the Transvaal, but I detested the idea of taking the same road we had travelled the year before, and my antipathy to it was strengthened by the prospect of our meeting the Adendorff party again, of whose sickening argumentation in favour of their so-called Banyailand Concession I had had more than enough. I was determined, though all my companions should have decided to leave me, not to return home *viâ* Transvaal—I wanted to travel with the light waggon through Khama's land and Bechuanaland. The pro's and con's of the two routes having been fully discussed, it was finally decided that we should all leave with the new little spring waggon at three the next morning. At first we had intended to leave at ten o'clock in the evening, but, as there was no moonlight, and as it was rather rainy, we had to postpone our departure till the morning.

The same evening we were invited to dinner by Captain Tye. The guests, most of whom were military officers, numbered about fifteen. At ten o'clock I returned to our waggons. Captain Tyson and Mr. Lange did not retire before twelve. Bandmaster had sinned against Mr. Lange in some way or other during the evening, and the latter so lost his temper about it that he kicked up a very unseemly row with the poor mortal, and it terminated in Bandmaster getting a severe thrashing—a punishment wholly undeserved. I was very cross with my friend, especially so because it was the last night that Bandmaster was to be with us —he was to quit our service the following day. And how could I sleep whilst such a noise was going on! No, with all due respect and love to our Epie, I must say he was very unreasonable that night. I had never seen him so turbulent before.

We left Fort Tuli on Monday morning at half-past four and had to travel in a very muddy road, as it had rained all the night. We sat, six of us, in the little waggon—Mr. Rhodes and myself at the back, Captain Tyson and Mr. Lange in the middle, and Tonie and Arri in front. The two waggons and the cart with which we had reached Tuli, our riding-horses with saddles and bridles, our bedding and a quantity of clothing, we left behind. We also bade farewell to Sergeant James, who was to return with Bosbok, Jas, Roeping, Zwartboy and Pikenin to Mashonaland with the waggons. Mr. van der Bijl was to follow us to Capetown with Bandmaster, Jan Kaapnaar and Matokwa. Thus, of all the Inhambane Kafirs, Matokwa was the only one who travelled through to Capetown. It had all along been understood that Pikenin should go with us to Capetown, and it was only on our arrival here that it was decided he should return to Salisbury, there to be employed by Dr. Jameson. At this decision I was naturally sorely disappointed, and Pikenin no less, not to mention the dissatisfaction Matokwa felt, who had virtually been deceived, for, I presume, he would never have left his comrades to spend his remaining days in a country entirely foreign to him if he had not relied on Pikenin* accompanying him. However, I did not oppose the Premier's desire lest I should appear disagreeable.

Our six oxen ran with the waggon as if some fiend were after them. I was afraid that before noon

---

* I am informed that after Pikenin had faithfully served the Rhodesian Administrator for a twelvemonth he fled, on the outbreak of the Matabele War, from Salisbury to Umtali, where Mr. Rhodes, on his next trip to Mashonaland (after the war) fortuitously saw him washing clothes at a stream. "Ah, Pikenin, is that you?" said the Premier, pleasantly surprised at the unexpected meeting, and then and there offered the Inhambane boy to take him to Capetown. In a moment Pikenin was ready to go, and at present both he and Matokwa are happy and faithful servants at the Prime Minister's residence, "Groote Schuur."—*Translator.*

some limb of the vehicle would break, for whenever our road was downhill all we could do was to cling to our seats and hold our breath.

At a quarter-past six we stopped at the Baobab River, and there had breakfast. At seven we left the stream, and, with a new team of oxen, fresh and vigorous, our waggon ran so fast with us that the wind hummed in our ears. The animals could not, however, keep up this speed for long, so we were soon again travelling like a sane party.

At half-past eleven we outspanned at Similali, a spot at which we spent nearly an entire day the year before, as there was plenty of grass and water, and a beautiful mimosa-tree. Having taken our midday meal, we proceeded again at half-past one, our road taking us into the Mapani Forest, where a large variety of birds was to be met with. Thunder-clouds meanwhile began to gather. At three we outspanned to allow the animals a little relaxation, and soon we set off again. Rain now came down in torrents, and peal after peal of thunder seemed to rend the air; but Arri, the driver, who paid but little heed to the state of the weather, advised us to travel as fast as we could; there was no need to fear the oxen failing, for at every outspan-place—that is, after every two hours' or two and a half hours' drive—there was a fresh team waiting for us. Rain fell throughout the night.

At one o'clock next morning we arrived before a river through which old Arri was afraid to drive. Mr. Rhodes, however, was determined to go through it. We bade him be more reasonable and not risk his life in a river of which his knowledge was next to nothing. In order to ascertain its depth, we made the leader of the oxen walk into the stream. The water reached a little above the middle of his body. We considered it shallow enough to cross, and through we drove.

Of sleeping was not to be thought. How Arri managed to pass all the trees growing by the roadside without running the waggon against any is to me a puzzle. At a quarter-past six we arrived at the Macloutsi Camp, where all were still apparently asleep. We wanted to prepare coffee, but the wood and the ground were so wet that we could hardly light a fire. We had outspanned in front of the shop of an English gentleman, a Mr. Howman, and we had not been there long when the shop-proprietor came to invite Mr. Rhodes, Captain Tyson and Mr. Lange to take coffee in his house. Me, however, though I was standing next to the other gentlemen, he did not invite. I felt more than insulted at this snobbish treatment. I believe I was as well-dressed as any of my fellow-travellers, and appeared as respectable. "Howman," I thought, "hills and mountains do not part and meet, but men do; the day may come when we shall meet again!"

This matter reminded me of a somewhat similar incident which took place when I was a young man, and was making my first trip to the Free State in company with a brother of mine. There was of course no railway at that time by which to travel. We journeyed by cart. As we were passing through the Murraysburg district we one night came to the farm of a Mr. Theron, who—very inconsistent with Boer hospitality—for some inexplicable reason deliberately refused to sell us either meat or bread or even forage for our tired and hungry horses. But we so humbly begged him to give us something, and offered him such high prices for what we asked, that he ultimately gave us some old dry bread, such as I would not give my dog, and a tough thin piece of meat, charging us five shillings for them; and for our horses he let us have two oat-sheaves for three shillings. I was then twenty years of age. Twenty-two years afterwards I met an aged farmer at the Middleburg Bond Congress, who came to me to make my acquaintance. We began talking to each other, and somehow the unpleasant night I had spent at Mr. Theron's came back to my mind, and, by questioning the gentleman as to who he was and where he lived, I discovered that he was the very Mr. Theron who had so shabbily treated us. I then reminded him of the incident and very politely, though not less frankly, told him—what I would fain have told him twenty-two years ago, but dared not—what I thought of men of his kind.

We had breakfast in a small restaurant, and at eight o'clock we were ready to leave Macloutsi. At this point a number of officers, who had just got out of bed and were still rubbing their eyes, came to the waggon and made a score of excuses to the Managing Director of the Chartered Company for not having known of his coming. Dressed in their military attire, they wished to honour the Premier by escorting him some distance out of Macloutsi, but the latter, who hated anything of that kind, bade them leave him.

Within the last twenty-four hours we had travelled seventy miles.

CHAPTER XXX.

We leave Macloutsi—Meet Khama—At Palapye—The chief's grievances—I do not enjoy the *rôle* of John Gilpin, and reproach my companions—A little excusable exaggeration in my complaints—Captain Tyson and Mr. Lange left behind—Matabele boys—Arrival at Notwani.

ON the 17th of November, at a quarter-past eight, we left Macloutsi. We travelled day and night, being supplied with a fresh team of oxen at regular intervals. We went like the wind. The oxen were all in excellent condition, but this was not surprising, seeing that they were well fed and that they had to draw only three or four times in a fortnight. To my admiration the leaders of the teams did not once let go the rope; they were generally young Kafirs who ran as lightly over the road as young bucks. Want of rest, however, soon began to tell upon us, and we became so drowsy that we could hardly keep our eyes open.

Just before we entered Palapye we met Khama and his son on some arable land. The chief had been engaged tilling his land with four ploughs. Immediately upon seeing us he came to greet us, courteously lifting his hat and making a low bow. We stopped the coach for a few minutes, exchanged a few words with the Bamangwato ruler, and drove on again, the chief promising to come and see us in his town. We outspanned near the telegraph-office at Palapye and carried on some communication by wire with our people at Capetown.

At five o'clock our little waggon was ready to leave Palapye; it had a new driver, Arri remaining behind in Khama's capital, where his family was living. Captain Tyson and Mr. Lange were to follow the waggon with a large tester-cart, and Mr. Rhodes requested them, before we left, not to tarry long in the town.

Khama, who had followed our waggon to his town shortly after we met him at his ploughs, and who was desirous to discuss some matters with the Chartered Company's Managing Director, but could not talk English, now came to ask Mr. Rhodes to go with him to his interpreter. To this request the Premier readily acceded. Mr. Rhodes, Khama, Mr. Moffat, junior, and myself then rode on horseback to the interpreter's, allowing our waggon meanwhile to proceed. Arrived at the interpreter's, the Premier and the chief entered his house, whilst Mr. Moffat and I remained outside. Khama complained of the conduct of Missionary Hepburn, who had faithfully worked among his people for twenty years but had latterly begun to play the master in the country. Khama, as ruler over his people, claimed that he knew his work well, and could not bear—perhaps reasonably so—to see another command his subjects. The natural result of Mr. Hepburn's behaviour was the growth of discord between the chief and the missionary, and the quarrel ended in Khama leaving Mr. Hepburn the alternative of submitting to him or of quitting the country. The missionary thereupon left the land, and, as I am informed, is now in London complaining to the authorities there about the conduct of the Bamangwato chief.

At seven o'clock we said good-bye to Khama. It was pretty dark then. Mr. Rhodes and Mr. Moffat had good horses; mine was a good-for-nothing brute that seemed to take delight in bringing its rider in contact with Mother Earth as often as possible. It was not very pleasant to ride on such a horse at such a speed as that at which we were going. Upon my word, we rode like three John Gilpins. Mr. Moffat was anxious to overtake the waggon and return to Palapye, whilst Mr. Rhodes was not at ease so long as the waggon remained out of his sight. I, though desirous of riding at a less speed, had to do as my companions did, for I would under no circumstances lag behind, being a perfect stranger to the road. The first time my horse stumbled, both it and I fell flat upon the ground, but we were soon up again. The second time it fell I flew over its head, my poor face sweeping the sand. I mounted again and rode as hard as I could to overtake the others, but my poor creature *would* lag behind. My companions did not trouble themselves at all about me, their mind being fixed on only one thing—the waggon. My horse and I now had our third tumble and this was the worst fall of all—the animal rolled right over me. I thought my spine was broken. I arose, wiped the sand from my eyes, and, as loud as my throat could yell, I shouted to my friends to stop. They fortunately heard me and turned back. I was busy putting the saddle right when Mr. Rhodes arrived at the scene.

"What is the matter with you?" he asked, rather unpleasantly.

"I have to ride a clumsy, rotten thing," I answered, with a deep groan, "which has now for the third time tumbled with me, and this time I've been seriously hurt. It is not over-kind of you and Mr. Moffat to leave me in the lurch in the dark in a country entirely unknown to me. My back has been so badly injured that I can go no farther."

Turning to Mr. Moffat, I told him he ought to be ashamed of himself for having made me ride such a miserable beast. "I have," I said, "much experience of horses, and I have trained at least a dozen, but never in my life did I sit upon an animal so undeserving the name of horse as this thing here. My neck is not quite so cheap, my friend, as you appear to think."

Both of them then appeared rather anxious about me.

"What is really the matter with you?" asked Mr. Rhodes again. "Why can you ride no farther?"

"My back is too painful!" I replied, with a pretence of great suffering. As a matter of fact, my back had not been so seriously injured as I feigned, but I knew that if I did not exaggerate a bit I would be thrown behind again and run the risk of losing my way.

My companions asked me to try to mount the horse again, promising they would not desert me. I had gained my object. I once more got upon my so-called horse, and we proceeded.

At length we came to Brakpan, the place at which Sir Henry Loch was met by Khama the previous year. According to agreement, we found our waggon awaiting us here, but Mr. Lange and Captain Tyson had not arrived yet. Mr. Moffat now parted with us and returned to Palapye, taking with him the horses Mr. Rhodes and I had ridden. Without much delay we resumed our journey in the little waggon, which was now inspanned with a fresh team of oxen, and, without stopping on the way, we travelled through the night. The road was wet and heavy, but, as our vehicle had not the weight of Captain Tyson and Mr. Lange to carry, the animals had not much difficulty to trot along with it. There being more room for us in the waggon now, we were able to enjoy a little sleep.

The next day, the 19th of November, we again set out without Captain Tyson and Mr. Lange, having no time to wait for them. The road was still wet and clayey. At one o'clock we came to the Crocodile river. Our two Kafir boys and I went to fetch some water at the stream, a little distance from where we had outspanned. Arrived there, I found the water so cool and tempting that, though I was aware that there were crocodiles in the river, I decided to take a swim. As it was some days since I had last had a bath, and as the weather was hot, it was a glorious treat to lie in the cold water, and I would certainly have stopped in it an hour had time allowed.

We soon again proceeded. Towards evening we had some rain accompanied by thunder, but we paid no attention to the elements, and we again journeyed through the whole night, still at regular intervals obtaining our new team of oxen, as well as a new leader. It was indeed a pleasure to see how the young leaders ran in front of the oxen. A good idea of the rate at which they were running can be formed by remembering that we left Macloutsi at a quarter-past eight on the eleventh, and arrived at Palapye at three o'clock on the eighteenth—a distance of one hundred and eighteen miles. Whether by night or by day, we could invariably tell when it was a Matabele boy who was leading the oxen, for he always sang whilst running, always seemed merry, and never ran slowly. Exposed to heat and cold though his naked body was, he seemed very content with his lot. It was always a pleasure to me to work with Matabele or Inhambane Kafirs; they never grumbled at anything I gave them to do, however difficult the task—whatever their master told them received their amen. But then, don't forget, these Kafirs were not brought up at mission stations, and had, therefore, not been impressed that they were in every respect the white man's equal.

The following day we arrived at Notwani, where a coach was awaiting us. The driver wished us to wait for Captain Tyson and Mr. Lange, but neither Mr. Rhodes nor I felt inclined to do so, for we did not know how far behind they were still, and we were anxious to reach home as soon as possible; besides, Mr. Rhodes had distinctly told them before we left them at Palapye to follow the waggon without delay, assuring them that he would not wait for them at Notwani. They had, therefore, themselves to blame for not being with us now.

CHAPTER XXXI.

Ox-waggon substituted by mail-coach—Lord Randolph and the mules—My anxiety not to disturb his lordship's rest—A rapid run to Mafeking—The troubles of fame—Mr. Rhodes makes a speech at Fourteen Streams—At Kimberley.

WE brought all our luggage over from the waggon to the coach. The waggon was still as sound and strong as the day we had started with it. At seven o'clock we left Notwani. We had now to give up all hope of enjoying on our further journey the company of Captain Tyson and Mr. Lange, because, now that we were to travel by a coach drawn by mules, it was impossible for these gentlemen to overtake us. I was very sorry to miss their pleasant society, especially as I knew that months would pass before I could meet them again.

The Premier and I had now six seats in the coach at our disposal. After travelling seventeen miles we allowed the mules a short rest at a little camp on Lindswi's territory. At five in the afternoon we stopped at another little station, and we were there given six fresh strong mules and two poor thin ones— two that Lord Randolph Churchill had had the grace to leave us, having appropriated for his own service two of the best mules designed for us. As was to be expected, the two weak animals caused much trouble and delay. Mr. Rhodes said not a word about it; he remained quiet, I daresay, for the sake of peace. I, however, felt too much annoyed to hold my tongue.

At the next station we came to we found that the very same thing had been done—Lord Randolph had coolly taken two of our best mules, and had left two of his fatigued creatures in their stead. Over the head, eyes and ears the innocent animals had been thrashed with a sjambok, a whip made of hippopotamus hide.

At two o'clock in the morning we arrived at Mashoudi, a Kafir town where there was a police-station and a telegraph-office. We would not have arrived there so early had I not offered the drivers between the last two stations a pound each if they drove as hard as they could. I had an object for doing so, and that object I gained. I had reason to believe that Lord Randolph would be spending the night in that Kafir town, and I was anxious that he should enjoy his rest undisturbed! I told the driver to create as little noise as possible when he drove into the town, and he obeyed capitally. The moment the waggon stopped my eye fell on the waggons of Lord Randolph, and a cold shock instantly ran through my body. I was very much afraid that we would accidentally arouse the nobleman and be compelled to finish the rest of our journey in company with him; but I had warned both the driver and the leader to keep as quiet as possible, and this they did admirably. When we had changed our mules for a new team and were on the point of departure, Mr. Rhodes asked the "watch" at the station whether he did not think it advisable to wake

Lord Randolph and intimate to him that we were there.

"Oh, no, sir!" was the ready reply; "he is very tired, and he particularly requested me not to disturb his rest."

"Well," said the Premier, "then I shall write him a note."

I felt as though I stood on heated coal while the speaking lasted, for I greatly feared that his lordship would thereby be aroused. Mr. Rhodes wrote him that he was sorry to pass him by without seeing him, that he had to be in time at Kimberley to meet Mr. Sivewright, who was on his way to the Transvaal, and that he had been requested by the "watch" at the station not to disturb his lordship, but he hoped that Lord Randolph would be his guest at Capetown.

Promptly at half-past two we left with eight fat strong mules. Half an hour later we arrived at the Notwani River, where we had to choose between venturing to ford the swollen river and taking a roundabout, but much safer, course of thirty miles. The drivers, who had crossed the river more than once before, were afraid of it. Fortunately we met a Kafir there who, upon Mr. Rhodes offering him a sovereign, was ready to walk into the stream to ascertain its depth and willing, if he did not find the water too high, to lead the waggon through. He stepped in quite fearlessly and found the water at its deepest reaching up to little below his waist. He then returned, took the rope, and ably led the coach safely through the river. The negro was extremely delighted with his pound.

For four hours in succession we drove through a fine

tract of pastural country, every now and then meeting with native cattle and sheep, all of which were in beautiful condition.

Near to Gaberones twenty of the Chartered Company's police came to meet Mr. Rhodes. We had to cross the Notwani a second time, and on this occasion we did not hesitate to do so, the river being low. We outspanned on its bank and took a bath in the pleasant water. At the telegraph office at Gaberones Mr. Rhodes received a wire from Lord Randolph stating that he was exceedingly sorry that we had passed him, and that he had never thought that we would travel so quickly with our oxen as we did.

We took breakfast at Gaberones and were well entertained by the officers there. At eight o'clock we sped on again, and at ten minutes past ten we arrived at Ramoetzi, a distance of eighteen miles from Gaberones. Ramoetzi is a pretty little Kafir town with a population of about 4500, including a few whites.

After partaking of lunch in the house of a very kind family—whose name, I am sorry to say, I have forgotten—we left Ramoetzi and were again going through fine country. We met several herds of cattle along the way, all fat and healthy, and now and then we passed a lakelet swarming with birds.

A little before one o'clock we came to a place called Aasvogelkop, which lay sixteen miles from Ramoetzi, a distance which we covered at the rate of ten miles per hour; this was by no means bad for mules, seeing that the road was very sandy.

The Chartered Company bored for water at Aasvogelkop, and at a depth of about forty feet they struck a formidable stream. They tried the same experiment at another station of theirs, with the result that at a depth of one hundred and five feet they met with copious water. These wells, I may mention, were sunk in the driest season of the year.

Leaving Aasvogelkop, we travelled over a very extensive valley, in which Mr. Rhodes shot some korhaans.

At midnight we arrived at Mafeking, one hundred and twenty-five miles from Mashoudi. Our coach stopped in front of an hotel, where a crowd of people had assembled to meet the Managing Director of the Chartered Company. We had expected that all would be in bed by that time—but how mistaken! Everyone of them had something to inquire about and something to tell. We felt more inclined to sleep than to talk, for we were really very tired, and we told our entertainers so, but it availed nothing. It was not before two o'clock that they allowed us to go to bed; and, had the Premier not reminded them that they could meet us the next morning, I dare say they would have kept us up a great deal longer. Mr. Rhodes and I decided to start from Mafeking at five in the morning at the latest. We did not make this resolution, as it might seem, with the set object of escaping the company of the Mafeking people—for their company would be as welcome as that of any other at the proper time—but it served that purpose, because the Mafekingans thought that, as the mail-coach was to leave at eight o'clock, we would not leave before that hour. They were, however, mistaken. We arranged with the postmaster of the place to have everything ready for our departure by four, so that our coach could leave a little before five; but when we were waked we felt so sleepy still that we decided to devote another half hour to repose. With a fresh team to our coach we set out at five minutes past five. The road was rather wet, but this did not prevent our coach from travelling at the rate of—well, a Portuguese train.

At half-past eleven we came to Settagoli, a small station, and there, at a neat little hotel—the only one there was—we had dinner.

A little before seven we entered Vrijburg, and were put down at the house of Sir Sidney Shippard, having covered that day at least a hundred miles. In seven days and six nights we had travelled, with oxen, mules and horses, a distance of not less than 625 miles, nearly half of which was accomplished by oxen. This was a record travel; no one else had before completed that distance in so short a time with only draught animals, and, I may pretty safely assert, no one ever will. A fair idea of the speed which we travelled at can be formed by bearing in mind that 625 miles is approximately the distance between Capetown and Kimberley, and that we covered it in less than a week.

We had now practically come to the end of our long journey, and could once more enjoy the comforts of a house. We felt very "at home" at the Administrator's, who did all he could to make our stay at his house a pleasant one. We had made his acquaintance and friendship the year before, when he was a fellow-traveller of ours for a portion of our trip, and we were now glad to enjoy his genial company once more. Miss Shippard, a very sociable and refined young lady, added considerably to the entertainment we received. Having partaken of a most enjoyable dinner, we indulged in cheerful conversation till late in the evening, when the Premier and I betook ourselves to our quiet bedrooms, a privilege we had not been permitted for some time. I need not add that our repose was of the sweetest.

The next morning—Monday, 23rd November—we bade our Vrijburg friends "Good-bye," the Administrator accompanying us to the station, which we left by the eight o'clock train. We had dinner at Taungs, the village where Sir Henry Loch met Mankoraan the previous year.

In honour of Mr. Rhodes the train in which we were travelling had been arranged to be the first passenger-train crossing Fourteen Streams. A loud cheer went up from the assembled crowd at the bridge as the train steamed over it. On the other side of the bridge the train was stopped, and the Prime Minister addressed the people in a few words suitable to the occasion, congratulated the workmen on the good piece of work they had done, and stood the latter a treat.

At four o'clock we arrived at Kimberley.

During my absence from home, which seemed to me thrice as long as it really was, some of my acquaintances had died, but, for the rest, I found all well and everything prospering. Considering that I had travelled about 4000 miles, the greater part of which through a wild country, I can be exceedingly thankful at having reached my home safe and sound after all our many adventures.

CPSIA information can be obtained
at www.ICGtesting.com
Printed in the USA
BVHW020404141222
654146BV00005B/101